AF352254

Women and Legislative Representation

Women and Legislative Representation

Electoral Systems, Political Parties, and Sex Quotas

Edited by
Manon Tremblay

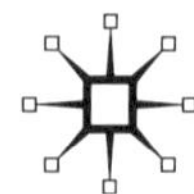

WOMEN AND LEGISLATIVE REPRESENTATION
Copyright © Manon Tremblay, 2008.
All rights reserved. No part of this book may be used or reproduced in any manner whatsoever without written permission except in the case of brief quotations embodied in critical articles or reviews.

First published in 2008 by
PALGRAVE MACMILLAN™
175 Fifth Avenue, New York, N.Y. 10010 and
Houndmills, Basingstoke, Hampshire, England RG21 6XS.
Companies and representatives throughout the world.

PALGRAVE MACMILLAN is the global academic imprint of the Palgrave Macmillan division of St. Martin's Press, LLC and of Palgrave Macmillan Ltd. Macmillan® is a registered trademark in the United States, United Kingdom and other countries. Palgrave is a registered trademark in the European Union and other countries.

ISBN-13: 978-0-230-60378-3
ISBN-10: 0-230-60378-5

Library of Congress Cataloging-in-Publication Data

Women and legislative representation : electoral systems, political parties, and sex quotas / edited by Manon Tremblay.
        p. cm.
Includes bibliographical references and index.
ISBN 0-230-60378-5 (alk. paper)
1. Women politicians. 2. Women in politics. 3. Legislators. 4. Sex role.
5. Representative government and representation. I. Tremblay, Manon.

HQ1236.W6335 2007
328.082—dc22

2007021993

A catalogue record of the book is available from the British Library.

Design by Macmillan India Ltd.

First edition: February 2008

10 9 8 7 6 5 4 3 2 1

Printed in the United States of America.

In memoriam

Wilma Rule
(1925–2004)

Contents

Subpart II   Majority

Part II   Proportional Representation

Subpart I   Closed Lists

**Subpart II   Preferential (Open) List Systems and
Single Transferable Vote**

Part III   Mixed-Member Systems

Subpart I   Proportional

Subpart II   Majoritarian with Partial Compensation

Subpart III   Majoritarian

Figures

Tables

Foreword

This year (2007) marks the centenary of the election of the first women to parliament anywhere in the world—in Finland. Finland was exceptional: not only were women elected in its first election with universal suffrage, but they were elected in considerable numbers. When its magnificent parliament building was finally built in 1931, it even included a special conference room for its women parliamentarians. Elsewhere, women had to wait much longer to be elected in significant numbers as legislators, and global progress was by no means linear. In the early 1990s the fall of communist and other authoritarian regimes led to an initial drop in the average parliamentary representation of women across the world. The decade of the 1990s also, however, saw the successful politicization of the absence of women from parliamentary bodies. Such absence became a marker of "democratic deficit." With the help of women mobilizing at home and abroad, the representation of women in parliament is now widely accepted as an indicator of the quality of democracy. It has become a proxy for equality of citizenship and equal opportunity and is seen as contributing to the legitimacy of parliamentary institutions and their capacity for inclusive deliberation.

Strategies to deal with this democratic deficit have included the adoption of electoral quotas for women in over 100 countries. A global focus on the representation of women in public decision making was reinforced by the Platform for Action adopted by the United Nations Fourth World Conference on Women in Beijing in 1995. According to the platform, women's equal participation in political life plays a "pivotal role in the general process of the advancement of women," and the UN Economic and Social Council subsequently endorsed the use of quotas to achieve it. The systematic monitoring by the Inter-Parliamentary Union of the level of representation achieved in national parliaments and, more recently, the monitoring of the adoption of quotas by the International Institute for Democracy and Electoral Assistance (IDEA) have helped raise awareness of exactly how and where gains are being made. Numerous nongovernmental bodies, often at the regional or international level and supported by multilateral bodies such as IDEA, have come into being to support women into politics. Above all, the level of women's movement mobilization, both nationally and internationally, and both inside and outside political parties, helps provide momentum for the adoption of mechanisms such as quotas, while pressure from aid donors also plays its part.

As a result of all these efforts the number of women in national parliaments has been rising in most parts of the world. In the ten years since 1997, average representation has risen from 11 to 17 percent, while the number of countries where women form over 30 percent of national legislators has risen from 5 to 17. Nonetheless, progress is still patchy and has even stalled in some of the older democracies. This means the question of the most effective means to increase the representation of women in parliament is very much a live issue and one that requires the attention and knowledge of experts in electoral politics and electoral systems. The significance of the type of electoral system for the representation of women and minorities has long been recognized, and valuable work was done over many years by a pioneer in this field, the late Wilma Rule.

Manon Tremblay has now taken on the mantle of Wilma Rule to take forward the study of how electoral system design can advance the representation of women. She has brought together an outstanding team of experts to assist her with the task of analyzing the full gamut of electoral systems and their interactions with specific national contexts in producing particular gender outcomes. She has organized the project around three main families of electoral systems: first, plurality and majority systems; second, proportional representation (PR), including closed and open lists and single transferable vote; and third, mixed systems, combining constituency and party list votes, and varying in accordance with whether the party list element is designed to be fully or only partially compensatory.

It has long been a central tenet of the electoral system literature that PR systems are more woman friendly than single-member electorate systems. This is because of differing incentives they create for candidate selection. As Wilma Rule and others have argued, PR systems give political parties an incentive to produce a balanced ticket to appeal to all sections of the community and to appease all sections of the party, rather than seeking a lowest common denominator candidate as in single-member systems. PR also means representation for smaller and newer parties such as the Greens, in which women play a major role, although it may also mean representation for small parties of the religious or populist Right, which tend to be male led. But perhaps, most importantly, PR makes it easy to introduce quotas, because representation is not a zero-sum game in which a male candidate must be replaced by a female one.

Women and Legislative Representation: Electoral Systems, Political Parties, and Sex Quotas takes us well beyond the existing state of knowledge concerning the impact of electoral systems on the representation of women and, indeed, challenges a number of existing beliefs concerning the significance of district magnitude or the supposed advantages of closed compared with open lists. An interesting aspect of open list systems that has been analyzed elsewhere by Anne Maria Holli is that they can give parliamentarians greater independence of political parties and hence facilitate cross-party cooperation by women parliamentarians. Such cooperation by women across Left-Right divisions in Finland in 1994 helped achieve a legally enforceable right to childcare for all children under three, despite the opposition of a right-wing Cabinet.

The spread of mixed-member systems has increasingly problematized easy assumptions about PR. Sarah Childs and her colleagues, writing about the United Kingdom, confirm that in the mixed electoral systems used for Scotland and Wales, equality measures in the constituency seats were more important than the list seats in increasing women's representation. In New Zealand, Jennifer Curtin finds that although the list seats have returned a higher percentage of women than the constituency seats, the move of a major party to the Right can swamp the incentives provided by PR.

This is not just a book for electoral system enthusiasts, but rather a contribution to knowledge that is of practical importance for all people working toward the greater electoral representation of women. Its 15 case studies are carefully chosen to illustrate the dynamics of the full range of electoral systems across all continents and in both developing and long-established democracies. The intersection of electoral systems with a range of other political factors forms a vital part in the explanation of gender outcomes, for example, the effects of incumbency or term limits in the United States or Mexico, the significance of personal support networks in Japan, the feminization of the Labour Party in New Zealand, or the influence of the Social International on the Spanish Socialist Workers' Party. While electoral systems may have a positive effect in terms of the representation of women, this will always be context dependent. This book increases our knowledge of both the nuances of electoral systems and their interplay with other political variables. It is an important step toward better understanding of what works for women in electoral system design.

Marian Sawer

Canberra, May 2007

Preface and Acknowledgments

Since the beginning of the 1980s, the invigoration of two historically marginalized fields of political science has resulted, among other things, in a publication boom: these fields are electoral studies and "women and politics" (sometimes called "gender and politics"). Although they share a similarly marginalized status within the discipline, these two fields have rarely intersected—or rather, to be precise, the works identified with electoral studies have rarely incorporated a gender perspective. The inverse is more frequent, as demonstrated by two collections edited by Wilma Rule and Joseph F. Zimmerman, *United States Electoral Systems: Their Impact on Women and Minorities* (Praeger, 1992) and *Electoral Systems in Comparative Perspective: Their Impact on Women and Minorities* (Greenwood, 1994). By contrast, electoral studies volumes published since the mid-1980s either completely ignore the representation of women or discuss women in a "sociodemographic representation in parliament" section, thereby treating 50 percent of the human species as a minority group. In addition, certain concepts used in electoral studies demonstrate little sensitivity to women. Thus, the concept of "proportionality," which is essential for defining the merits of a voting procedure, applies to the relationship between the proportion of valid votes cast for a political party and the proportion of seats obtained in parliament, but it does not take into account the relationship between the proportion of women in the population and the proportion in parliament. The latter, however, is a key measure of political representation, known as microcosmic or descriptive representation; it is concerned with proportionality between the whole (i.e., the population) and a sample (i.e., the group of female and male representatives).

The present work aims to reconcile two fields of political science: "electoral studies" and "women and politics." Naturally, some researchers have already explored these two perspectives, notably in *Electoral Systems in Comparative Perspective: Their Impact on Women and Minorities* (edited by Wilma Rule and Joseph F. Zimmerman, Greenwood, 1994) and *Women's Access to Political Power in Post-Communist Europe* (edited by Richard E. Matland and Kathleen A. Montgomery, Oxford University Press, 2003). However, the former is now outdated and the latter is limited to a specific region. In contrast,

Women and Legislative Representation: Electoral Systems, Political Parties, and Sex Quotas adopts an international perspective by touching upon each and every continent.

I began this project while I was a visiting researcher in the Department of Political Science at the Australian National University (ANU) from January to June 2006. I wish to thank Dr. Alastair Greig, who was Head of the School of Social Sciences at the time, as well as Dr. Gwendolyn Grey. These two people made my visit to Canberra possible. ANU offers a visually stunning and intellectually stimulating environment and it seems that anything is possible there.

I would also like to express my sincere gratitude to the colleagues who accepted my invitation to write a chapter for this book. Their expertise and professionalism, their enthusiasm for this project, their respect for the, at times, demanding specifications, and, finally, their willingness to respond to my numerous questions all contributed to enabling *Women and Legislative Representation* to see the light of day. I am deeply indebted to Marian Sawer who agreed to write the Foreword. It was truly an honor to have her participate in this endeavor.

Manon Tremblay

Montréal, September 2007

Notes on Contributors

Gretchen Bauer is professor and chair in the Department of Political Science and International Relations at the University of Delaware. She teaches African and comparative politics and gender and politics. She is the author of *Labor and Democracy in Namibia, 1971–1996* (Ohio University Press, 1998), the coauthor, with Scott D. Taylor, of *Politics in Southern Africa: State and Society in Transition* (Lynne Rienner, 2005), and coeditor, with Hannah E. Britton, of *Women in African Parliaments* (Lynne Rienner, 2006). In 2002, she was a visiting researcher at the Institute for Public Policy Research in Windhoek, Namibia.

Hannah E. Britton is an associate professor of political science and women's studies at the University of Kansas, Lawrence. Her research interests include gender and African politics, democratization and development, and civil society–state relations. Her articles have been published in *Africa Today, International Feminist Journal of Politics, International Politics,* and the *Journal of South African Studies.* She is the author of *From Resistance to Governance: Women in the South African Parliament* (University of Illinois Press, 2005) and the coeditor, with Gretchen Bauer, of *Women in African Parliaments* (Lynne Rienner, 2006).

Rosie Campbell is a lecturer in research methods in the School of Politics and Sociology, Birkbeck College, University of London. Her research examines gender and politics, particularly voting behavior, representation, and participation. Her book *Gender and the Vote in Britain* (ECPR, 2006) compares men and women's political attitudes and behavior from 1997 to 2005. Her most recent research includes a study of elite and mass political opinion, interest in politics, and how morale frameworks relate to vote choice.

Sarah Childs is a senior lecturer in politics at the University of Bristol, United Kingdom. Her research explores the relationship between sex, gender, and politics. In particular, it addresses the key question of what difference women's political presence makes, in both theoretical and empirical terms. Her book *New Labour's Women MPs: Women Representing Women* (Routledge, 2004) provides the first academic analysis of the attitudes and experiences of Labour women MPs first elected in 1997. Her most recent publication is the 2005 Hansard Society Report *Women at the Top*. Her next book, *Women in British Party Politics*, will be published in 2008 (Routledge). She has also published widely in numerous academic journals, including the *British Journal of Political Science*, the *British Journal of Politics and International Relations*, the *European Journal of Women's Studies*, *Parliamentary Affairs*, and *Political Studies*.

Ray Christensen is an associate professor of political science at Brigham Young University. His research is in the area of Japanese electoral politics, including campaign strategies, electoral coalitions, malapportionment, gerrymandering, and women in politics. His articles have been published in several journals, including the *American Journal of Political Science, Comparative Political Studies*, the *Japanese Journal of Political Science*, and *PS: Political Science and Politics*. In 2000 he authored *Ending the LDP Hegemony, Party Cooperation in Japan* (University of Hawai'i Press).

Dr. Jennifer Curtin is a senior lecturer in policy and politics at the University of Auckland, New Zealand. She is the author of *Women and Trade Unions: A Comparative Perspective* (Ashgate, 1999) and *Voicing the Vote of the Bush: Rural and Regional Representation in the Australian Federal Parliament* (Department Parliamentary Library, 2004) and coauthor of *Rebels with a Cause: Independents in Australian Politics* (UNSW Press, 2004). She has published numerous articles and chapters on women, politics, and policy, and she recently coedited a special issue of the *Australian Journal of Political Science* (June 2006) entitled "Globalising the Antipodes? Policy and Politics in Australia and New Zealand."

Andrea Fleschenberg is currently working as a research consultant on gender and politics in Afghanistan. She has been working, in 2007, as visiting professor at the University of the Punjab (Lahore, Pakistan). From 2003 to 2007, she was a research fellow at the University of Duisburg-Essen, a lecturer of comparative politics at the Universities of Cologne and Duisburg-Essen, and (in 2006) a visiting professor, International Masters Peace and Development Studies, University Jaume I, UNESCO Chair of Philosophy for Peace (Castellon, Spain). She is a member of the board of the German Asia Foundation and Watch Indonesia. Her recent publications include "Asia's Women Politicians at the Top—Roaring Tigresses or Tame Kittens?' (in *Women's Political Participation and Representation in Asia: Obstacles and Challenges*, edited by K. Iwanaga, NIAS Press, forthcoming) and "Elections in the 'New' Afghanistan. Commanders, 'Quota Women' and Missing Political Parties" (with C. Derichs, in German, in *ASIEN*, no. 98 [January 2006]).

Yvonne Galligan is reader in politics and director of the Centre for Advancement of Women in Politics at Queen's University Belfast. She is coeditor of *Sharing Power: Women, Parliament, Democracy* (with M. Tremblay, Ashgate, 2005). She is coauthor of "A Job in Politics Is Not for Women: Analysing Barriers to Women's Politics Representation in CEE" (with S. Clavero, *Czech Sociological Review*, 2005), "Measuring Gender Equality" (with E. Breitenbach, *Policy and Politics*, 2006), "Equalising Opportunities for Women in Electoral Politics in Ireland" (with K. Knight and U. N. G. Choille, *Women and Politics*, 2004), and *Gender Equality Indicators for Northern Ireland: A Discussion Document* (with E. Breitenbach, OFMDFM, 2004). She was Fulbright Scholar and Distinguished Scholar in Residence at the School of Public Affairs, American University, Washington, D.C., for 2005–2006.

Magda Hinojosa is assistant professor of political science at Arizona State University. She received her PhD from Harvard University in 2005. Before joining the faculty at Arizona State University, she was an assistant professor in the Political Science Department at Texas State University. She is currently working on a manuscript that assesses the effects of party candidate selection procedures on women's municipal representation in both Mexico and Chile. She was a visiting researcher at the Instituto Tecnológico Autónomo de México in Mexico City in 2003 and was a Fulbright-García Robles International Scholar in Mexico in the same year.

Dr. Gabriella Ilonszki works for the Institute of Political Science at Corvinus University of Budapest and heads the Elite Studies Centre there. Her research focuses on the working of parliamentary government and the role of elite groups in democratic politics, including the role of women politicians. Her English language publications most relevant to this volume include *Women in Parliamentary Politics. Hungarian and Slovene Cases Compared* (with Milica G. Antic; Peace Institute, 2003); "Weak Mobilization, Hidden Majoritarianism, and Resurgence of the Right: A Recipe for Female Under-Representation in Hungary" (with Kathleen Montgomery; in *Women's Access to Political Power in Post-Communist Europe*, edited by R. E. Matland and K. A. Montgomery, Oxford University Press, 2003, pp. 105–129); and "Women in Politics: The European Union and Hungary" (in *Changing Roles. Report on the Situation of Women and Men in Hungary*, edited by I. Nagy, T. Pongrácz, and I. Gy. Tóth, TÁRKI, 2005, pp. 57–69).

Joni Lovenduski is anniversary professor of politics at Birkbeck College, University of London. Her most recent published work on gender and politics includes *Feminizing Politics* (Polity Press, 2005), *State Feminism and Political Representation* (edited with Claudie Baudino, Maria Guadagnini, Petra Meier, and Diane Sainsbury, Cambridge University Press, 2005), *The Hansard Report on Women at the Top* (with Sarah Childs and Rosie Campbell, Hansard Society, 2005), and *Gender and Political Participation* (with Pippa Norris and Rosie Campbell, Electoral Commission, 2004). She is also the author of many articles and essays in edited collections on issues of gender and politics. Her current research is on gender and the state, including equality policy, political representation, and public policy debates.

Ian McAllister was professor of politics at the University of NSW from 1985 to 1996 and professor of government at the University of Manchester from 1996 to 1997. From 1997 to 2004 he was director of the Research School of Social Sciences at the Australian National University and is now professor of political science there. He is the coauthor of *How Russia Votes* (Chatham House, 1998) and *The Australian Electoral System* (UNSW Press, 2006) and coeditor of *The Cambridge Handbook of the Social Sciences in Australia* (Cambridge University Press, 2003). He is currently completing a book on the Northern Ireland conflict.

Petra Meier is assistant professor at the Department of Political Sciences at the University of Antwerp (Belgium), working especially in the fields of gender and politics (including electoral systems and their impact on women) and gender and equal opportunities policies. Since October 2003, she is also attached to the Politics Department at the Radboud University of Nijmegen (the Netherlands). She has published extensively on elected women and electoral systems, including "The Belgian Paradox: Inclusion and Exclusion of Gender Issues in Politics " (in *State Feminism and Political Representation*, edited by J. Lovenduski et al., Cambridge, 2006) and "The Contagion Effect of National Gender Quota on Similar Party Measures in the Belgian Electoral Process" (*Party Politics* 10, no. 3 [2004]). She is the coeditor of *Genre et science politique en Belgique et en Francophonie* (with B. Marques Pereira, Academia-Bruylant, 2005).

Marian Sawer is an adjunct professor in the School of Social Sciences at the Australian National University and chairs the International Political Science Association Research Committee on Gender, Politics and Policy. Her most recent books include *Us and Them: Anti-Elitism in Australia* (edited with B. Hindess, API Network, 2004) and *The Ethical State? Social Liberalism in Australia* (Melbourne University Press, 2003). Together with M. Tremblay and L. Trimble, she has been convening a four-country comparative project that was published by Routledge in 2006 under the title *Representing Women in Parliament: A Comparative Study*.

Gregory D. Schmidt is a professor of political science at the University of Texas at El Paso, where he serves as chair of the department. He also has taught at Northern Illinois University and several leading Peruvian universities. Professor Schmidt has published extensively on Peru in leading journals and for prestigious presses, focusing on development, decentralization, electoral rules and administration, executive-legislative relations, and gender. Among his publications are "All the President's Women: Fujimori and Gender Equity in Peruvian Politics" (in *The Fujimori Legacy: The Rise of Electoral Authoritarianism in Latin America*, edited by Julio Carrión, Pennsylvania State Press, pp. 150–177) and "Effective Quotas, Relative Party Magnitude, and the Success of Female Candidates: Peruvian Municipal Elections in Comparative Perspective" (*Comparative Political Studies* 37, no. 6 [2004]: 704–734, with Kyle L. Saunders).

Mariette Sineau is political scientist and research director at the Centre National de la Recherche Scientifique. Based in Paris, she works at Centre de Recherches Politiques de Sciences Po. Her main research fields are women's political behaviors and women politicians. Her work is also concerned with family policy and child care system. Her recent publications include *Profession: femme politique. Sexe et pouvoir sous la Cinquième République* (Presses de Sciences Po., 2001), *Genderware. The Council of Europe and the Participation of Women in Political Life* (Council of Europe Publishing, 2003), *Who Cares? Women's Work, Childcare, and Welfare State Redesign* (coauthored with Jane Jenson, University of Toronto Press, 2001), and "Candidats et députés français en 2002. Une approche sociale de la représentation" (with Vincent Tiberj, *Revue française de science politique*, 57, no. 2 [2007]: 163–185).

Donley T. Studlar is Eberly Family Distinguished Professor of Political Science at West Virginia University, where he teaches courses in comparative politics and public policy. Over the past 20 years his work on gender politics and electoral systems has been published in leading international journals and books, most recently *Representing Women in Parliament: A Comparative Study* (edited by M. Sawer, M. Tremblay, and L. Trimble, Routledge, 2006). Two of his contributions were awarded best paper prizes at the conferences where they were first presented. The author of an award-winning PhD dissertation, four books, and over 100 articles, he has served in various professional roles, including 11 years as executive secretary of the British Politics Group and on editorial boards for internationally oriented journals.

Manon Tremblay is professor at the School of Political Studies at the University of Ottawa. Her research interests are women and politics, electoral studies, the Canadian parliamentary regime, social movements and pressure politics, sexual identities and politics, as well as art and politics. She has extensively published in academic journals, notably *Australian Journal of Political Science, Canadian Journal of Political Science, Democratization, International Political Science Review, Journal of Commonwealth and Comparative Politics, Journal of Legislative Studies, Party Politics, Politics & Gender,* and *Political Science.* Her most recent publication is *Representing*

Women in Parliament: A Comparative Study (coedited with M. Sawer and L. Trimble, Routledge, 2006). She has been the French coeditor of the *Canadian Journal of Political Science* (2003–2006). She was honored with the Wilma Rule Award for the best paper on gender and politics at the 2006 International Political Science Association Congress (Fukuoka, Japan).

Celia Valiente is associate professor in the Department of Political Science and Sociology at Universidad Carlos III de Madrid. Her main research interests are gender-equality policies and the women's movement in Spain from a comparative perspective. Her most recent book is *Gendering Spanish Democracy* (with M. Threlfall and C. Cousins, Routledge, 2005). She has published articles in *Gender & Society, European Journal of Political Research*, and *South European Society & Politics* and has contributed chapters in *Women's Movements Facing the Reconfigured State* (edited by L. A. Banaszak, K. Beckwith, and D. Rucht, Cambridge University Press, 2003) and *State Feminism and Political Representation* (edited by J. Lovenduski et al., Cambridge University Press, 2005).

Introduction

Manon Tremblay

At the beginning of 2007, 17.2 percent of all members of the lower or single houses of some 190 national parliaments are women.[1] Thus, women's share of seats in parliament remains very much lower than that required for parity between the sexes. In fact, only two parliaments—those of Rwanda and Sweden—comprise almost an equal number of women and men. Although these countries clearly have very different cultural, socioeconomic, and political profiles, they have in common an important feature: proportional representation (PR) voting systems. For many years now, studies have identified the primary role that electoral systems play in ensuring a sizable proportion of women parliamentarians (Larserud and Taphorn 2007; Matland 2003; McAllister and Studlar 2002; Norris 1987: 123, 1997a, 2004: 187; Norris and Inglehart 2005; Paxton 1997; Reynolds, Reilly, and Ellis 2005: 60–61; Rule 1987, 1994a, 1994b; Rule and Norris 1992; Sawer 1997; Schwindt-Bayer and Mishler 2005). However, things are rarely so simple. The Inter-Parliamentary Union's figures also show that many countries using PR systems achieve only modest proportions of female legislators and, moreover, that many such countries are outperformed by those with majoritarian systems. In addition, more and more scholars argue that previous studies may have exaggerated the extent to which voting systems[2] can promote or hinder the achievement of a substantial presence of women in parliaments. Salmond (2006), for example, contends that "previous work has overstated, by factors of between two and three, how much of a difference an electoral system can make" (175). The relative influence of voting systems on the election of women remains a significant area of debate in the field of women and politics and is the reason for this book.

The overarching objective of *Women and Legislative Representation: Electoral Systems, Political Parties, and Sex Quotas* is to examine the effects of voting systems on the proportion of women in national parliaments, while also taking into account the roles of other variables (cultural, socioeconomic, and political). To do this, it examines 15 countries, which are divided among the three following electoral families: (1) plurality/majority systems: First Past the Post (FPTP), Single Nontransferable Vote (SNTV), Two-Round System (TRS) and Alternative Vote (AV) System; (2) PR systems: Closed List PR, Preferential (Open) List PR, and Single Transferable Vote (STV) systems; and finally (3) Mixed-Member (MM) systems: Proportional (MMP), Majoritarian with Partial Compensation, and Majoritarian (MMM) systems. More specifically, *Women and Legislative Representation* pursues three secondary objectives. First, the work aims to assess and explore the contention that PR systems favour women's entry into parliaments. This idea is widely taken for granted in works studying the election of women in politics. A critical examination involves identifying and evaluating the validity of effects that could create such a relationship, such as the hypothesis that closed lists encourage the election of women. It also requires us to assess the corollary argument that majority voting systems do not favour the election of women. Second, *Women and Legislative Representation* aims to evaluate the role of other variables—cultural, socioeconomic, and political—in women's election to parliamentary seats, with particular attention to both political parties and sex quotas. This secondary objective explores the idea that voting systems do not automatically determine the proportion of women in parliaments, but they do contribute to determining it, albeit in combination with other factors, notably political parties' demand for candidates and sex quotas. If voting systems concern interparty competition (i.e., the conversion of votes into seats in parliament and their allocation to the different parties), it is the political parties that are responsible for the intraparty competition (i.e., which candidates will sit in parliament). Further, when properly designed and implemented, sex quotas (legal and party quotas) may play a key role in the feminization of parliamentary arenas. The third and final objective of the work is to present relevant case studies.

In the following sections of this introduction, I will first develop the concept of representation and how it relates to voting systems. Second, I will review relevant literature on the factors influencing women's legislative representation, with special attention to electoral systems, political parties, and sex quotas. Third, I will describe the analytical framework used by the contributors in their case studies. Finally, I will explain the rationale for the choice of countries and outline the shared format in which all chapters are structured.

Political Representation and Electoral Systems

In her book, which nearly four decades after its release is still an authority on the subject, Pitkin (1967) distinguishes between four meanings of political representation: symbolic representation, which embodies an idea or an entity (e.g., a flag or a king represents the nation); formal representation, which refers to institutional rules and procedures by which representatives are designated (i.e., the electoral regulations and the voting system); descriptive representation, which refers to the similarities and differences between representatives and the represented; and substantive representation, which evokes the activities of representation (and more specifically the responsiveness of representatives to the represented). The present study is firmly anchored in the descriptive and formal conceptions of political representation, as they apply to women in parliamentary assemblies. It does not, therefore, attempt to examine what happens once women achieve access to political arenas (women's substantive representation).

In terms of descriptive representation, a legislative assembly is said to be representative if its makeup constitutes a miniaturized model or a microcosm of society. Consequently, it is argued that women are equal citizens and therefore should share, equally with men, public decision-making positions; otherwise, there is a representation deficit. While this is not a new view of representation, it has gathered momentum in recent years. If, historically, the discussion of political representation excluded women, today it is impossible to imagine it proceeding without addressing the political representation of women. In fact, the proportion of women in parliament is increasingly perceived as an indication of a state's quality of political representation.

Formal representation refers to the institutional rules and procedures through which representatives are chosen. The voting system, as the primary mechanism for this choice, is the process through which the will of the people is converted into seats in parliament (Farrell 2001: 4; Gallagher and Mitchell 2005a: 3). There are three basic types of electoral systems: plurality/majority (or majoritarian) systems, PR systems, and mixed systems (Massicotte and Blais 1999; Norris 2004: 41; Reynolds, Reilly and Ellis 2005: 27). Each type of electoral system is based on a particular concept of political representation. McLean (1991) suggests that voting systems be classified according to the distinction between the "microcosm" and "principal-agent" conceptions of representation. Lijphart (1984: 150) stresses the same point. PR systems find their ideological justification in the "microcosm" conception of representation. Such systems are intended to represent both the majority and the minorities proportionally translating party votes into party seats in parliament. Consequently, PR systems are those most likely to give rise to multiparty arrangements. By contrast, majoritarian systems, which are based on the "principal-agent" conception of representation, not only bestow victory on the majority while ignoring minorities, but they also give further power to the victorious party by accentuating its representation in parliament (to the detriment of other political groups). Such systems give rise to a smaller and less diverse range of parties than do PR systems. This is, of course, a general description; a closer look at the evidence reveals several nuances: some PR systems behave like majoritarian systems (in Hungary, for instance), while some majoritarian systems do allow for minority representation (for example, in India, where representation is supported by a system of reserved seats for members of depressed classes). Nevertheless, the general pattern illustrates a persistent conflict between principles of universality and particularity in political representation. Mixed systems, to borrow from the title of a book by Shugart and Wattenberg (2001a), are an attempt at bringing together the best of both worlds, although some writers, such as Sartori (1994), feel that they actually combine the weaknesses of the two contributing formulas (for a contrary opinion, see Shugart 2001). In any case, the choice of voting system is not neutral: in one sense, it corresponds with a conception of political representation while, in another, it determines how the people's will is represented in parliament.

The plurality single-seat constituency system (also called the FPTP system) is in some ways the basic electoral model: one individual is elected per constituency and this is the person who receives the greatest number of valid votes cast in her or his favour. The elector is granted only one vote and goes to the polls only once (a one-round system). This system is used in many countries, including Bangladesh, Canada, Great Britain, India, Malawi, Malaysia, Sudan, Uganda, and the United States. Plurality voting may also occur in multimember electoral districts (this is called the block vote [BV]). In this case, the elector is granted as many votes as there are seats to be filled,[3] and the winners are the candidates who receive the greatest numbers of votes in their favour in each electoral district. This formula is used in countries including Kuwait, the Lao People's Democratic Republic, Mauritius, Palestine, Tonga, and Tuvalu. The BV can also be implemented at the party level (as in Djibouti): the elector receives one vote to choose a party (not candidates) and the political party that receives the most votes wins all of the seats in the district. This is called the party block vote (PBV).

Some countries with majoritarian systems require an absolute majority (at least 50 percent plus one) of the valid votes cast in a district in order for a candidate to be declared the winner. At least two formulas exist. The first, the TRS, involves summoning the electorate to a second election if no absolute majority is obtained by any candidate in the first round. In the second round, one of two processes is used: the two candidates who received the most votes during the first election run against each other, the winner being the one who receives the absolute majority of valid votes cast (this, the runoff election, is the method used for presidential elections in France); alternatively, a few candidates selected according to the electoral rules compete again, the winner being the one who receives the most votes, but not necessarily an absolute majority (this process is used for the legislative elections in France and Hungary). The second absolute majority formula, the AV, asks the elector to rank candidates in order of preference. Once the first-preference votes are tallied, if no candidate has received an absolute majority of the valid votes cast, the second-choice votes for the least popular candidate are redistributed among the other candidates; this is repeated until one of them achieves an absolute majority. The election of the members of the House of Representatives in Australia is carried out in this fashion. Fiji and Papua New Guinea also use the AV. Except for the PBV, all plurality/majority systems require the elector to vote for one or more candidates and not for political parties.

Proportional representation is an attempt to match the proportion of seats assigned to a political party in the legislative assembly to the proportion of the valid votes cast for that party. Essentially, there are two types of proportional systems: STV—also called the Hare system, after its inventor, Thomas Hare— and the list proportional representation system (list PR). Under STV, the voter must rank all or some of the candidates whose names appear on the ballot in decreasing order of preference. In other words, the elector marks "1" on the ballot next to her or his favourite candidate, then, if required to do so, a "2" next to her or his second-choice candidate, and so on. This is typically a vote for an individual and not a party (although the party option is available for the Australian Senate and is used by more than 95 percent of electors). An electoral quota is established,[4] which determines the minimum number of valid votes required for a seat in the assembly. The ballot count initially considers each candidate's first-preference votes, and those who reach the quota are elected. If the first count does not fill all of the seats, additional counts are held that consider and allocate three types of votes: the first preference votes assigned to unelected candidates; the next preferences (second, third, fourth place votes, etc.) of ballots that gave higher preference to candidates already elected; and, finally, the next preferences of ballots that gave higher preference to any candidate eliminated because she or he received the lowest number of votes in a given round[5] (for an excellent description of the STV calculation process, see Farrell 2001: 121–152; Gallagher and Mitchell 2005b: 593–596). This procedure continues until all the seats are assigned. Ireland and Malta used the STV, as does the Australian Senate.

List PR is the most common procedure used in proportional representation systems. In this procedure a country is either designated as a single electoral district (Israel and the Netherlands) or divided into several multimember districts. On polling day, the voter selects one of the lists created by the political parties in the race (as in Costa Rica and South Africa) or one or more candidates whose names appear on the lists (as in Brazil, Finland, and Indonesia). In other words, the lists may be open (vote for a candidate) or closed (vote for a party), so that the voter may or may not have the option of changing the order of names determined by the parties.[6] Seats are assigned to political parties according to various procedures (there are two main categories of electoral formula, the highest average method and the largest remainders method[7]) and then to candidates according to their ranking on the list.[8] To avoid proliferation of parties represented in parliament, list PR systems usually impose a threshold for representation. This threshold is the minimum proportion of valid votes required for a political party to win a seat in parliament (for instance, 5 percent of the national vote in Germany). A wide array of countries in all regions (with the exception of Oceania and the Pacific islands) use the list PR system.

Apart from plurality/majority and PR systems, a third variety of voting system has recently gained popularity in the electoral sphere: the mixed system. Bolivia, Germany, Italy, Japan, Lesotho, Macedonia, Mexico, New Zealand, Russia, Senegal, and Venezuela are among the countries that use the Mixed-Member System. Essentially, this hybrid electoral formula pursues two ideals: stable effective government (a characteristic of the majority governments typically formed in plurality/majority systems) and sociodemographic representation in parliament (a characteristic of PR). The typical MM System operates as follows: one portion of the seats in the legislative assembly is allotted by plurality/majority representation (usually FPTP) and the other portion by the PR system (usually by list PR in multimember districts). The voter has two ballot papers, one for the majoritarian tier and the other for the PR tier, in order to elect representatives who will sit in the same legislative assembly.

In terms of the plurality/majority tier, usually the candidate who receives a simple plurality of the valid votes cast in her or his district is declared the winner after only one round. This is the case in Mexico, New Zealand, and Thailand, for example. Sometimes, however, the requirements are more demanding and the election continues into a second round, in which the candidate who receives the absolute majority (in a runoff, as in Georgia) or a plurality (as in Hungary) is elected. While the PR tier is most often in lists (usually closed), sometimes there are no lists, and the seats are assigned by the parties to their highest-polling unsuccessful candidates, or "best losers" in the majoritarian tier. This list may be national (as in New Zealand) or by electoral district (as in Mexico).

While MM systems combine the principles of majority and proportional representation to elect the members of the legislative assembly, the assigning of seats may or may not take into consideration the interaction of these principles. Mixed-Member systems are known as compensatory when the distribution of seats in one tier (usually the proportional tier) depends on the parties' gains in the other tier (usually the majoritarian one). This is the case in Bolivia, Germany, New Zealand, and Venezuela. MM systems in which the distribution of seats in both tiers is carried out in an independent manner are known as parallel. This is the case, for example, in Armenia, Japan, Monaco, Russia, and Ukraine. These two approaches result in different distributions of seats in the assembly: the compensatory method favours the proportional principle, while the parallel method favours the majority principle. Usually, a party must win a minimum proportion of the valid votes cast to participate in the distribution of seats in the PR tier. Although this threshold is generally set at 4–5 percent on a national scale (such as in New Zealand, where the threshold is 5 percent unless a party has won one constituency member), it ranges greatly across countries. If the threshold is too low the government's efficiency could be endangered, and if the threshold is too high "wasted votes" will accumulate, depriving large segments of the electorate of legislative representation. The selection of an electoral threshold does not adhere to strict norms but is rather determined on a case-by-case basis (Lijphart 1994: 149). Another form of the mixed system provides for any party to participate in the distribution of seats in the PR tier as long as the party achieves the election of a certain minimum number of candidates to the majoritarian tier, notwithstanding the level of electoral support earned on the national level. This is the case in Germany (where the minimum is three candidates) and in New Zealand (where the minimum is one). This is, however, only a brief overview: electoral engineers have developed an extensive range of principles and procedures to ensure that their creations will thrive (see Ferrara, Herron, and Nishikawa 2005; Shugart and Wattenberg 2001a).

In short, there is a large range of mechanisms through which the people select their parliamentary elite. This spectrum can be organized into three main categories: plurality/majority systems, PR systems, and MM systems. As previously mentioned, each electoral system is based on a conception of political representation, which is expressed in the actual makeup of the parliamentary assemblies. Thus, analysis of the proportion of women parliamentarians in 88 free countries in 2005, based on the Freedom House's Gastil index, reveals that the average proportion of lower-or single-house representatives who are women is 10.8 percent in plurality/majority systems, 17.7 percent in MM systems, and 21.1 percent in PR systems (see also Norris 1997a, 2004: 187). In other words, legislative assemblies that are derived from a PR system include proportionally twice as many women as parliaments elected through a plurality/majority system.

Review of the Literature

How can we explain the apparently disadvantageous impact of plurality/majority single-seat systems on the election of women? In these voting systems, each political party designates one—and only one—person per electoral district, unlike in list PR systems in which every party nominates several names per district. At the point of candidate selection in a plurality/majority single-seat constituency system, the aspiring candidate is assessed as an individual and not as a member of a team (such as a candidate list).

Consequently, the local party association selects the aspiring legislator who it perceives to be the median candidate—in other words, the candidate it thinks is the most broadly acceptable to the largest number of voters. Not all candidatures are equally assessed in this process, given that an informal model of the "winning candidate" guides the selectorates (i.e., the small group of local party activists) when making their choice. According to Norris and Lovenduski (1989), this informal model, which they call "homo politicus," disadvantages women (see also Carroll 1994: 158–159 for the United States; Sineau 2001: 45–56 for France; Studlar and McAllister 1991 for Australia; Reynolds, Reilly, and Ellis 2005: 37, 61, more generally).

While PR systems are generally more favourable to the election of women, this pattern is not universal, as illustrated by Inter-Parliamentary Union data collected from over 190 countries. Analysis of those countries ranked highest for the proportion of women in lower or single houses reveals that, although most countries with at least 25 percent women parliamentarians have a PR system, many countries that fall below this level also use PR systems to elect their parliamentarians. This is the case, for example, in Chile (where, incidentally, many political parties use quotas), Colombia, Israel, Poland, and Portugal, among others. In terms of STV, Galligan (2005; see also Engstrom 1987; Rule 1996) argues that this system does not favour women's access to the Irish Daíl. Others argue that, in fact, list PR is the method most likely to contribute to the election of women to parliaments, because parties benefit from offering their electorate lists that are sociodemographically and ideologically diverse (Matland 2003; Norris 1987: 129).

Other elements of PR systems also support the election of women. The threshold of representation is the most powerful tool with which voting procedures can influence proportionality (Lijphart 1994: 139). When set at a relatively high level, the threshold reduces the number of parties between which parliamentary seats are shared, giving each party more seats. Parties can therefore assign more seats to women, whether voluntarily (i.e., to balance its representation) or mechanically (because the number of seats to be filled reaches further down the list to where female candidates are often placed; Mateo Diaz 2005: 87–93; Matland 2003, 2005).[9] Many studies have shown that district magnitude, the other mechanism responsible for a PR voting system's degree of proportionality, also influences women's ability to be elected: the more seats there are to fill in an electoral district—and, especially, the more a party can hope to win—the stronger are women's chances of entering parliament (Engstrom 1987; Matland 1993; Matland and Brown 1992; Reynolds, Reilly, and Ellis 2005: 121; Rule 1987; Studlar and Welch 1991). According to Rule and Norris (1992), a district must have seven or more representatives (with preferential vote) in order to constitute an electoral context that is favourable to women. Moreover, a high proportionality of seats to votes contributes to a higher proportion of women MPs (Farrell 2001: 157–159, 166; Norris 1992; but see Caul Kittilson 2006: 127).

If several studies find that PR systems produce assemblies with a higher proportion of women than do plurality/majority systems, many also present a more complicated view of the association, too frequently assumed, between PR and a substantial presence of women in parliaments (Beckwith 1992; Darcy, Welch, and Clark 1994: 147; Kunovich and Paxton 2005; Mateo Diaz 2005: 51, 81; Norris 1992). Indeed, voting systems do not act independently of their contexts; how else could we explain parliaments formed through the same voting system that show different proportions of women lawmakers, or the fact that the percentage of women in any given parliament varies across time even if the voting system remains constant? This is the critical perspective subscribed to in the present work. Of course, the intrinsic features of voting systems have the potential to affect the proportion of women parliamentarians. But voting systems interact with a wide array of cultural, socioeconomic, and political factors, creating an entire dynamic that influences the feminization of parliaments.

In fact, studies have shown that a range of factors influence women's access to legislative arenas. These factors can be grouped into three broad categories: cultural, socioeconomic, and political. While such categorisation simplifies analysis, these factors actually combine and overlap in influencing women's access to power. They therefore pose a problem in terms of causality: do cultural factors precede socioeconomic, and political factors, or is it the opposite? For example, must there first be a culture of gender equality before women in large numbers can access legal careers and achieve economic independence, which are both major advantages in stepping into the political arena? Because such questions remain unresolved, it is probably more instructive to assume that cultural, socioeconomic, and political factors interact to create a dynamic that acts as a global incubator for the election of women.

Culture refers to the values, standards, beliefs, and attitudes that underpin a society and its institutions and that animate the population's ways of being, talking, and doing. Religion, education, and views of gender-based social roles are the primary cultural factors identified as determinants of the proportion of women in parliaments. Generally, Protestantism as dominant religion (as opposed to other religions), women's access to university education, and egalitarian gender roles are variables positively associated with women's access to parliaments (Norris 1985, 1997b; Norris and Inglehart 2001; Nowacki 2003; Paxton 1997; Peschard 2003; Reynolds 1999; Rule 1987; Saint-Germain 1994). Moreover, Inglehart and Norris (2003: 140–141), Mateo Diaz (2005: 64), and Paxton and Kunovich (2003) have all shown that culture, especially a conception of equality between women and men, is a more influential variable than voting systems in determining the proportion of women in parliaments.

Despite the apparent importance of cultural factors, a quick glance at the Inter-Parliamentary Union data on women in parliaments encourages us to be cautious in analysing the impact of culture—and particularly of traditional or egalitarian conceptions of gender roles—on the feminization of parliament. In terms of the proportion of single or lower-house members who are women, Afghanistan, Burundi, and Rwanda, societies where Catholicism and Islam dominate, are ahead of Australia, France, and Great Britain, societies where the idea of equality between women and men enjoys support from the general public (Inglehart and Norris 2003: 29–48). It must be noted, however, that Afghanistan and Rwanda have constitutional quotas to promote women's access to parliament, and Burundi uses a system of list PR (with quotas), while Australia, France, and Great Britain all use plurality/majority system known to be less favourable to the election of women. Moreover, the cases of Afghanistan, Rwanda, and Iraq brilliantly demonstrate that institutional strategies (i.e., quotas) can be justified not only in terms of basic justice but also to overcome the hostility of the population toward the political participation of women.

Socioeconomic factors shape the conditions that lead women to envision careers in politics. As Norris and Lovenduski (1995: 14–15) note, we are talking here about the supply of candidates. One theory is that if there are only a few women in politics, it is because women are underrepresented in the milieus where parties identify and recruit their potential candidates (Darcy, Welch, and Clark 1994: 104–105). An improvement in women's socioeconomic conditions should therefore favour an increase in their presence in parliaments. Variables considered in this category include the type of society (agricultural, industrial, or postindustrial), the Human Development Index, the birth rate, the proportion of women in the labour market, the female/male revenue ratio, the per capita GNP, public expenditure on education and healthcare, and the urbanization rate. Studies show that the proportion of women in parliaments is positively influenced by factors such as participation in the labour market (particularly in specialized employment), a high Human Development Index, a postindustrial society, and a developed welfare state (Matland 1998a, 2005; Moore and Shackman 1996; Norris 1985, 1987: 122, 2004: 186; Oakes and Almquist 1993; Reynolds 1999; Rosenbluth, Salmond, and Thies 2006; Rule 1987, 1988; Siaroff 2000; United Nations Office at Vienna 1992: 30–31).

Once again, the data collected by the Inter-Parliamentary Union suggest that a nuanced approach is required when analyzing the contribution of socioeconomic factors to the parliamentary representation of women: Mozambique (34.8 percent), South Africa (32.8 percent), the Seychelles Islands (29.4 percent), Guyana (29 percent), or even Namibia (26.9 percent), countries devoid of socioeconomic privilege, outdo G8 member countries such as the United Kingdom (19.7 percent), the United States (16.3 percent), France (12.2 percent), and Japan (9.4 percent) when it comes to the feminization of their parliaments. Again, the unexpectedly higher representation of women in the former group may partly be explained by the presence of quotas (both legislative and party based), measures to which their Western counterparts seem allergic.[10] The influence of socioeconomic factors proves to be very unstable, to the extent that this influence is often crushed under the weight of other variables in multivariate analysis (Inglehart and Norris 2003: 140; Kenworthy and Malami 1999; Norris and Inglehart 2001; Paxton 1997).

Political factors shape the demand for candidates. More specifically, these factors influence the selection (that is, the choice of which citizens from the "eligible pool" will contest the election) and election of candidates. In terms of women's representation, political factors belong to two dimensions: the political rights of women and the political regime. The first dimension refers to the political citizenship of women. It is primarily measured by the year women achieved the right to vote in national legislative elections. A large number of studies have demonstrated a connection between this measure and the proportion of women in parliaments (Kenworthy and Malami 1999; Mateo Diaz 2005: 67; McAllister and Studlar 2002; Norris 2004: 186; Siaroff 2000; United Nations Office at Vienna 1992: 99). Unfortunately, few variables have been developed to understand the specific mechanisms by which the political rights of women affect the proportion of women in parliaments. However, many aspects of women's political rights may influence women's presence in parliaments. These include the year women won the right to run for office in a national election, the year the first woman was elected to parliament and the year a woman joined government for the first time, whether a woman has already held the position of president or premier, and so on.

Unlike the political rights of women, the political regime (the second dimension of political factors discussed here) has received extensive attention from researchers. Here, researchers have drawn on a wide range of variables to explore the impact of the political regime on the proportion of women parliamentarians. These variables include the structure of parliament (the number of seats and the maximum term of a legislature), the nature of the legislative career (the "turnover rate" of legislators), the party system (the number of parties contesting elections, the number of effective parliamentary parties, the ideology of the parties that form the government, how candidates are selected, and so on), and obviously the electoral system itself (the type of voting system, the district magnitude, the nature of the lists—closed, open or free, and so on). Matland (2003) as well as Oakes and Almquist (1993) and Antić (2003) support the idea that the number of seats plays a role in the proportion of women in parliaments. A low turnover rate of MPs has long been identified as an obstacle for women's access to legislative assemblies (Andersen and

Thorson 1984; Darcy and Choike 1986; Schwindt-Bayer 2005). Norris and Inglehart (2001; see also Norris 1992) believe that parliaments where many parties are represented offer female candidates more possibilities to be elected than bipartisan parliaments. Political formations tending toward the Left and Centre on the ideological spectrum offer better possibilities for women wishing to obtain a seat in parliament than do Right-tending ones, particularly where parties of the dominant ideological position form the government (Caul 1999, 2001; Caul Kittilson 2006: 60–66; Mateo Diaz 2005: 76; Siaroff 2000). If quotas appear to have a direct and immediate impact on the feminization of parliaments, it is important to note that many criteria must be present for quotas to achieve their objectives. For example, they must preempt resistance by mandating a gender-sensitive order for classifying candidates on lists and by imposing penalties for offences against the law (Dahlerup 2006a; Htun and Jones 2002; Mateo Diaz 2005: 76–80; Matland 2006; Peschard 2003).

The role that parties play in the election of women to parliaments has been the subject of many studies, which is not surprising since they are the true superintendents of the parliamentary representation of women. According to Matland and Montgomery (2003a: 31–32), "The electoral system directly effects [*sic*] female legislative representation, because it shapes the recruitment strategies of party gatekeepers at the nomination phase." In other words, the voting system shapes parties' strategies for selecting candidates. This perspective is endorsed by Farrell (2001: 167), who argues that "it is not the electoral system which is at fault [for the underrepresentation of women in parliaments] so much as the party selection committees" (see also Gallagher 2005; Norris, Carty, Erickson, Lovenduski, and Simms 1990). Here, the argument is that the feminization of parliaments depends less on the voting system than on the will of political parties to feminize their parliamentary ranks, as Maurice Duverger noted in his early work *The Political Role of Women*, published more than 50 years ago, in 1955. More recently, Caul Kittilson (2006) has convincingly documented this idea.

In almost all electoral systems, it is the parties and not the electorate that control the selection of candidates—and therefore the composition of parliaments. However, the nature of the control that the parties exercise over the selection of candidates varies greatly according to the voting procedure and its particular characteristics (Carey and Shugart 1995; Gallagher and Marsh 1988; see the case studies in Norris 1997c). In terms of proportional representation, closed lists and lists without preferential voting give political parties absolute control over the composition of parliament, as opposed to open lists with preferential voting (and *panachage*) in which the voters play a role in designating the people, and not only the parties, who will represent them. There is, however, no consensus as to which list (closed or open) best fosters the election of women (for closed lists, see Htun and Jones 2002; Matland and Montgomery

2003a; for open lists, see Caul Kittilson 2006: 106, 116–117, 132; Rule 1994a; Rule and Norris 1992; Rule and Shugart 1995; Schmidt 2003a; Siemieńska 2003). In the STV system, parties have indirect (in other words, preliminary) control over the composition of parliament: female and male candidates must obtain endorsement from the party for which they are campaigning, but votes for endorsed candidates are preferential votes entrusted by the electorate to the individual. These votes, and not the ranking established by the parties, will therefore determine who will hold a seat in parliament. The few countries that use an STV system (notably Ireland and Malta) show low proportions of women in their parliaments (Galligan 2005; Hirczy 1995; Lane 1995; Rule 1996).[11] As for plurality/majority representation, the American system of primaries does not confer any power on the parties to select candidates for Congress, while the Australian and British[12] parties firmly hold the reins of the candidate selection process. Women may benefit from having a standardized and centralized selection process, as this would allow national elites to more easily adopt positive affirmative measures and quotas (Caul 1999; Matland and Studlar 1996; Norris 1992; Randall 1982: 141–142). Furthermore, a standardized and centralized process of selection enables the women's movement to more easily pressure political parties to select women as candidates.

Many studies have brought to light how important it is for the women's movement to mobilize in the electoral sphere if the number of women parliamentarians is to increase (see the case studies in Lovenduski et al. 2005). As Matland (2003) notes, any group that aspires to parliamentary representation must mobilize in the electoral sphere. This is especially crucial "for those groups that are important within the parties, but are not at the centre of power" (p. 333). Rule (1987) goes so far as to argue that this kind of mobilization can be a counterweight to the resistance of certain voting systems to the election of women: "Negative electoral system features have been overcome by women's political mobilization" (p. 495). Caul (1999; see also Caul Kittilson 2006: 60–66) has shown that the mobilization of women within party structures can have positive effects on the legislative representation of women, although Tremblay and Pelletier (2001) document a less straightforward relationship. Outside of parties, Paxton, Hughes and Green (2006) have revealed that the mobilization of the women's movement on the international scene and global pressure in favour of women's access to political representation are important variables in explaining the growing feminization of legislative arenas around the world.

Analytical Framework

From the literature review presented here, the following analytical framework emerges. Figure 0.1 presents the analytical framework that guides each of the contributors in their case studies in this book. Its objective is

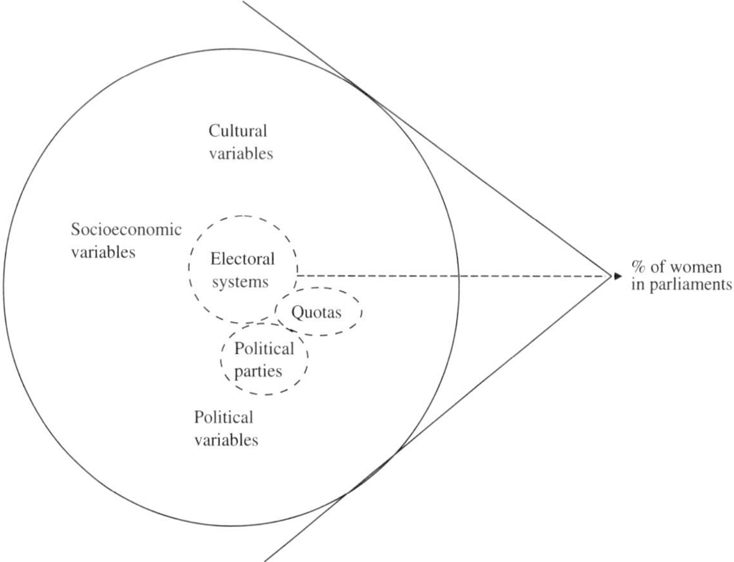

Figure 0.1   The global dynamic influencing the proportion of women in national parliaments

twofold: first, to schematize and summarize the dynamic created by the many factors that influence the percentage of women in parliaments; and, second, to emphasize the central role that electoral systems play in this dynamic (a role widely recognized in previous studies) while also considering the contribution of political parties and sex quotas. Thus, the analytical framework postulates that the presence of women in parliaments is not the product of one isolated variable—not even such an influential variable as the voting system. Electoral systems do not act in isolation; instead, they interact with a host of cultural, socioeconomic, and political variables to create a global dynamic that in turn influences the proportion of women in legislative assemblies.

In more technical terms:

- the dependent variable (or the phenomenon to be explained) is the proportion of women legislators;
- the independent (or explanatory) variables refer to cultural, socioeconomic and political factors. These three groups of factors are taken from the literature review given earlier. Cultural factors include, among others, the female literacy rate; the proportion of women enrolled in tertiary education; gender role values (traditional or egalitarian); and

religion. Socioeconomic factors include, for example, the Human Development Index; the gender empowerment index; the fertility rate; gross domestic product per capita; the level of poverty; the rate of female economic activity rate as a percentage of the male rate; the ratio of female to male earned income; the percentage of all professional and technical workers who are female; the urban population as a percentage of the whole; the level of public expenditure on education and health; and so on. Political factors refer to both the state framework of governance and the achievements of women in politics. The former encompasses indicators such as the structure of the state (unitary or federal); the structure of the national legislature (e.g., the number of houses, the maximum term of the legislature, and the number of seats in the lower or single house); the party system (e.g., the effective number of electoral and parliamentary parties); the conditions of candidacy (whether a monetary deposit is required for candidacies; whether candidates' campaign costs are subsidized); and electoral turnout. Variables referring to the political achievements of women include the year women secured the right to vote and to stand for national elections; the year the first woman was elected to the lower or single house; and whether there has ever been a woman head of state (as president) or chief of government (as prime minister).

This analytical framework preserves a place for the electoral system that recognizes its special status, as established by the broad consensus emerging from studies that have examined the impact of this variable on the percentage of women legislators. This special status is conveyed by the central position occupied by the electoral system in the model, presented, as it is, in the middle of the constellation of independent variables. This preponderant influence on the feminization of parliaments is expressed by the extending dotted line that indicates the dependent variable. This line is also intended to convey the fact that, although the voting system exercises a major influence on the feminization of parliament, this role is not divorced from the wider societal context in which it is anchored. In this perspective, the analytical framework highlights the contribution of two variables intimately connected to voting systems that also exercise an influence on the number of women parliamentarians: political parties and sex quotas. These variables appear as dotted lines adjacent to the voting system, in order to express the relationships through which they are intimately related. Thus, the proportion of women in parliaments ought to be seen as an interactive function of electoral systems, political parties, and sex quotas as well as a host of cultural, socioeconomic, and political variables. In addition, electoral systems in themselves constitute a very complex universe; their impact on the election of women depends on their specifics (such as the level of proportionality, the number of electoral districts, district magnitude, whether the party list is closed or open, the electoral threshold, the electoral formula—d'Hondt, Hare, or St. Laguë, etc.), and so on. For example, electoral rules that favour a high party magnitude are likely to assist in the election of women. Therein lies a major contribution of this work: its focus on these details of electoral systems in order to identify which ones influence the election of women, and how. Finally, the dotted circle around "electoral systems" indicates that this variable is not only immersed in a wider context of cultural, socioeconomic, and political variables, but that these variables and the voting system interact to create an overall dynamic that affects the access of women to parliaments. The solid lines connecting the circle created by all the independent variables to the dependent variable illustrate this holistic effect.

This, therefore, is the general analytical framework that I proposed to the contributors of this book. The model entails qualitative rather than quantitative analysis; it does not intend to establish statistical relationships between variables. The strength of this analytical framework is its flexibility. In theory, it includes the whole range of independent variables that influence the proportion of women in parliaments. However, not all of these variables are relevant in every case study. For example, the female literacy rate is certainly not a significant variable in explaining the level of feminization of the French Assemblée nationale or the British House of Commons. It was left to contributors, based on their own electoral expertise and in-depth knowledge of the country they were studying, to draw from this analytical framework the variables they judged to be relevant to their case study. However, one variable, the voting system, was included in every study, given the purpose of the book and the central place that this variable occupies in the analytical framework. Consequently, the case studies presented in this book do not systematically use the same independent variables; all, however, take the voting system (as well as political parties and sex quotas) into account. In sum, the analytical framework designed for this book provides a flexible approach to discovering how a dynamic constituted by an array of cultural, socioeconomic, and political variables, dominated by the voting system, determines the percentage of female parliamentarians.

Case Studies and Structure of the Chapters

This book analyzes the impact of voting systems on women's legislative representation in 15 countries whose systems are divided between the three aforementioned electoral families: plurality/majority systems, PR systems, and mixed systems. Each electoral family takes up a section of the book.

Four criteria were used in the selection of countries for inclusion in this book. The first criterion applied was the type of electoral system: it was important to cover the broadest possible spectrum of voting systems. Thus, the majoritarian systems covered are: First-Past-the-Post, Single Nontransferable Vote, Second Ballot, and Alternative Vote. The section on PR systems includes case studies of Closed Lists, Preferential [Open] List, and Single Transferable Vote systems. Finally, the cases of Mixed-Member systems were selected to represent Mixed-Member Proportional, Majoritarian, and Majoritarian with Partial Compensation. The second criterion was that of geographic diversity. Since the issue of women's presence in parliaments is now on the international agenda, and in order to free the book from the restrictive Western and Northern perspective to which too many works are confined, it was important to ensure a broad representation of countries across all continents. The third criterion, intimately connected to the preceding one, was to ensure that the countries selected reflected cultural, socioeconomic, and political diversity. Finally, the fourth criterion is that countries were selected to include several typical cases. For example, Ireland is one of the rare countries that uses STV and Afghanistan SNTV; Mexico has sex quotas that apply to the PR tier, of course, but also to the constituency tier, which is quite rare. The remainder of this section lays out the rationale under which each country was selected.

The section on majoritarian systems discusses six countries. In the first group of countries are the plurality systems, some of which use single-seat constituencies (Uganda, the United Kingdom, and the United States of America), while others use multimember districts (Afghanistan, where the SNTV is in effect). In the other group are the majority systems, used in France (the TRS) and Australia (where the members of the House of Representatives are elected by the AV). Spread across several continents, the countries covered in this section exhibit a wide range of cultural conditions (for example, varying attitudes to gender equality and materialist/postmaterialist values) and socioeconomic positions (for instance, Afghanistan has an agricultural economy while four other of the countries are G8 members). Some countries are well-established democracies while others are developing democracies. In addition, four of these countries (Afghanistan, France, Uganda, and the United Kingdom) have specific mechanisms in place to encourage the election of women to parliament. As of February 2007, the proportion of women parliamentarians varies between 12.2 percent (France) and 29.8 percent (Uganda).

Each of these countries also has particular characteristics that warrant closer study as part of this book. Uganda has a reserved seats policy for women. In the United Kingdom, after the Labour Party's all-women shortlists policy was deemed discriminatory, the Labour government brought in legislation permitting positive discrimination in the selection of parliamentary candidates. The United States uses an electoral system with several characteristics judged to be negative for the election of women, such as a very strong two-party system and a low turnover rate of representatives. Afghanistan and Australia use the SNTV and the AV, respectively, voting systems that are little seen elsewhere in the world. Finally, France has adopted a law on female/male parity in political representation (requiring a 50/50 quota of candidates), which has had extremely disappointing results in feminizing the Assemblée nationale.

The five case studies in the second section of the book—PR cases—are divided into two categories: first, closed-list PR voting systems (two countries), and second, preferential (open) list PR systems and STV (three countries). The countries using the closed-list PR can be found on two continents and offer significant cultural, socioeconomic, and political diversity. Both are equipped with specific measures to increase the proportion of women parliamentarians (i.e., party quotas), which explains in part—but only in part, as shown by many chapters in this book—their high proportions of women legislators (between 32.8 percent and 36 percent). South Africa clearly illustrates the important role played by the mobilization of the women's movement in securing the presence of women in the legislative institutions of a new regime. And, as in South Africa, the progress made in Spain shows what a sympathetic political party can accomplish for the legislative representation of women.

Countries using preferential (open) list PR voting systems and STV can be found in South America and Europe. Two of the countries covered in this section are long-standing democracies while the other is a more recent one. In this group, which is also made up of very culturally, socioeconomically, and politically diverse countries, the proportion of women parliamentarians (varying between 13.3 percent and 34.7 percent) is generally more modest than in the closed-list PR voting systems group. Ireland and Peru are interesting for reason of their use of open lists. More specifically, Ireland is an important case because of its STV system, the effects of which on the proportion of women in parliaments remain little understood. Belgium is equipped with a legal quota to increase the proportion of women parliamentarians, but it also seems that the feminization of the lower house has been affected by other unexpected developments within voting system itself.

The third and final section of the book deals with Mixed-Member systems. Two countries (Mexico and New Zealand) belong to the MMP voting systems category, one (Japan) to the MMM systems category, and one (Hungary) is considered to be in the MMM system category with partial compensation (using votes instead of seats to link the tiers and make the proportion of seats held by a party in parliament reflects the proportion of votes received by that party; Ferrara, Herron, and Nishikawa 2005: 23). Spread across four continents, the countries in this last section also show great cultural, socioeconomic and political diversity. The proportion of women legislators varies between 9.4 percent and 32.2 percent. Only two of the countries in this section (Hungary and Mexico) have measures designed to improve the proportion of women in parliament. Mexico is particularly significant as its legal quota for women in politics is a unique case in North America. The electoral system change that New Zealand has experienced from 1993 to 1996 renders this country an unavoidable case in any study of women's representation and voting systems. In addition, in New Zealand, the MMP system has not assisted the legislative representation of women as much as certain theoretical analyses had promised. Hungary has one of the most complex voting systems in the world, making it important to analyse the effects of this system on women's access to the Orszaggyules. Finally, the case of Japan illustrates the importance (maybe even the precedence) of cultural variables over socioeconomic and political factors in understanding the proportion of women in parliaments.

Analysis of each of the countries examined in this work shares a common format of four sections, in addition to the introductions and conclusions:

- *Description of the voting system*: The objective of this section is to describe the voting system used to elect members to the lower or single house of the national parliament. In each chapter this section is intended to outline the rules of the electoral game through which women are elected to parliament;
- *Analysis of the evolution of the proportion of women legislators*: The second section, which deals with the dependent variable in the analytical model underpinning this work, is intended to sketch out the evolution of women's presence in the lower or single house of each national parliament since World War II. In doing so, these accounts demonstrate that countries with similar voting systems can have very different proportions of women parliamentarians;
- *Analysis of the impact of the voting system on women's legislative representation*: This section is intended to identify how the voting system influences the proportion of women in the lower or single house of the national parliament. The voting system is the variable at the heart of the analytical framework that guides this book. These analyses scrutinize the various characteristics of each voting system that might explain the proportion of women parliamentarians;
- *Analysis of other variables that might influence the percentage of women in legislature*: The last section of each chapter elucidates the fundamental idea on which this work is based: that voting systems do not act

mechanically or in isolation to determine the proportion of women in parliaments. Rather, their effects combine with the effects of a range of societal factors acting together. As previously shown, the research results carried out to date on the determining factors in the election of women help to separate these factors into three broad categories: cultural, socioeconomic, and political (the political rights of women and the political regime). This section gives particular attention to both political parties and sex quotas.

Women and Legislative Representation is an important contribution in the field of electoral studies as well as gender/women's studies for several reasons. First, since the 1990s, under the momentum created by several events (such as the adoption of the Beijing Platform in 1995), and responding to pressure from several international and regional organizations (such as the United Nations and the Southern African Development Community) as well as women's movements, many countries have adopted new electoral rules to satisfy the requirements of representative democracy, while others thoroughly revisited their electoral systems. One of the objectives sought by these reforms was to establish parliaments that reflected more closely the profile of the community. In this context, there was a call for an increased presence of women in parliaments. Hence, this book seeks to understand a profound political shift, that of the democratization of political regimes, through the particular perspective of female representation in parliaments. In addition, this book provides those who are interested in constitutional and electoral design the tools they need to understand key features of voting systems and the potential impact of these on women's access to parliamentary representation. The other volumes currently available on constitutional and electoral engineering either completely ignore the representation of women or discuss women in a "sociodemographic representation in parliament" section, implying that women (half of the human species) are just a minority group.

Second, this book is important because it evaluates the idea that PR systems are women-friendly. Too frequently, studies present this idea as an authoritative argument, thus obscuring the fact that many countries with PR systems have low proportions of female legislators. This idea has become a kind of dogma that is unthinkingly repeated to explain the level of women's legislative representation, in a similar way to that in which critical mass is presented as a precursor to the substantive representation of women. The latter idea, however, is increasingly questioned (see the "Critical Perspectives on Gender and Politics" section in *Politics & Gender*, December 2006). This book calls for a more nuanced approach to the contribution of PR systems to the feminization of parliaments and sheds light on the particular characteristics of PR that are most likely to render parliaments women friendly.

Third, this book is important because it revisits the questions considered by *Electoral Systems in Comparative Perspective: Their Impact on Women and Minorities* (Westport, Connecticut: Westview Press), edited by Wilma Rule and Joseph F. Zimmerman in 1994. Rule and Zimmerman's text is an authoritative work on the impact of voting systems on the presence of women in parliaments. Considering the speed and complexity of the changes brought about by electoral engineering in the last ten years, however, *Electoral Systems in Comparative Perspective* is now outdated and, until now, no other text has sought to replace it.

Although many articles have been published in scholarly journals on the factors influencing women's access to parliamentary representation, unlike those articles the chapters included here share a common analytical framework. Herein lies one of the original contributions of this work. The study of different cases using a common analytical framework allows for parameters that promote consistency in analysis from one case to another. Another original contribution of *Women and Legislative Representation* is that it considers countries on all continents that are very diverse in cultural, socioeconomic, and political terms. Too often, comparative works concentrate on Northern and Western countries, neglecting Southern and Eastern ones. The sad consequence of this narrow perspective is that initiatives undertaken in these Southern or Eastern areas to increase the proportion of women in parliament have too often escaped the attention of Western readers.

One final word: *Women and Legislative Representation* acknowledges the remarkable work of Professor Wilma Rule, a pioneer and a dedicated scholar in the field of "women and electoral systems." For several years, she was the only specialist to study the impact of voting systems on women's legislative representation. Today, her work is highly respected by scholars of electoral reform. Professor Rule left us in January 2004. This book is dedicated to her memory.

Notes

* I wish to thank Gretchen Bauer and Sarah Childs for their helpful comments. I would also like to thank Merrindahl Andrew (Australian National University) for her linguistic assistance.

1. See www.ipu.org/wmn-f/world.htm; accessed February 14, 2007.
2. In the Introduction and Conclusion, the terms "voting system" and "electoral system" are used interchangeably.
3. If the voter can use all of her or his votes for a single candidate, it is called a cumulative vote. For an argument in favour of this system, see Guinier (1991). It is possible for the voter to be given fewer votes than there are seats to be filled. This voting system, used in Gibraltar, is called the limited vote. It is also possible for each elector to receive only one vote in a multimember electoral district. This voting system,

called the Single Nontransferable Vote, has been adopted in Afghanistan and was used in the Japanese House of Representatives from 1947 to 1993.

4. According to the LR-Droop quota.

5. STV elections are largely, but not exclusively, determined by first preference votes, depending on whether subsequent rounds of counting are required. A variant of the STV system is STV with Borda elimination, which weights the voters' complete and initial rankings; see Geller 2005.

6. Reynolds, Reilly, and Ellis (2005: 84, 90) also mention free lists, used in Luxembourg and Switzerland. This is a preferential vote because the voter may change, in several ways, the list that a party submits—by entering a candidate's name more than once, by crossing out some names, and even by adding the names of candidates from other parties to that party's list.

7. The highest average method allocates seats sequentially: the number of votes a party won is divided by a sequence of divisors. Varieties include the d'Hondt system (the sequence of divisors is 1, 2, 3, 4, 5, etc.), the Sainte-Laguë formula (1, 3, 5, 7, etc.), the modified Sainte-Laguë formula (1.4, 3, 5, 7, etc.), the Imperiali method (1, 1.5, 2, 2.5, 3, etc.), and the Danish method (1, 4, 7, 10, etc.). The largest remainders method calculates a quota (Q) based on the numbers of votes cast (V) and the number of seats to be allocated (S). There are various formulae: the Hare quota ($Q=V/S$), the Hagenbach-Bischoff quota ($Q=V/(S+1)$)), the Droop quota ($Q=V/(S+1)+1$), and the LR-Imperiali quota ($Q=V/(S+2)$).

8. It is possible, as in Finland, for the number of seats assigned to a political party to be determined by the sum of votes received by candidates on an individual basis. The elector is then voting for a candidate and not a party (Raunio 2005; Taagepera 1994).

9. The opposite effect can also be argued: a low threshold of representation favours the parliamentary representation of small parties for which women are often candidates. However, this argument suffers from an important weakness: since small parties achieve only a few seats each, it is likely that these seats will be given to men, as men are more likely to be the party leaders and thus at the top of each list.

10. France is an exception, where both voluntary (for the plurality/majority elections) and compulsory (for List PR elections) measures encourage parties to present an equal number of female and male candidates in legislative elections (see Scott 2005: 124–146), as in Great Britain, where, in 2002, legislation was passed to give political parties who adopted such measures protection from antidiscrimination law (see Childs 2004: 204–211).

11. However, STV is not associated with low women's representation in the seven legislative chambers using it in Australia. In addition, the Australian Senate, which has used STV since 1949, has always had a higher proportion of women than the House of Representatives (which uses the majoritarian Alternative Vote). I thank Marian Sawer for her comment on this point.

12. However, it should be mentioned that the Conservatives used primaries in a few instances in 2005 and hope to have more next time around. I thank Sarah Childs for bringing this to my attention.

Part I

Majoritarian Systems

Subpart I

Plurality

Reserved Seats for Women MPs: Affirmative Action for the National Women's Movement or the National Resistance Movement

Gretchen Bauer

Introduction

In February 2006 Uganda held a fourth set of national elections since a political transition two decades earlier, sending 89 women to its eighth national parliament. Within six months an additional 10 women were elected to parliament for a total 99 women out of 332 members.[1] With 29.8 percent women members of parliament (MPs), Uganda ranks in the top 20 worldwide in early 2007, well above the African and world averages of 17 percent women in a lower or single house of parliament. This is an impressive accomplishment for a country that endured a series of brutal military and civilian regimes for the first 25 years of independence and ranks among the poorest in the world. Indeed, after independence from the British under a federal constitution in 1962, Uganda experienced a mere four years of relative peace before Prime Minister Milton Obote seized power from the president in 1966. Obote's regime did not last long; in 1971 he was overthrown by army officer Idi Amin. After eight devastating years Amin was deposed by the Tanzanian army. Elections in 1980 brought Obote back to power in 1981 only to be ousted in a military coup in 1985. Meanwhile, in 1981, the National Resistance Army (NRA), led by a young former defense minister named Yoweri Kaguta Museveni, declared a liberation war for the country. In 1986 Museveni and the NRA seized power, and the army's political wing, the National Resistance Movement (NRM), formed a new "movement" government with Museveni as president. From the start, the NRM banned political parties though it held elections. Over time, "movement" rule was contested by a growing opposition, and in 2000 a national referendum was held on the matter. When the multipartyists boycotted the referendum, however, they also lost it. Finally, in 2003, under continuing pressure from the opposition and the international donor community, Museveni announced a transition to a multiparty political system. This was approved by the electorate in a 2005 referendum, and the country's first multiparty elections were held in 2006, still dominated by the NRM political party (EIU 2006).

Uganda's early political decline was accompanied by an equally steep socioeconomic demise. By the time that the NRM took power in 1986, the country's once vibrant economy was in ruins. A combination of largely liberalizing policies led to a stabilization of the economy and return to growth by the 1990s, however. Today agriculture remains the most important sector of the economy, accounting for about 40 percent of gross domestic product (GDP). Moreover, subsistence agriculture forms the core of food production in the country and is about one half of total agricultural output. The southern and southwestern portions of the country remain the most prosperous because of greater rainfall and political stability in contrast to the war-ravaged north. With a per capita GDP (at purchasing power parity) in 2005 of about US$ 1,450 too few Ugandans have benefited from the apparent economic recovery. The situation has been further exacerbated by a significant HIV/AIDS epidemic that, while it has been significantly addressed, still poses many challenges (EIU 2006).

A number of factors have coalesced to produce an increasing number of women in Uganda's parliament and are discussed in the remainder of this chapter. First, however, the chapter outlines the electoral system used to elect members to parliament in Uganda since 1986 and describes the evolution of women's representation in national legislative bodies in Uganda over time. Next, the chapter considers the impact of the electoral system on women's parliamentary representation in Uganda and other factors that have influenced their growing presence in the National Assembly. The chapter concludes that the method by which women are elected to Uganda's National Assembly has had a profound, potentially negative, impact on their role in parliament and government but that the existence of a mobilized women's movement has mitigated that impact in some ways.

The Voting System

When the NRM gained power in Uganda in 1986, it introduced a "no-party" political system that prohibited the activities of political parties and allowed only those of "the Movement" (the ruling NRM). The NRM leadership defended the "no-party" or "movement" political system with the argument that in the past Ugandan political parties had been built on the basis of religious or ethnic ties and in so doing had contributed to the country's history of division and conflict (Nordstoga Hanssen 2005). An initial set of elections was held in 1989 for a National Resistance Council (NRC) that would serve for seven years. A constituent assembly convened in 1994 drafted a new constitution that was adopted in 1995 and provided for a unicameral parliament, the National Assembly. Regular presidential and parliamentary elections were held every five years from 1996 onward. Candidates were allowed to stand for election and campaign freely but not as members of a political party (Nordstoga Hanssen 2005). NRM leader Yoweri Museveni was elected president in 1996 and 2001 and again in 2006 after the constitution was amended to abolish the presidential two-term limit.[2] Under the no-party system the parliament was thoroughly dominated by "the Movement." In 2006, the first multiparty presidential and parliamentary elections were held in the country; the NRM as political party dominated the 2006 parliamentary elections as it had earlier elections (www.ipu.org/parline-e/reports/2329.htm; July 2006).

Uganda uses a simple majority vote, or first-past-the-post electoral system, for 215 directly elected "constituency seats" in the National Assembly. In addition, 105 members are indirectly elected into reserved seats, at least 85 of whom must be women. The reserved seats for women include 80 district seats for women and one of five reserved seats for the youth, one of five reserved seats for workers, one of five reserved seats for persons with disabilities, and two of ten reserved seats for the army. Finally, there are currently 13 nonvoting ex officio members drawn from among ministers not elected to parliament, for a total of 333 members.[3]

While the 215 MPs in constituency seats are directly elected by universal adult suffrage, the 80 women MPs in women's seats are indirectly elected by district-based electoral colleges from all-female lists of candidates. The electoral colleges are constituted from members of local councils and the parallel women's councils in each district. The local councils and the women's councils are five-tier structures that operate from the village level through the district level. Only councilors from the three lower levels of both councils participate in the electoral colleges (Nordstoga Hanssen 2005). More importantly, the electoral colleges are male-dominated and closely tied to the ruling NRM. Indeed, the local councils and the women's councils, from which members of the electoral college are drawn, are regarded by many simply as "decentralized [National Resistance] Movement structures" used by the government to spread its ideas and bring development to the people (Nordstoga Hanssen 2005; Tamale 2004: 38). Finally, the district-based women MPs represent a district that may include three or four constituencies, whereas directly elected MPs represent one constituency only. Thus, the indirectly elected women MPs operate in a much larger area than their directly elected colleagues and they must contend with other—most likely male—MPs who are also from their district (Tamale 2004: 41).

By contrast, members of parliament in the 25 reserved seats for the youth, workers, persons with disabilities, and the army (of whom totally five must be women) are selected differently. As Anne Marie Goetz (2003) notes, the Ugandan Constitution distinguishes in important ways between the reserved seats for women and the reserved seats for the other four groups. Seats for the army, youth, workers, and the disabled are national- rather than district-level seats, and the members are selected directly by their national organizations rather than by district local-level officials. Moreover, the constitution describes MPs in seats for the army, youth, workers, and the disabled as "representatives of" those special interests, while MPs in the women's seats are described not "as representatives of women, but as representatives for each district" (Goetz 2003: 119).

Women in the Legislature: Historical Trends

In many respects, women's significant political representation in Uganda today can be traced back to their early organization into women's voluntary associations. According to Aili Mari Tripp (2000: 34), the earliest women's voluntary associations were formed by Christian missionaries and the wives of colonial administrators and businessmen shortly after Uganda became a British protectorate in 1894. While many early women's organizations were church based with an emphasis on instilling Christian principles and Christian living, others, such as the Girl Guides and the Uganda Women's League (with a focus on enhancing nursery schools and building maternity wards), were secular. During the 1940s and 1950s local-level women's groups or community clubs were established throughout the colony by the Ministry for Social Development; the clubs provided an opportunity for women to learn a variety of domestic skills and to socialize with one another (Tripp 2000: 34). Over time new women's groups, such as the Young Women's Christian Association, took on other issues such as school leaving at the primary level or housing for young girls working in urban areas. All of these groups, whatever their stated goals, succeeded as well in providing women members with leadership and organizational skills (Byanyima 1992: 132; Tripp 2000: 35).

As in many British colonies, Uganda was governed with the assistance of an Executive Council and a Legislative Council (Legco). The Legco Council was established in 1921. In 1945 the first three African representatives were nominated to the Legco; it was clearly stipulated, however, that the Africans on the Legco "should be *men* of substance and authority" (Ahikire 2004; italics in the original). From 1958 onward representatives to the Legco were elected as well as nominated. According to Tripp (2000: 39), "Women were poorly represented in the Legislative Council, even though they showed a keen interest in voting." Indeed, in the first Legislative Council elections in 1958, women outnumbered men at polling stations in many parts of the country. This interest among women in electoral politics encouraged the Uganda Council of Women (UCW) to focus its efforts on women's political representation, according to Tripp. The UCW emerged out of the Uganda Women's League in 1946 and marked the beginning "in earnest" of the movement to promote women's rights in Uganda (Tripp 2000: 37). As Tripp (2000: 39) further notes, "Many of the first women in the Legislative Council had been leaders in the UCW." The first women representatives were nominated to the Legco in 1954 and numbered 2 out of 60 members. The first two African women representatives to the Legco were not appointed until 1956 and 1958, with a handful more joining the body in the years before independence. The presence of even these few African women on the Legco can be attributed to pressure by the UCW on the colonial administration (Tripp 2000: 39). Only one woman stood in the 1958 Legco election and she lost; the few African women who served on the Legco were all nominated, "as it was virtually impossible for women to be elected to this legislative body" (Tamale 1999: 11).

While women turned out in large numbers for the first national Legco election in 1958, their franchise was still a limited one with literacy, property, income, or employment prequalifications excluding most women voters (Ahikire 2004; Tamale 1999). Whether or not women should be allowed to vote was still being fiercely debated as late as 1961. Only with independence and a new constitution in 1962 were women aged 21 years and older granted the right to vote (Tripp 2000: 46). Also, at independence in 1962, a unicameral national legislature, the National Assembly, was established. The first National Assembly had two women members out of 90 and that would be the most women members until 1989. Only two more elections were held before the NRM came to power in 1986; in 1967 no women were elected to the National Assembly and in 1980 one woman was elected (see table 1.1). Following the 1967 election the Uganda Association of Women's Organizations decided to help ten women candidates stand for the next

Table 1.1   Women in Uganda's parliament, 1962–2006

Election year	1962	1967	1980	1989	1996	2001	2006*
Number of women MPs/total MPs	2/90	0/82	1/126	42/238	50/276	75/305	89/322
Number of women in district reserved seats	NA	NA	NA	34	39	56	69
Number of women in other reserved or ex officio seats	NA	NA	NA	**	**	6	6
Number of women in constituency seats	NA	NA	1	2	8	13	14
Percent women MPs	2.2	0	0.7	17.6	18.1	24.6	27.6*

* In July 2006, 11 new districts and women's district seats were created such that women are now 99 of 332 (29.8 percent) members (one women's seat is vacant).
**Data unavailable.
Note: Table does not take into account changes after an election.
Sources: Tripp 2006, 116; Inter-Parliamentary Union parline database. www.ipu.org/parline-e/reports/2329_A.htm (March 2007). Table does not take into account changes after an election. NA: not applicable.

scheduled National Assembly election; the election never came to pass, however, as the government was overthrown in a military coup in 1971 (Tripp 2000: 40). During Amin's eight-year reign of terror, all potential sources of opposition were proscribed, including all women's organizations, which were banned in 1978; in their place Amin installed a state-sponsored National Council of Women (NCW) (Tamale 1999: 15). In spite of its lowly status in the Amin years, the NCW "kept the embers of the women's struggles smoldering until 1986 when the government stranglehold on NGOs was removed" (Tamale 1999: 15). During the second Obote regime in the early 1980s, the NCW demanded, unsuccessfully, that a full-fledged ministry for women be established. After the 1989 elections, the parliament comprised 17.6 percent women, 18.1 percent after the 1996 elections, and 24.6 in 2001.

For the multiparty parliamentary elections in early 2006, reserved seats for women in each of the country's districts were retained, with the women MPs in those seats selected in the same manner as in the past (www.ipu.org/parline-e/reports/2329.htm; July 2006). As noted, by the time of the 2006 election there were 69 district reserved seats for women and 5 additional reserved seats for women from the 25 seats designated for workers, the youth, persons with disabilities, and the army, for a total of 74 reserved seats for women (a 22.9 percent quota). In the event, six women were elected to the other reserved seats—two rather than only one of the worker seats went to women. In the 2006 election women were also directly elected to 14 constituency seats. In July 2006, 11 new districts were created in Uganda and in August 2006 ten more women district representatives were elected to parliament (with one seat still vacant as of early 2007). Thus, women hold 99 seats (29.8 percent) in Uganda's eighth parliament.[4] Interestingly, during the early 2006 election, there was fierce competition for some of the district reserved seats, with some prominent women MPs losing to lesser-known women candidates. This prompted speculation that more women might be persuaded in the future to run for directly elected seats, although many challenges of doing so remain (Muhumuza 2006). Indeed, the number of women directly elected into constituency seats has increased slowly over time, albeit only by one from 2001 to 2006 (see table 1.1).

The Impact of the Voting System on the Proportion of Women in the Legislature

Electoral systems are important to women's representation in legislatures primarily because the type of electoral system determines the type of affirmative action, if any, that can be utilized with that system. As Pippa Norris (2000: 350) notes, "By itself the electoral system is neither a necessary nor a sufficient condition to guarantee women's representation. Nevertheless, the electoral system functions as a facilitating mechanism, which expedites implementation measures within parties—affirmative action, for example—for female candidates." Indeed, the electoral system is the "gateway" to women's presence in legislatures with "the choice of a particular model (PR [proportional representation] or majoritarian) maximi[zing] or minimi[zing] the ability of political parties to manipulate the slate of candidates and representatives" (Meintjes and Simons 2002a: 167). With plurality-majority systems the most common type of electoral gender quota is a reserved seat of some kind, whereas with proportional representation electoral systems, an electoral gender quota is imposed by requiring a certain percentage of women candidates on a party list (and, ideally, their dispersion throughout the party list). There are clear differences—at a number of levels—in the two types of electoral gender quotas and their effect on the women who are elected through them (Matland 2006).

Indeed, in Uganda, the system by which women are elected to reserved seats has significant consequences. At a most fundamental level, as Goetz (2003: 118) points out, the "add-on" mechanism used in Uganda, whereby "new public space reserved exclusively for women: new bureaucracies, new parliamentary and local government seats for women-only competition, new ministerial positions" is created, is highly problematic. Rather than "giving women advantages in political contests with men," thereby allowing them to compete on an equal footing with men, district-based reserved seats for women only "have negative implications for the perceived legitimacy, and ultimately the political effectiveness, of women politicians" (Goetz 2003: 118). The add-on mechanism, in Goetz's view, reinforces a politics of patronage: it is based "on a principle of extending patronage to a new clientele, and indeed of 'extending the state'—creating new representative seats, new political offices, and where possible, new political resources" (2003: 120). In addition, she observes that the add-on mechanism influences the relationship between the Ugandan women's movement and women in office. Goetz (2003: 120) argues that the electoral college process for electing women to reserved seats requires "no further screening processes beyond ascertaining the candidate's gender, no process of winnowing out likely candidates according to their effectiveness in promoting any particular party platform or social programme, and no process to enable the women's movement to review candidates."

Tripp finds several disadvantages to the use of electoral colleges for selecting women to the district seats as well. For example, she cites one critic of the system who argues that "women MPs cannot legitimately speak on behalf of their constituents if they only represent the views of the electoral college" (Tripp 2000: 232) that elected them. Other critics argue that a small body such as an electoral college is especially susceptible to bribery and intimidation and other corrupt methods of persuasion. Moreover, there is a widespread feeling, as noted above, that the local bodies from which the electoral college members are drawn are NRM dominated and thus, as one opposition press release stated, "In a country where the local councils have become appendages and organs of the NRM, it would appear as if all the Women District Parliamentarians have been truly given to the NRM with both hands" (Tripp 2000: 231–232).

Miria Matembe, one of two women members of the 1989 Constitution Commission, former MP and former Minister of Ethics and Integrity, argues that women in Uganda "have been trapped and have become hostages to the quota system, which was originally introduced to liberate them" (2006: 8). In Matembe's view, rural and urban women in Uganda have failed to embrace the women's seats in parliament as a political right; rather, they perceive them as a privilege bestowed by a benevolent president. As a consequence, Matembe continues, women activists and politicians are unwilling to interrogate or challenge President Museveni and his government. In addition, Matembe argues, as a patronage opportunity, the quota system "does not necessarily attract qualified and competent women to espouse the cause of gender equality … but any woman who needs employment" (Matembe 2006: 9).

Finally, there are some potential negatives inherent in reserved seats, no matter how the election is conducted, as a mechanism for increasing women's legislative representation (Matland 2006: 289). A reserved seat system runs the risk of creating a two-tiered system of legislators, one that relegates representatives in "women's seats" to an inferior status and diminishes their legislative accomplishments. In addition, there is the danger that reserved seats act as a ceiling rather than a floor. Parties may be reluctant to stand female candidates for constituency seats when there are plenty of district seats available. As noted, the number of women in constituency seats in Uganda seems to have reached a plateau over the last two elections.

The Impact of Other Variables on the Proportion of Women in the Legislature

A number of recent studies have examined the phenomenon of large numbers of women MPs in several African parliaments, sometimes elected overnight as in Rwanda, where 49 percent of Chamber of Deputies members are women following the 2003 election, sometimes elected over the course of two or three consecutive elections. Several of these studies identify a common set of circumstances contributing to the influx of women into primarily east and southern African parliaments in the 1990s and beyond. These include postconflict situations; the use of electoral gender quotas; mobilized national women's movements; receptive, often left-leaning, political parties; and the influence of an international women's movement, foreign donors, and regional organizations and networks (Ballington 2004; Morna 2004; Bauer and Britton 2006a; Tripp, forthcoming). Many of these factors have been at work in Uganda.

Clearly, from 1986 onward, Uganda was in a postconflict situation, just beginning the recovery from decades of brutal dictatorial rule and civil war. As Donna Pankhurst (2002) notes, conflict can open up possibilities for women: "Countries which have experienced violent conflict have also been through major disruptions to gender relations. Sometimes this has provided new opportunities to articulate debate about gender politics as well as for individual women to live in a different way" (2002: 127). Pankhurst argues that the NRM, like liberation movements in southern Africa, "took serious steps to work against discrimination on the grounds of ethnicity, religion, education and sex," although she concedes that in the NRM, as elsewhere, "the women's project was often seen as potentially delaying the achievement of the bigger political project" (2002: 124–125). Pankhurst also credits NRM leader Museveni with helping to "keep open the political space to push for political change" (2002: 125). In an early retrospective on women in the NRM, Winnie Byanyima (1992: 140) suggests that while "seeking empowerment through participation in the NRM was far from easy for Ugandan women … there is no doubt that the guerilla war provided women the best opportunity, since Uganda's borders were first drawn, to be politically active." She notes that the climate in the NRM during the war years was favorable for women to take part in discussions and decision making. Once the war was over and reconstruction of the country had begun, women were formally included in decision making, though in a very limited fashion, through reserved seats starting at the resistance council level (Byanyima 1992: 141). Matembe (2006: 4–5) also credits the role of women in the "bush war" and positive actions on the part of the NRM in its early years in power with advancing the political position of women in Uganda.

Sylvia Tamale (1999: 17), in her book on women MPs in Uganda, asks to what "the dramatic changes favoring women introduced by the NRM," including reserved seats at the local and national level, can be attributed. She speculates that a number of factors were at work. These include "political expediency" in the sense that affirmative actions for women could be used to persuade the international community that the NRM was committed to democracy while at the same time cultivating favor with an influential half of the electorate. Tamale (1999: 17–19) also mentions the ideological influences of southern African liberation movements on Museveni as a student and exile in the 1960s and 1970s and suggests, finally, that affirmative action measures for women may have been a "token reward" for their participation as combatants in the five-year NRM guerrilla struggle for power.

In her book on women and politics in Uganda, Tripp focuses on the pressure exerted by the Ugandan women's movement on the NRM regime to "elevate women to key positions in the government as ministers, cabinet ministers, permanent secretaries, members of special commissions, and other key posts" (Tripp 2000: 23). As she notes, the women's movement in Uganda was also pivotal in the process of revising the 1995 constitution, "which adopted extensive provisions to enhance the position of women," and in pursuing key legislation affecting women (2000: 23). According to Tripp, the most important factor explaining the successes of the Ugandan women's movement is the autonomy of Uganda's women's organizations, "an autonomy that did not come easily and remains a struggle to maintain" (2000: 23). Among other things, this relative autonomy of the Ugandan women's movement has "allowed it to expand its agenda, to become a political force in the country, and, perhaps most remarkably, to seriously challenge clientelistic (i.e., ethnic and religious) bases of mobilization that have plagued the country since independence" (Tripp 2000: xvii).

In the final analysis, the vast majority of women in Uganda's parliament today are there because of the district-based reserved seats provided for in the constitution, with the factors given earlier contributing to the inclusion of such an electoral gender quota in the constitution.[5] Reserved seats for women in parliament were first introduced in the 1989 NRC election, although a limited number of reserved seats for women had been introduced at the local level in 1986.[6] Already, in 1964, Ugandan women's organizations made a plea for reserved seats for women in the National Assembly—a request that was rejected with the admonition that women "educate themselves so that they could become able politicians" (Tripp 2000: 40). Tamale suggests that after the NRM assumption of power in the mid-1980s, the Ugandan women's movement, "dissatisfied with the token representation in both local and national decision-making institutions" and inspired by the 1985 United Nations conference on women held in neighboring Kenya, demanded a greater role for women in politics and decision making (2004: 38). "Partly because of this pressure," she continues, "but also as a result of political expediency and calculation, the NRM, in 1989, opened the door further to women's participation in politics, expanding parliament to include 39 reserved seats for women (one from each district)." The quota system that provided for a number of reserved seats for women in parliament equal to the number of districts in the country was institutionalized in the new 1995 constitution. The 1995 constitution clearly states that affirmative action measures will be taken in favor of marginalized groups "for the purpose of redressing imbalances which exist against them" (Tamale 2004: 38). The number of districts (and therefore women's reserved district seats) was increased to 56 for the 2001 election, 69 for the 2006 election, and to 80 in July 2006.

As such, Uganda has taken the path of a growing number of countries around the world—opting for a "fast track," rather than an "incremental track," to women's equal representation in parliament (Dahlerup and Freidenvall 2005). The fast track, utilized today by an increasing number of African, Latin American, and other countries, means using gender-based electoral quotas to dramatically increase the number of women in legislatures, often overnight—in the course of one election. By contrast, the incremental track, exemplified best by the Scandinavian countries (for decades the world leaders in women's legislative representation), means waiting more than half a century from the time of women's enfranchisement until women comprise 20 or 30 percent of members of a legislature (Dahlerup 2006b: 7–8).[7] Though several Asian, European, and Latin American countries have utilized gender-based electoral quotas with success, nowhere in the world has the rate of increase in women's representation been as fast as in Africa (Dahlerup and Freidenvall 2005: 33). Primarily in east and southern Africa, electoral gender quotas are being used with great success today to rapidly increase the number of women in parliament (Bauer 2008).

It should be noted, however, that many obstacles facing women running for constituency and even district seats in Uganda remain. According to Tripp (2006: 116–117), these include a "myriad of cultural prohibitions" not faced by men, such as having to project an image of being a devoted wife and mother, having to dress in a certain way, or having to behave in a certain way. Single and divorced women face an especially tough time campaigning for public office in Uganda. Women candidates face other clear disadvantages as well, such as having fewer resources at their disposal in situations where a certain amount of largesse is expected of candidates and not being incumbents in office and so not being able to win votes through past favors and services to constituents.

Conclusion

The vast majority of women in parliament in Uganda today are in district reserved seats, and, it has been argued in this chapter, the method by which women are elected to these reserved seats appears to have limited the overall impact of these women MPs on Ugandan society. Indeed, the question has been posed whether Ugandan women MPs in reserved seats are serving the national women's movement or the NRM. Tripp (2006: 130) concludes that "the presence of women parliamentarians in reserved seats has ended up serving the Movement [NRM] rather than the women's movement." She argues that aside from the 1995 constitution, women in Uganda have little legislation that they can point to "that suggests a sustained commitment to advancing women's status." Matembe (2006: 8), herself a former MP, elaborates that, despite so many women in parliament, the body has failed to enact "good laws" on marriage, divorce or inheritance, domestic violence, and sexual offenses or to establish an equal opportunities commission as mandated by the constitution, among other things. Finally, those women MPs loyal to President Museveni, Tripp argues, have been less likely to embrace women's causes if they conflicted with the NRM, while those women MPs most outspoken (such as Miria Matembe) have been "warned, demoted, or thrown out of their positions" (Tripp 2006: 130–131).

At the same time it is important not to underestimate the impact of a powerful and dynamic women's movement. As Wilma Rule (1987: 495) observed early on in the case of 23 democracies, "Negative electoral system features have been overcome by women's political mobilization." Clearly, nearly one-third of parliamentarians in Uganda today are women because of remarkable strides by an autonomous women's movement that took advantage of political openings generated by the NRM government and that pushed for a host of measures to ensure women's greater political participation and representation, among other things. At mid-decade, a new opportunity for the Ugandan women's movement lies ahead. In early 2006 Uganda experienced another important transition—from a no-party or movement political system to a multiparty political system. It remains to be seen how the women's movement takes advantage of this political transition to influence the way in which women continue to be elected to parliament in Uganda and what they are able to do once they get there.

Notes

1. Six months after the 2006 election, 11 more districts were created in Uganda, making for 11 more district seats for women in the parliament. As of early 2007 one of the 11 new seats was vacant (Hiroko Yamaguchi, Inter-Parliamentary Union, personal email communication, January 16, 2007).

2. The abolition of the presidential term limit in Uganda required a two-thirds majority in parliament and was highly contested. Demonstrations were held in the capital city Kampala and Minister of Ethics and Integrity Miria Matembe was sacked for her outspoken opposition to the move (see Majtenyi 2005; Mulumba 2005; Tabe 2006).

3. See www.ipu.org/parline-e/reports/2329_A.htm (March 2007). According to the Inter-Parliamentary Union, the president of Uganda may appoint as many ex officio members as he/she wishes, and thus the statutory number of members may vary over time.

4. Hiroko Yamaguchi, Inter-Parliamentary Union, personal email communication, January 16, 2007.

5. According to Goetz (2003: 117–118), 18 percent, or 52, of the delegates to the constituent assembly were women, nine of them in directly elected seats and the rest in reserved seats: "The large number of women in the CA [Constituent Assembly] enabled women to act as a distinct negotiating and voting bloc. Most of them joined a non-partisan women's caucus, which was very strongly supported by the women's movement, particularly when it came to lobbying for gender-equity clauses in the constitution. The women's caucus was instrumental in ensuring that a number of key provisions were included in the constitution: a principle of non-discrimination on the basis of sex; equal opportunities for women; preferential treatment or affirmative action to redress past inequalities; provision for the establishment of an equal opportunities commission; as well as rights in relation to employment, property and family."

6. The practice of including at least one women's representative had already begun during the war years. "As a guerrilla movement, the National Resistance Movement/Army (NRM/A) developed unique structures of governance and participation, the kernel of which was formed by the resistance councils and committees (RCs). A significant advance to their operation was achieved with the mandatory inclusion of a women's representative on each committee" (Tamale 1999: 16).

7. As Dahlerup (2006b: 7) points out, while the Scandinavian countries are often cited as using electoral gender quotas to bring more women into parliament, this was not actually the case. In most cases, gender quotas were only introduced after women had attained 20 to 30 percent of seats in parliaments, and the quotas were always voluntary at the party level and typically used only by the left-leaning parties.

The "Mother of All Parliaments": Westminster's Male Face

Sarah Childs, Rosie Campbell, and Joni Lovenduski

Introduction

The "Mother of All Parliaments" is overwhelmingly male (and pale): 128 women MPs—just one in five of all members of the UK parliament—were elected at the 2005 general election. Moreover, the upward trend in women's representation at Westminster began only in the mid-to-late 1980s and it was not until the 1997 general election that a sea change occurred. At that election, the numbers of women in Parliament doubled overnight—from 60 to 120.

The number of women MPs returned since 1997, and the accompanying interparty imbalance—Labour women currently constitute 77 percent of all women MPs at Westminster—demonstrates, beyond reasonable doubt, that the levels of women's representation in the UK parliament reflect demand- rather than supply-side explanations of women's political recruitment (Childs, Lovenduski, and Campbell 2005; Norris and Lovenduski 1995): the biggest single reason for the current levels of women MPs in Westminster is the use of equality guarantees—measures that require an increase in the number or proportion of particular categories of candidates—by the Labour Party for both the 1997 and 2005 general elections (Lovenduski 2005). In their absence it is likely that Labour would have returned far fewer women MPs in 1997 and seen more lose their seats in 2001 and far fewer women selected for vacant party-held seats in 2005 when the number of Labour women MPs increased from 95 to 98 *despite* the party experiencing a net loss of 47 seats. The higher percentage of women sitting in the new devolved institutions of the Scottish Parliament and the National Assembly of Wales—where they represent 42 and 50 percent, respectively—similarly questions any straightforward relationship between majoritarian systems of election and lower levels of women's representation: women sit in greater numbers in the constituency seats, elected by a majoritarian system, than in the regional seats, elected by proportional representation. It also provides additional evidence, albeit in different electoral arenas, of the difference equality guarantees can make, ceteris paribus, to women's numerical representation.

The Voting System

The UK parliament at Westminster is elected by a Single-Member Simple-Plurality (SMSP) electoral system, often referred to as the "first past the post" (FPTP) system. The country is divided up into geographic entities (constituencies or seats) that return a single MP. Each voter has one vote. The candidate who receives the most votes (a plurality) in each constituency is returned as its representative; that the winning candidate need only have one more vote than the second-placed candidate to be declared the winner means that many MPs (this was some two-thirds at the 2005 election) are unlikely to receive 50 percent or more of the vote in their constituency when more than two parties compete.

Basis upon which Constituencies Are Drawn Up

At the 2005 general election the United Kingdom was divided up into 646 constituencies of roughly equal size: 529 in England, 59 in Scotland, 40 in Wales, and 18 in Northern Ireland (Leonard and Mortimore 2005: 23). This was a reduction from the 659 constituencies at the previous general election and reflects the establishment of the Scottish Parliament that supersedes the basis for the historic overrepresentation of Scotland (Budge, Crewe, Mckay, and Newton 2004: 373; Norris and Wlezien 2005: 673).[1] Because of population movement, constituency boundaries become outdated. Hence they have the potential to favor particular parties; in recent years this has been in Labour's direction, a consequence of urban-rural flight and the particular distribution of constituency votes.[2]

How the Voter Votes

At all elections in England, Scotland, and Wales, voters (i.e., those on the electoral register)[3] can vote in person at a polling station, by post, and, subject to certain legal requirements, by proxy vote[4] (Department of Constitutional Affairs 2005; Rallings and Thrasher 2005: 17). Most vote in person; increasing numbers vote by post; and less than a fraction of 1 percent vote by proxy. The proportion of electors with postal votes trebled at the 2005 election to 12 percent (Rallings and Thrasher 2005: 13), a consequence, in part, of the move to postal voting "on demand," which was introduced, under the 2000 Representation of the People Act, to assist electoral turnout.

In advance of the general election, each voter is allocated a voting station close to his or her residence and receives a polling card with information about the voting station's location and the date of the election, by convention (since 1935) a Thursday (DCA 2005). Polls are open from 7 a.m. until 10 p.m. When the voters arrive they will be asked their name—although neither their polling card nor any other ID is required—which is then ticked off against a register. They are then handed a ballot paper that has a list of the names of the candidates contesting the election. Where a candidate is from a party, the party's name is written underneath the candidate's name.[5] The act of voting occurs in a small booth, where the voter marks a single cross in the box next to one of the names to signal his or her vote and then places the folded ballot paper in a ballot box.

Voting Behavior in the United Kingdom

Predicting the choice that individual electors' make is a much more complex task than previously was the case in the United Kingdom. In part this is a result of the changing nature of British politics—following the post-1997 devolution reforms, which, have increased the number of elections—but it is also because of the declining importance of the once-dominant theory of British voting behavior: class. The authors of the 2001 and 2005 British Election Studies contend that not only is the role of class in voting declining (reflecting an increasingly de-aligned electorate and changing class structure), but also that it never had the overwhelming influence on determining vote choice that was often suggested (Clarke, Sanders, Stewart, and Whiteley 2004; Whiteley, Stewart, Sanders, and Clarke 2005). Rather, voters make "summary judgments" based on valence—"their perceptions of the likely competence of competing parties" managerial teams in the face of the "complex political and economic issues facing the country" (Clarke, Sanders, Stewart, and Whiteley 2004: 321). The reelection of Tony Blair in 2005 has, according to this perspective, more to do with the electorates' perception that Labour was best placed to maintain a healthy economy and improve public services and that Blair would make a better prime minister than his Conservative opponent, although Labour also benefited from higher levels of partisanship and an electoral system biased in its favour (Whiteley, Stewart, Sanders, and Clarke 2005). Thus, on a turnout of 61.4 percent, the 2005 general election saw Labour receive approximately 9.5 million votes, compared with the Tories' 8.7 million and the Liberal Democrats' 5.9 million—35.2 percent, 32.4 percent, and 22 percent of votes, respectively (Norris and Wlezien 2005). This translated into 355 seats for Labour, 197 for the Conservatives, and 62 for the Liberal Democrats. While Blair's third consecutive election victory was historic—no other Labour leader has managed a hat trick of victories—it was achieved on the back of the votes of only 21.6 percent of the electorate and a decline in its vote share of 5.5 percent (Norris and Wlezien 2005: 660). However, for the first time in the post-war period, more women than men voted Labour: 38 percent compared with 34, respectively (Campbell and Lovenduski 2005: 193).

Nature of Party Competition in the United Kingdom

The United Kingdom was long considered an example of a two-party system—postwar British politics (Northern Ireland excepted) was dominated by two major parties, the Conservative and Labour parties, contesting elections across the whole country in order to form a single-party government—but it is now more appropriate to acknowledge that it has a multiple-party system (Webb 2005). The two-party system began to transform in the 1970s as a consequence of class and partisan de-alignment and the emergence of postmaterialist issues (such as environmentalism and gender equality) and the question of Europe, which crosscut the traditional party divide. The reemergence of the third party (the Liberal Democrats) saw the erosion of the old two-party duopoly, even as the Conservatives and Labour continued to monopolize control of government. The establishment of devolved institutions under New Labour and elections by proportional electoral systems (table 2.1) have further transformed the structures and "rules of the game" of British politics.

Only the executive arena at Westminster remains largely indifferent to these changes protected as it is by the constraining effects of the SMSP electoral system. Yet, even here, the presence of smaller parties (such as the British National Party, the UK Independence Party, Greens, and Respect) indicates that a more competitive and open electoral arena may well be emerging. For example, the mean number of candidates fighting each constituency at the 2005 general election was 5.5, compared with an average of 5 in 2001, while the two main parties received only 67.6 percent of the vote, the lowest combined share since 1923 (Rallings and Thrasher 2005: 2). These developments should, however, not be overstated (Childs 2005): at Westminster, the SMSP electoral system continues to prop up the two-party system and will do so until a system of proportional

Table 2.1   Electoral systems in the United Kingdom

Level of jurisdiction	*Type of electoral system*	*Brief explanation*
Westminster	Single-Member Simple Plurality	646 single-member constituencies; the candidate gaining a plurality of votes is elected
Scottish Parliament	Additional Member System	73 Members of the Scottish Parliament elected using SMSP, with an additional 56 chosen from regional lists to assist reasonable proportionality.
National Assembly for Wales	Additional Member System	40 assembly members (AMs) elected using SMSP, with an additional 20 chosen from regional lists to assist reasonable proportionality
Northern Ireland Assembly	Single Transferable Vote	A voting system in which voters rank candidates in order of preference; votes from elected or eliminated candidates transfer to the voter's next favored candidate. In Northern Ireland, each of the 18 Westminster constituencies elects six MLAs
Greater London Assembly	Additional Member System	14 AMs elected using SMSP, with an additional 11 chosen from a London-wide list to assist reasonable proportionality

representation is introduced, something that looks remote, given the antipathy toward electoral reform by both the two main parties.

Women in the Legislature: Historical Trends

Since 1918, when women were granted the right to sit in the House of Commons, a total of 253 women have been elected to Westminster, constituting a mere 6 percent of all members of Parliament (House of Commons 2006). As shown in figure 2.1, in the period between 1945 and 1983, women averaged approximately 4 percent of MPs. In 1987 this rose to 6.3 percent and in 1992 to 9.2 percent before the watershed election of 1997 saw both the number and percentage of women double to 120 (out of 659 MPs) and 18.2,

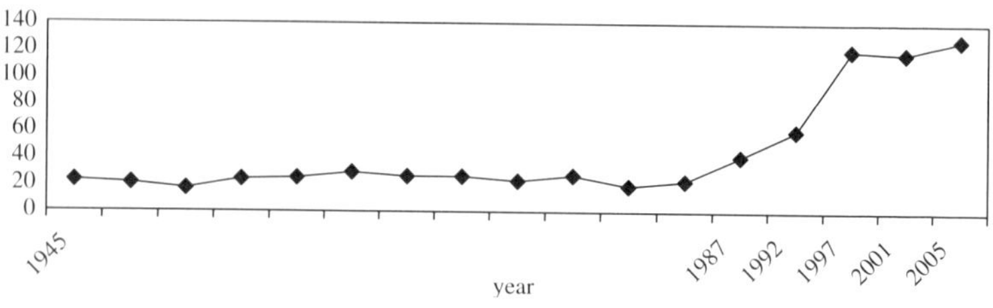

Figure 2.1   Numbers of women MPs elected to the House of Commons, 1945–2005

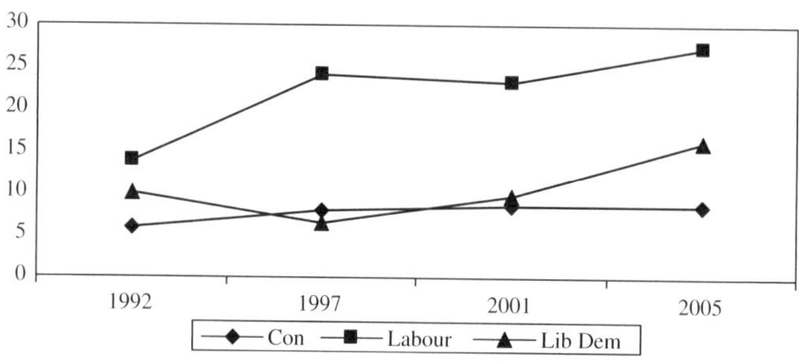

Figure 2.2   Percentage of women MPs, by party

respectively. The general election of 2001, however, delivered the first decline in a generation: the number of women decreased by 2 to 118 and the percentage fell to 17.9. The upward trend returned in 2005—at the general election 128 women were elected to the House, although two of these women died and were replaced by men. In the current Parliament (as in the 2001 one) there are only two black and minority ethnic women MPs, both representatives of the Labour Party.

The interparty imbalance in women's numerical representation currently witnessed in Parliament—a Labour woman MP looking across the floor of the chamber would see only 17 Conservative and 10 Liberal Democrat women, along with one woman each from the Ulster Unionist Party, the Democratic Unionist Party, and Sinn Fein—is a long-standing phenomenon. In only two elections in the postwar period—those of 1970 and 1983—has the Conservative Party elected more women MPs than Labour. In 1997 the Conservative Party's 13 women MPs constituted 11 percent of all women MPs and in the 2005 Parliament this had only increased to 13 percent. Moreover, as a proportion of their respective parliamentary parties in 2005, Labour's 128 women MPs constituted 28 percent; the Tory women 9 percent, and the Liberal Democrat's 16 percent (see figure 2.2). Upward trends in both the Labour and Liberal Democrat parties in 2005 are, then, not matched by the flatlining Conservative Party.

The Impact of the Voting System on the Proportion of Women in the Legislature

Majoritarian electoral systems are widely considered to be less favorable to women's descriptive representation than proportional representation systems (Norris 1997c). Westminster's single-member constituencies, the continuing importance of the two-party system with its large number of safe seats, and political parties' decentralized selection practices all inhibit the selection of women candidates (Norris and Lovenduski 1995).[6]

The overwhelming majority of MPs in the United Kingdom are representatives of political parties, most from the three main parties. Candidate selection in these parties is devolved to local constituency parties. To be sure, the central parties have national rules and standard selection procedures, as well as a role in "approving" aspirant candidates, and can shape decisions. But, for the most part, they leave the choice to local constituency selectors. The process of selecting candidates for all 646 constituencies is, then, the responsibility of local selectorates in discrete constituencies and, collectively, occurs over an 18-month or longer time frame. A key consequence of this is that women's underrepresentation only becomes fully apparent at the time of the election—when the individual choices of hundreds of constituency parties are aggregated—at which point local parties may assert that they have objectively selected the "best" candidate and/or regret that the outcome nationally is that in eight out of ten cases MPs are male. Leaving aside accusations of selectorate discrimination for the moment, it is worth noting that because each Westminster constituency selects a single candidate, candidate selection is a zero-sum game—the selection of a woman candidate means that a male candidate is not selected. Contrast this with multimember constituencies, where the tendency is to select a balanced ticket of women and men, younger and older, majority and minority ethnic candidates, or open lists, where voters can choose to prioritize particular candidates.

The New Devolved Institutions: The Myth of Proportional Representation

A cursory comparison of the levels of women's representation in the Scottish Parliament and the National Assembly for Wales (although not Northern Ireland, where a history of militarism and sectarianism limits women's representation) appear to support the claim that proportional systems of election are more favourable to women's descriptive representation than majoritarian ones: elected under systems of mixed proportional representation, these institutions currently return significantly higher percentages of women than Westminster (table 2.2).

The story is, however, more complex and, arguably, counterintuitive: in both Scotland and Wales women were returned disproportionately in the SMSP rather than List seats (see tables 2.3 and 2.4 which show the results of the latest elections). These outcomes reflect a number of factors: new electoral and party systems with accompanying new interparty dynamics; intercountry

Table 2.2   Women's numerical representation in British politics

Institution	Percentage of women
National Assembly for Wales	50
Scottish Parliament	42
Greater London Assembly	36
European Parliament	24
Westminster	20
Northern Ireland Assembly	17

Table 2.3   Members of the Scottish Parliament (MSPs), 2003

Party	Constituency		Regional		% Women
	Women	Men	Women	Men	
Labour	26	20	2	2	56
SNP	2	6	7	10	36
Conservative	0	2	4	13	21
Liberal Democrat	1	11	1	4	12
Other	1	1	6	9	41
Total	30	40	20	38	39

Source: CAWP (http://www.qub.ac.uk/cawp/UKhtmls/MSP.htm; May 2007).

Table 2.4   Members of the National Assembly for Wales (AMs), 2003

Party	Constituency		Regional		% Women
	Women	Men	Women	Men	
Labour	19	11	0	0	63
Plaid Cymru	1	4	5	2	50
Liberal Democrat	2	1	1	2	50
Conservative	0	1	2	8	18
Other	0	1	0	0	0
Total	22	18	8	12	50

Source: CAWP (http://www.qub.ac.uk/cawp/UKhtmls/AM.htm; May 2007).

dynamics, not least lesson learning; and the prior mobilization of women, especially in Scotland, that demanded greater gender equality in the new polities (Chaney 2004: 291; Russell, Mackay, and McAllister 2002: 73; Mackay, Myers, and Brown 2003).

Moreover, and fully in line with the argument outlined below emphasizing the importance of political parties creating an artificial demand for women candidates in respect of Westminster, the increased levels of women's representation in Scotland and Wales also reflect the use of equality guarantees, especially by the Labour Party. Expecting to win most of its seats in the constituencies rather than from the regional lists, the Labour party "twinned" constituencies in 1999 in Scotland and Wales and used "All-Women Shortlists" (AWS) in Wales four years later (Chaney 2004; Mackay, Myers, and Brown 2003).

The Impact of Other Variables on the Proportion of Women in the Legislature

Westminster: Equality Guarantees

Comparisons of the numbers of women elected over a relatively short period of time to a single institution, such as the House of Commons, minimize the likely impact of changes in socioeconomic and cultural determinants of women's representation (which take longer to change) while revealing the impact of what Norris and Lovenduski (1995) term systemic (the legal, electoral, and party systems) and party context factors (parties' organizations, rules, and ideology).

As the recent elections (1992–2005) to the House of Commons demonstrate—contra expectations of correlations between higher numbers of women and proportional electoral systems found in comparative studies (Norris 1997c)—it is possible for a political party to increase dramatically the numbers of women representatives elected under a majoritarian electoral system. In the UK parliament, like other party democracies, MPs are overwhelmingly party representatives: all bar one of the current MPs are representatives of political parties, and MPs from the three main parties constitute 95 percent of all MPs. This means that the question of who gets elected to Parliament is one of *whom our political parties select* as their parliamentary candidates, particularly in vacant party-held and winnable seats. Consequently, the focus shifts onto the various determinants that might engender the selection of women candidates by parties.

At the general elections of 1997 and 2005, Labour artificially created a demand for women parliamentary candidates among its party selectorate. This took the form of AWS—the list of candidates from which a local association can choose that comprises only women. For 1997 the party decided that there should be AWS in 50 percent of all vacant Labour-held seats and 50 percent of all its key seats (winnable on a 6 percent swing from the incumbent party). In 2005, and aiming for 35 percent women in the Parliamentary Labour Party, it designated 30 vacant held seats AWS. In terms of outcome, these measures translated, in 1997, into 35 "AWS selected women" out of its total of 101 women elected to Parliament and, in 2005, 23 "AWS selected women." Indeed, half of all Labour's women MPs currently sitting at Westminster were selected on an All-Women Shortlist in either 1997 or 2005. The hiatus of the 2001 general election, where the number of Labour women MPs declined, can be explained by the failure of the party to employ equality guarantees and instead rely upon only equality rhetoric (exhorting women to seek selection, for example) and equality promotion measures (such as women-only training and sex-specific funding) (Lovenduski 2005), neither of which guarantees women's (s)election.[7] The party could not use AWS in 2001 because to the Labour government had not changed the law in view of a legal challenge that had declared AWS illegal in 1996 (Childs 2004). The Sex Discrimination Act (2002) was duly, if belatedly, passed after the 2001 general election. It permits, but does not prescribe, the use of equality guarantees. However, with a "sunset clause," the legislation will expire in 2015 unless Parliament decides to extend its life.

Demand for greater numbers of women MPs among parties' leaders, the wider membership, and/or gender equality advocates within the parties depends on whether there is acceptance—for principled or instrumental reasons—of the claim that there *should* be greater numbers of women in politics. All of the three main political parties in the United Kingdom have made public statements to this effect, most often for reasons of justice and fairness (Childs 2003). Nonetheless, women's representation, and the politically more tricky question of equality guarantees, has become an issue over which the main parties are now competing. This "belated contagion effect" is most evident in the transformation of the Conservative Party under its new leader David Cameron (Campbell, Childs, and Lovenduski 2006). Cameron's reforms of Conservative Party selection procedures, arguably, reflect the party's failure to make significant electoral gains at the last three general elections. Increasing the number of women in the Conservative Parliamentary Party— or at least signaling the desire to do so—symbolically represents the shift from a "nasty" and unelectable party to a modern "compassionate Conservative Party" ready for a return to government; there are also women's votes to be won.

Yet, even when a political party wishes to introduce equality guarantees, its freedom to do so is constrained by the nature of the party's wider ideological position vis-à-vis gender and its party organization, not least in terms of intraparty democracy and the nature of center-local relations. As stated above, in the United Kingdom, political recruitment in the main three political parties is largely devolved to local constituency parties. Local party autonomy in respect of candidate selection is widely prized and robustly defended. Introducing centrally led equality guarantees is, therefore, dependent upon either a convergence in the goal of, and means for, selecting greater numbers of women by the center and local parties or sufficient political will to override and ride out any opposition on the part of party leadership. In the latter case, any action is unlikely to be cost free. Notwithstanding the ultimate success of AWS in increasing the number of women MPs at the 1997 general election, the policy had its critics within the party (and the leadership for that matter) and following an industrial tribunal ruling— brought by two disgruntled male members of the Labour party and which had found AWS illegal—Blair chose not to contest the outcome. And in 2005, the Labour safe seat of Blaenau Gwent was lost to an independent but ex-Labour-Party member, who stood on an explicitly anti-AWS (and implicitly anti-party-headquarter) ticket (Childs, Lovenduski, and Campbell 2005). Importantly, though, Blaenau Gwent was the exception rather than the rule (Cutts, Childs, and Fieldhouse 2007). Similarly, the recent reforms of Conservative Party selection—in particular, the creation of "priority candidates" of whom 50 percent are to be women and from amongst whom local constituency associations in Conservative-held and 'target' seats are expected to choose—reveal the constraints imposed by powerful local associations; local Conservative associations will be "persuaded" rather than forced to select a greater diversity of candidates as the leadership seeks to avoid overt confrontation (Campbell, Childs, and Lovenduski 2006).

The available opportunities to use equality guarantees—under Westminster's FPTP the number of vacant party-held and winnable seats— reflect rates of electoral turnover, through either the death or retirement of sitting MPs or the transfer of a seat from one party to another at an election. The opportunities at any single election to the House of Commons to increase dramatically the numbers of women elected are, then, likely to be limited, although it is possible to create openings artificially. It is, for example, accepted that ageing MPs are offered a move to "another place" (the House of Lords) in exchange for a timely retirement. Other mechanisms to facilitate retirements, such as the early retirement rule employed by Labour for the 2005 general election, can also encourage the "freeing" up of seats, which can then be subject to equality guarantees (Childs, Lovenduski, and Campbell 2005). Despite this, Westminster's turnover rate suggests that a party's commitment to the use of equality guarantees needs to be medium to long term rather than "one off."

Recommending that all political parties use equality guarantees to increase the numbers of women first selected and then elected to the UK parliament (and other political institutions for that matter) (Childs, Lovenduski, and

Campbell 2005) does not imply a lack of concern for supply-side factors of women's political recruitment. Women's gendered socialization, the sexual division of labour, and women's employment patterns are all likely to cause women to have, on average, fewer resources than men—whether that is the necessary free time to engage in politics, money to fund a selection and election campaign, and/or lower levels of political ambition and confidence. Indeed, a recent summary of women's presence in key areas of public, political and economic life—senior civil servants, members of the legal profession, directors of FTSE (Financial Times Stock Exchange) 100 companies, key actors in the media, and individuals holding senior university positions—finds only incremental improvement in recent years (Childs, Lovenduski, and Campbell 2005). Neither does a focus on demand-side factors ignore the importance of ensuring that a wider range of women are able to acquire these resources and to enter into the supply pool from which political parties select their candidates—it has already been noted only two black and minority ethnic women currently sit in the House of Commons, a situation that all the parties need to redress.

Nevertheless, an emphasis on demand-side explanations suggests that belief in the "incremental track" to women's representation—the optimistic assumption that women's representation will inevitably increase significantly over time as their presence in the roles and occupations characteristic of male politicians increases—is misplaced (Dahlerup 2006a). At the 2005 general election the three main parties selected over 400 women as candidates. All three parties had, therefore, more than enough women to fill half their vacancies with women—that is, the seats they already held where the sitting MP was retiring and/or half their target seats (Childs, Lovenduski, and Campbell 2005). Unless one is happy to accept that these women candidates were of a universally lower standard than their male peers, it is likely that selectorate discrimination (most likely indirect discrimination, where ideas of what constitutes a good MP count against women) was operating to direct the majority of these women toward seats that were difficult to win.

Conclusion

The underrepresentation of women in the UK parliament is a good example of how the presumption of a linear relationship between countries' economic or social development and the levels of women's political representation is misguided. For much of the postwar period the numbers of women MPs remained static at about 4 percent and when the sea change occurred in the 1990s it was party specific and a consequence of a political decision: it was equality guarantees introduced by the Labour Party in 1997 and again in 2005 that first delivered, and then protected, the unprecedented numbers of women sitting in the House of Commons. The impact of these quotas in transforming the sex balance among MPs is beyond dispute and, importantly, acts to negate the disadvantages associated with the majoritarian electoral system. Recent constitutional reforms, which have seen the establishment of a Scottish Parliament and National Assembly for Wales, provide additional evidence against those who contend that there is always a positive relationship between proportional electoral systems and higher levels of women's numerical representation. In both Scotland and Wales it was the use of equality guarantee measures in the majoritarian seats that delivered the higher levels of women's representation. This is, of course, not to say, that improvements in women's socioeconomic position—and particularly a rebalancing of women's life/work balance—would not enhance the numbers and range of women seeking selection to our political institutions; neither is it to suggest that a reformulation of what constitutes politics and greater numbers of women connecting to and engaging in party politics would not be a good thing in itself and might also encourage women to seek party candidature. But these changes are not, in themselves, sufficient to deliver elected women representatives at Westminster. In the United Kingdom, like other party democracies, the question of who are our representatives is one of whom our political parties select as their candidates. Their choice is, in turn, determined by the parties' internal organization, the nature of their selection processes, and their wider beliefs about the role of women and men in public life. With the political will, parties can introduce equality guarantees. Indeed, the United Kingdom's system of majoritarian election may be particularly conducive as it is unlikely that voters will choose not to vote for the party of their choice just because its candidate is female.

Such conclusions suggest, then, that rather than a passive optimism that women's representation will inevitably increase over time as their presence in the roles and occupations characteristic of male politicians increases, gender equality advocates should campaign for political action to ensure that the legislative framework allows political parties to use equality guarantees. They should do this first by ensuring that the Sex Discrimination (election candidates) Act is extended and that all political parties introduce measures to guarantee the selection and election of women MPs.

Notes

1. For the 2009–2010 general election, the expectation is that the number of constituencies will increase slightly to about 650 (personal correspondence with Michael Thrasher).
2. In 1997 the average size of the electorate in Labour-won seats was 65,708. This compares favourably with the 72,021 in Conservative-won seats (Budge, Crewe, Mckay, and Newton 2004: 373.)

3. It is an offence, punishable with a £1000 fine, to refuse to provide information requested by one of the electoral registration officers who are required to create an annual electoral register.
4. On the basis of physical incapacity or overseas residence, or because they are attending an educational course or making a journey on election day, or are employed in certain occupations such as those in the armed forces (Electoral Commission: www.electoralcommission.gov.uk/your-vote/waystovote.cfm; May 2007).
5. To be so registered, the candidate's nomination paper must be accompanied by a certificate authorizing his/her candidature issued by or on behalf of the nominating officer of the registered political party. Alternatively, the candidate may have the word "independent" or have no description on the ballot paper (DCA 2005). According to the Political Parties, Elections and Referendums Act 2000, any organization wishing to put up candidates at a relevant election must be registered as a political party with the Electoral Commission. Some 321 parties are registered with the Electoral Commission, almost half of which are single-issue parties or represent special interest groups (www.electoralcommission.gov.uk; May 2007).
6. Since 1945 Labour has continuously held 150 seats and the Conservative Party 105. The average turnover in the last three elections is 92 (184 in Labour's first landslide in 1997, 29 five years later, and 62 in 2005). At the 2005 general election, incumbents constituted 16 percent of all candidates and only 9 percent of them failed to win a seat (Rallings and Thrasher 2005: 9). Though women constitute fewer incumbents, their number in 2005 reflected their presence in the 2001 Parliament (17.7 percent and 17.9 percent, respectively) (Rallings and Thrasher 2005: 10).
7. Admittedly, AWS only guarantee women's election when they are used in vacant party-held seats and when the electorate vote in the same way as in the previous election.

Feminist Society, Paternalist Politics: How the Electoral System Affects Women's Representation in the United States Congress

Donley T. Studlar

Introduction

Women's representation in the United States Congress is a paradox. By socioeconomic and cultural indicators, conditions in the United States are among the best in the world. Yet comparative studies have consistently shown that women's representation in Congress trails that in other advanced industrial democracies and even several developing democracies (see table 3.1). This is a chronic problem. While women's representation has increased over the past quarter century, the United States has not advanced in this respect as have other established democracies and, in fact, has been passed by several other countries. The evidence points to political institutions, particularly the single-member plurality (SMP) electoral system, as the major influence on this state of affairs.

The Voting System

This chapter will concentrate on representation in the U.S. House of Representatives, since that body is the most comparable to the lower houses of other democracies in being based on direct election by the citizenry.

Table 3.1   Women in legislative elections, Western democracies, 2006

World ranking in % women legislators, Country	Current electoral system	% Women legislator 2006	Mean district magnitude	Number of Seats	Mean incumbency return rate
2. Sweden	Proportional representation (PR) List	45.3	12.0*	349	74.1
4. Norway	PR-List	37.9	8.5*	169	60.7
5. Finland	PR-List	37.5	13.3	200	65.0
6. Denmark	PR-List	36.9	7.9*	179	74.6
7. Netherlands	PR-List	36.7	150	150	63.7
11. Belgium	PR-List	34.7	13.6	150	69.5
12. Austria	PR-List	33.9	4.3*	183	61.4
13. Iceland	PR-List	33.3	9	63	66.4
15. New Zealand	PR–mixed-member proportional (MMP)	32.2	1, 51	120	72.5
16. Germany	PR-MMP	31.8	1, 18.6*	598	78.7
30. Australia	Plurality–Alternative Vote	24.7	1	150	80.0
34. Luxembourg	PR-List	23.3	15	60	64.7
44. Canada	Plurality–First Past the Post (FPTP)	20.8	1	308	53.1
50. United Kingdom	Plurality-FPTP	19.7	1	646	75.7
60. (t)Italy	PR-List, with bonus for first place	17.1	23.7	630	64.5
69. USA	Plurality-FPTP	16.3	1	435	84.9
74. Israel	PR-List	14.2	120	120	63.8
78. (t)Ireland	PR–Single Transferable Vote (STV)	13.3	4.0	166	76.1
86. France	Plurality-second ballot	12.2	1	577	57.7
103. Japan	Semi-PR Parallel	9.0	1, 16.4*	480	74.9

* More than one tier of seats.

(t) = tied for ranking.

Sources: International IDEA, www.idea.int; Inter-Parliamentary Union, www.ipu.org; Matland and Studlar (2004); Gallagher and Mitchell (2005c); Gallagher, Laver, and Mair (2005).

Elections to the U.S. House occur every second year, in November, making each individual House a short-lived body. Turnout for House elections varies considerably, depending on whether it coincides with a presidential election occurring every four years. In presidential election years it may range up to 60 percent of the voting age population, in "off year" elections it is usually about 40 percent.[1]

In the U.S. House, the electoral system has varied little. Single-member districts have been the rule since 1842. In the past there have been a few individual at-large House seats by state, but a 1967 law mandated every legislator to represent a specific and nonoverlapping district. The number of seats was set at that time at 435, unlike some other countries where the number of legislators is allowed to rise with population growth.[2] Vacancies are filled through "special elections" (by-elections) in a particular district.

Since the U.S. population, and therefore the number of citizens per district, has increased substantially over time, every seat has the potential to attract multiple candidates. Nevertheless, in general elections, the number of competitive, marginal seats has declined because of partisan redistricting and the power of individual incumbency. Some legislators even run unopposed.

Redistricting (reapportionment) of these SMP seats is carried out on a state-by-state basis after each decennial census, with some states gaining seats, others losing them, and most remaining the same. Almost all states utilize partisan methods of redistricting, usually by state legislatures. Such decisions may be challenged in the courts, but not solely on the basis of their partisanship. Partisan redistricting by state legislatures means that to some degree there are trade-offs of a few safe seats for the minority party in return for more safe seats for the majority party in the state. These conditions have led to technically sophisticated geographic mapping procedures and intense battles over redistricting of existing seats. Recently the U.S. Supreme Court ruled that state legislatures can reapportion seats more than once after the census, which may encourage even more partisan redistricting strategies.

The U.S. has a nearly universal two-party system, with practically every representative being elected as either a Democrat or a Republican. Nevertheless, the U.S. party system is decentralized, with little central or even state party organization control over candidate choice. This applies to the Congressional parties as well. Candidates run under the party label but may have very diverse views, not only within party caucuses, but also in voting behavior in the legislature. This is often done to court constituents "back home" and rarely incurs any major sanctions from the party. Although aided by national party organizations, U.S. Congressional campaigns are focused on individual candidates. The individualistic basis of U.S. elections has resulted in large incumbency advantages, with reelection rates per election at around 90 percent, including those who retire (Matland and Studlar 2004). Thus, we have the paradoxical result that no matter how unpopular the institution of Congress may be, voters tend to love their own individual Congressional representative (Hibbing and Theiss-Morse 1995). The difficulties of raising enough campaign financial support and of gaining name recognition, plus partisan redistricting, have made it difficult for challengers pitted against incumbents (Jacobson 2004). Unless a Congressional election campaign can be "nationalized," with similar sentiments affecting voting countrywide, it is difficult to unseat many sitting legislators of either party.

Many states, however, allow competition for party nominations through primary elections. These contests do not limit participation to active party members or, in some states, even party registrants. Especially in districts with ideological divisions within the dominant party, this results in a few incumbents being replaced through losing primary elections.

There has been no significant movement for a reform of the electoral system (electoral formula) in the United States, although one group, the Center for Voting and Democracy, has carried on the struggle. The only recent instance of electoral reform coming to a legislative vote concerned term limits for Congressional representatives, which was part of the Republican "Contract with America" in 1994. After being defeated once on the floor of the House, this issue has never been resurrected. The U.S. Supreme Court has ruled that term limits for Congressional representatives cannot be imposed by states. Given this environment, little study has been devoted to the effects of U.S. electoral practices in comparative perspective. Instead, scholarly and public attention has been devoted to redistricting, candidate qualities, political ambition, campaign finance, and other characteristics associated with candidate emergence and competitiveness (Jacobson 2004).

Women in the Legislature: Historical Trends

The summary of women's progress in Congressional elections after receiving the federal vote through a constitutional amendment in 1920 has been summarized as "extremely slow and incremental" (Kohn 1980). As table 3.2 shows, after 60 years of equal suffrage, women were barely 5 percent of the candidates and winners for the House of Representatives. Typically, there were only small increases in numbers, if any, from one election to the next. In partisan terms, the balance was relatively equal between Democrats and Republicans, with elected women legislators following general partisan tides.

These relationships, however, changed somewhat in 1992. A redistribution of seats coincided with a major increase in women being nominated by the Democratic Party and the political drama of how Anita Hill's testimony in the Supreme Court confirmation hearing of Judge Clarence Thomas was treated by a Senate committee made up exclusively of men. The "Year of the Woman" resulted in women's representation in the U.S. House jumping from 6.5 to 10.8 percent (Berch 1996). Subsequently, however, increases have returned to incremental levels.

The 1992 election also represented the beginning of a change in the partisan distribution of women representatives. Since 1992 Democrats consistently have had about twice as many women as the Republicans. This is

Table 3.2   Women's representation in U.S. House elections, 1974–2006

	Nominees			Winners			
	Total	Dem	Rep	Total	Dem	Rep	Totals (%)
1974	44	30	14	18	14	4	4.1
1976	54	34	20	18	13	5	4.1
1978	46	27	19	16	11	5	3.7
1980	52	27	25	19	10	9	4.4
1982	55	27	28	21	12	9	4.8
1984	65	30	35	22	11	11	5.1
1986	64	30	34	23	12	11	5.3
1988	59	33	26	25	14	11	5.7
1990	69	39	30	28	19	9	6.4
1992	106	70	36	47	35	12	10.8
1994	112	72	40	47	30	17	10.8
1996	120	77	43*	51	35	16*	11.7
1998	121	75	46	56	39	17	12.9
2000	122	80	42	59	41	18	13.6
2002	124	79	45	59	38	21	13.6
2004	141	88	53	65	42	23	14.9
2006	136	94	42	71	50	21	16.3

* Includes one woman who ran and won as an Independent but then joined the Republican party in Congress.
Source: Data from the Center for American Women and Politics, Eagleton Institute of Politics, Rutgers University (www.cawp.rutgers.edu/; May 2007).

partly due to the fact that women are more likely to contest and to win Democratic primary elections than Republican ones (Matland and King 2002). In contrast to what occurred previously, the overall national electoral tide of the period (toward Republicans until 2006) has not affected the partisan distribution of women representatives. This coincides with an earlier developing but continuing "gender gap" in the electorate, especially among the majority white population, with women being more inclined to vote Democratic and men more Republican (Studlar, McAllister and Hayes 1998). The Democratic gains in 2006 only led to further incremental numerical gains for women although Nancy Pelosi did become the first female Speaker of the House of Representatives.

The Impact of the Voting System on the Proportion of Women in the Legislature

As previously noted, lack of variation in the electoral system used for the House of Representatives has led several U.S. analysts to look for other influences explaining women's low representation. The most prominent exception was Wilma Rule, who argued that changing the electoral formula was a "priority variable" for getting more women into Congress (Rule 1994b, 2000; Rule and Norris 1992). Comparative research into the effects of electoral systems has confirmed this conclusion many times over the years (Duverger 1955; Darcy, Welch and Clark 1994; McAllister and Studlar 2002).

In general, women fare better in candidacies and election where there are more seats per district, even in proportional representation systems. Women winning seats especially depends on "party magnitude," that is, the expected number of seats each party anticipates to win (Matland 1993). Where there is only one seat, it is, literally, "winner take all." While U.S. parties can encourage the selection of women candidates through exhortation and special training, they cannot mandate women's selection by any constituency. A quota system for women candidates is unthinkable in the decentralized party system and individualistic political culture of the United States. The lack of an enforcement mechanism to encourage or compel the choice of women is a chronic problem in single-member electoral systems, in which candidate selection is a zero-sum game.

The role of the voting system in limiting the numbers of women in the U.S. House of Representatives is obvious. However, other political institutional, cultural, and socioeconomic variables should also be taken into account.

The Impact of Other Variables on the Proportion of Women in the Legislature

Political variables

Several political variables have been examined in studies of women's representation in Congress, especially as the number of women legislators has increased over the past 25 years. These analyses have been hampered by the fact that women's numbers are still small, some relationships have changed over time, some seats have never had a woman representative, and some states are stronger in generating women candidates and winners than others. Recently, women are more likely to be elected when they are Democrats running in a favorable partisan district, when they are incumbents or are not opposing an incumbent (open seats), when they can match their opponent in campaign finance, and when they are running outside the southern region of the United States (Palmer and Simon 2006; Ondercin and Welch 2005).

For many years the most reliable way for a woman to attain a Congressional seat was to run as the widow of a Congressman who had died in office. Although this phenomenon has declined, it has not entirely disappeared (Kincaid 1978; Gertzog 2002; Palmer and Simon 2006).

Incumbency is significant for women as well as men, but as an underrepresented group, women suffer from the fact that most incumbents are male.

The power of incumbency is further demonstrated by women being more likely to win special elections occurring for open seats than they are at regularly scheduled elections (Nixon and Darcy 1996).

Party has become an increasingly important factor. Since 1992 the Democrats consistently have nominated almost twice as many women as Republicans, and in more favorable seats for election as well (Palmer and Simon 2006). Similar to leftist parties in other countries, the Democratic Party has been more receptive to women's demands for representation than their more ideologically conservative rival.

In the U.S. federal system, state legislatures are a major recruitment pool for Congressional candidates. Recently Democrats also have had about twice as many women state legislators as Republicans. As in Congress, this partisan disparity has been increasing since the early 1990s (Sanbonmatsu 2006).

Although often having persistent effects, political institutions sometimes can be changed, with different behavior resulting. The adoption of terms limits for legislators in some 15 U.S. states, however, has not improved women's numerical representation as expected, even though it reduced the individual incumbency barrier (Carey, Niemi, Powell, and Moncrief 2006; Carroll and Jenkins 2001).

The women's social movement and its now-established interest groups in the United States have been an inspiration for similar groups elsewhere in the world. They have also entered the realm of U.S. electoral politics. The political finance gap for women candidates has been eliminated, largely owing to the efforts of a few groups that direct their support to women candidates, especially if they hold a liberal opinion on abortion. This means that most of the money flows to women candidates in the Democratic Party (Burrell 2005). The most prominent of these groups is EMILY's List (for "Early Money Is Like Yeast, which helps raise the dough"). Yet the increases in women's representation in Congress remain incremental.

In comparative perspective, the significance of U.S. political institutions in hindering women's representation is clear. There are other formidable barriers to substantial change: one winner per district in a two-party system, partisan redistricting, decentralized nominations and campaigns, heavy campaign spending, and incumbency advantage. The linchpin of the whole operation, however, is the electoral system.

Social and Cultural Variables

How do these conclusions about the role of political institutions, especially the electoral system, stand up when measured against socioeconomic and cultural influences? We begin with cultural factors. Cultures evolve slowly, but over time can result in fundamental changes in political attitudes.

Rochon (1997) gives several examples of this in the United States, including attitudes toward women's role. But public opinion and political culture (longer-term value shifts) usually change in response to repeated patterns of events, social movements, and/or underlying socioeconomic change. In the case of women's political roles in the United States, the increased divorce rate, the availability of artificial birth control, and women's greater entry into the postwar labor force were precursors to the rise of the women's social movement in the 1960s (Schmidt 1993). The women's movement also drew inspiration from the struggle for racial equality and other social movements of the time. Thus, both longer-term social trends and political movements and events moved the public toward greater willingness to consider women politically equal to men in their office-holding ability, as shown in figure 3.1 (Rochon 1997; Dolan 2005).

These attitudes toward women's political involvement compare favourably to those in other advanced industrial democracies (Norris and Inglehart 2005). While the problem of whether actions follow or contradict attitudes is an old one, these particular findings are reinforced by others that show no demonstrable bias among voters in support for women candidates (Darcy, Welch, and Clark 1994; Dolan 2005).

Do these findings justify referring to the United States as a "feminist" society? It all depends on what one means by "feminism," which is a highly contested term. But findings indicate that even women who do not consider themselves to be "feminists" hold many opinions consistent with a reasonable definition of this term. In other words, even if they may not like the connotations of the term "feminist," their attitudes about women's role show many of the components of feminism. We can define the term minimally as advocating equal rights for women, including in the elite political sphere, and being willing to encourage change in this direction (as opposed to paternalism, or

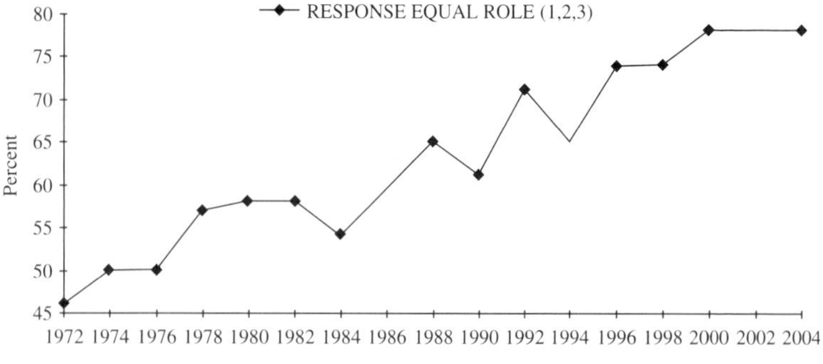

Source: Graph 4C.1.1, The American National Election Studies, November 30, 2005

Figure 3.1 Equal role for women, 1972–2004

male dominance). Then it would appear that the U.S. public is highly, although nowhere near unanimously, feminist in orientation and has moved strongly in this direction over recent decades (Huddy, Neely, and Lafay 2000). In fact, public attitudes are more favorable toward feminism in the United States than in several countries with *more* women as a percentage of legislators (Hayes, McAllister, and Studlar 2000).

The lingering but declining impact of cultural resistance to women in political office is shown by the fact that the South lags behind other regions in nominating and electing women. This may be because of more traditional views of male/female social distinctions in that area (Welch and Studlar 1996; Ondercin and Welch 2005). Thus, although there may be pockets of resistance to women as political leaders, this is not widespread enough to be able to explain the overall laggard U.S. performance in women's Congressional representation.

Socioeconomic Factors

If cultural factors do not provide a good explanation for why women should be so underrepresented in the U.S. Congress, what about socioeconomic ones? Broadly, greater socioeconomic modernization can help explain women's representation across the globe, but differences among developed polities are less susceptible to these influences (Matland 1998a; Norris and Inglehart 2005). Some changing socioeconomic factors that should favour more women candidates and legislators, namely the percentage of women in the labour force and the percentage of women holding tertiary degrees and professional occupations, especially in law (a major professional qualification for legislators in the U.S.), have not had the anticipated effects (Ondercin and Welch 2005; Norris and Inglehart 2005).

Compared with male candidates, there is a continuing tendency for women who run for Congress to be older and to be either childless or to have grown children (Ondercin and Welch 2005). Some argue that this is a manifestation of lack of equality in household labor between men and women.

Palmer and Simon (2006) find that there are "women-friendly" districts for nominating and for electing women, differing for black and white women, Democrats and Republicans. For blacks, men's and women's districts are much the same socioeconomically. Among white women representatives, Democrats tend to come from districts that are more liberal, urban, ethnically diverse, educated, and wealthier than their male counterparts. Female Republican representatives tend to come from constituencies that are less conservative, more urban, and more ethnically diverse than their male counterparts. The dilemma for Republicans is that, in socioeconomic terms, the districts where their women can compete well are also those likely to elect Democrats, especially men. Although the number of socioeconomically women-friendly districts has increased, women candidates in the Democratic Party have benefited disproportionately.

The failure of women to continue their forward march in numbers of candidacies in recent years has led to a renewed search for individual-level characteristics, especially self-confidence and political ambition, which can explain why women do not stand for election (Bledsoe and Herring 1990; Lawless and Fox 2005). But once elected, women are as ambitious and long serving as men (Palmer and Simon 2006).

Conclusion

The evidence for the influence of the electoral system and its associated political institutions in explaining the low proportion of women in the U.S. House of Representatives has become more compelling as other explanations have lost force. General socioeconomic conditions affecting women's candidacies have improved, yet over the past decade the growth in women's representation has returned to its incremental path.

Cultural expectations about women's roles have liberalized dramatically over the past half century, perhaps especially due to generational change, but women's share of the U.S. House has only slightly improved, in contrast to several other advanced industrial democracies. Women are no longer disadvantaged, if they ever were, by campaign financial support, thanks to active feminist support groups for them. On the state legislative level, term limits have not benefited women.

Given these findings, what factors are left? In the individualist culture of the United States, with the overwhelming dominance of the SMP electoral system, it is perhaps no surprise that many researchers have turned inward, to social psychology, to explain why women do not contest elections more frequently. In fact, systematic studies of the political ambition of politicians have been undertaken mainly in the United States. This reflects the orientation of the culture and of its academic researchers. But why have women in other countries not been found to have similar problems? The institutional configuration of multiple seats in one district and stronger, more centralized parties may encourage greater collective solidarity and less competitive behavior among potential candidates within the same party.

Among Western democracies, the United States is exceptional in its low representation of women in the central legislature. In fact, that ranking has been falling, not improving, in relation to other countries, especially established democracies. In 2004 the United States ranked fifty-seventh in the world in proportion of women in the lower house (Lawless and Fox 2005); by 2006 it had fallen to sixty-ninth (www.ipu.org). Because of ties on percentages, in fact there were 82 countries ranking higher than the United States in 2006.

As noted in table 3.1, among 20 advanced industrial democracies, the United States ranks seventeenth (the mean for these 20 countries is 26.5 percent women), and its relative standing in that group has fallen over the past half century as well (McAllister and Studlar 2002). Furthermore, in comparison with other industrialized democracies, there are proportionally fewer women candidates in the United States as well (Welch and Studlar 1996).

In comparative perspective, the dominant impact of the electoral system and its associated features in explaining the low proportion of women in the U.S. House of Representatives is evident. Women's representation continues to lag in SMP systems in comparison with those based at least partially on proportional representation, especially party-list PR. Conditions of a low district magnitude, strong incumbency bias, partisan redistricting, a shrinking number of marginal seats, a two-party system, and self-starting nominees in a decentralized party system and individualistic political culture stunt the possibility of developing processes of contagion among parties for women candidates, as has occurred in some PR systems (Matland and Studlar 1996).

As noted previously, even the Democratic success in the "nationalized" Congressional election of 2006 did not lead to a second "Year of the Woman" as some had hoped. Unless Democrats nominate even more women or the Republicans increase their share, a Republican victory in a future Congressional election might even reverse the overall incremental improvements for women. It is doubtful whether the success of Nancy Pelosi or other high-profile women in either party will lead to large increases in women's candidacies.

The safest conclusion is women will continue to make only limited and slow progress in descriptive representation in the U.S. House. This was predicted in mathematical and computer models originally developed two decades ago, which still serve well as explanations of the numbers of women in Congress (Andersen and Thorson 1984; Darcy and Choike 1986). To paraphrase Shakespeare: "The fault, dear Brutus, lies not in us, but in the electoral system."

Notes

* Thanks to Arnita Sitasari, Rachael Rudolph, David Mastro, and Kyle Christensen for research assistance.

1. The U.S. Senate is an equally important body in the U.S. system of government and is also directly elected, but on the basis of a fixed ratio of two representatives per state, with staggered terms of six years each. Thus, both its power and method of election render it different from most other upper houses in the world, even among democracies.

2. In 2007 legislation was introduced to give the District of Columbia a seat, along with an extra one for Utah. If the bill is successful, that would give the U.S. House 437 seats, probably with Eleanor Holmes Norton, the longtime nonvoting delegate from D.C., as an additional woman member.

4 Afghanistan

From Misogynist Theocracy to Gender-Inclusive Democracy?

Andrea Fleschenberg

Introduction

When it comes to women's representation at the intersection of election systems and politics, Afghanistan is one of the most challenging and particular case studies in point. Under the rule of the Taliban and its subsequent overthrow in 2001 by U.S.-led forces in the aftermath of 9/11, the misogynist conditions and the sociopolitical exclusion to which Afghan women have been subjected for long years, if not decades, came to be known to the international public and on the agenda of international policy-making. The "war on terror" on Afghan soil was not only about the fight against Al-Qaida and its fellow *jihadis*. It was also justified by "liberation" and subsequent "empowerment" of Afghan women in the process of armed regime change, aimed at introducing a democracy model according to "international standards" with the help of the international community and its governmental and nongovernmental representatives on the ground (Abirafeh 2005: 3; Kandiyoti 2004: 134; Kreile 2005: 104).

So far, the study of electoral systems and their impact on a given electorate or on specific social groups, such as women or minorities, has commonly focused on states with a functioning apparatus, that is, historically developed and working political institutions such as a party system, a parliament, a judiciary, and electoral procedures. To all of these components a certain understanding and definition are attributed, mainly derived from competitive liberal democracies, which then structure international democratization interventions in postconflict societies. These perceptions of procedures, institutions, and their composition and functions are then translated and transferred to a context—not only in the case of Afghanistan—that is completely different with regard to key characteristics such as systemic legacies, current political power structures, and interest aggregation. These "translated" instruments or procedures are applied to a postconflict scenario of a so far "failed state" coming out of three decades of political conflict; a state-building process still in the making within a society whose fragmented population segments and leading actors champion divergent views of "state," defend their "traditional" forms and means of political organization, or try to capture the newly built institutions for their own purposes and means of decision-making.

The question arises, What kind of authoritative resources, policy-making capacity, and self-determination the government of President Hamid Karzai has to implement a representative political order and to guarantee its citizens political participation rights? As the United Nations Special Rapporteur on Violence Against Women, Yakin Eturk, highlighted in 2005, the country faces perhaps the most daunting challenge in terms of women's rights, given its unique physical and social destruction with no working system in place through which to address gender discrimination (Esfandiari 2005a).

But some important steps have been taken during the last few years in Afghanistan. In recent postconflict contexts in different parts of the global south, electoral gender quotas have become a marker of good, modern governance and were included in several founding constitutions and electoral laws with Afghanistan (single nontransferable vote [SNTV]) and Iraq (proportional representation [PR]) being the most current examples in the Muslim world. As a consequence of its constitutional provision, Afghanistan now ranks twenty-fifth (out of 188) with its 27.3 percent female representation in the lower house, the Wolesi Jirga, well ahead of consolidated democracies such as the United Kingdom (rank 53), the United States (rank 68), or India (rank 109) (www.ipu.org/wmn-e/classif.htm; April 2007). At the same time, women willing to participate in elections still face a challenging, precarious, and highly contested sociopolitical environment in which their rights and the country's gender regimes will remain at the core of Afghan power and identity struggles for years to come. Therefore, we need to take a closer look at the realities, institutional structures in place, and dynamics generated for women candidates (and voters) before, during, and since last year's parliamentary elections on September 18, 2005—with the SNTV election system being one symptom of current Afghani politics, but not the predominantly decisive factor for female parliamentary representation and participation.[1]

The Voting System

SNTV, categorized as a majoritarian system, is currently only used in a handful of countries worldwide. Each voter has one vote for a candidate in multimember districts, that is, those candidates with the highest number of votes win a given number of parliamentary seats (Reynolds, Reilly and Ellis 2005: 113). The SNTV has a set of advantages: it is perceived to facilitate the representation of minorities and independents, to be more proportional than other majoritarian systems for reason of larger district magnitude, and to be less complicated to use in societies with high level of illiteracy or low level of political knowledge (Reynolds, Reilly and Ellis 2005: 113; Carey 2005: 9; Norris [n.a.]: 4).

But the SNTV is more frequently understood as an election system with more disadvantages, in particular in countries with embryonic or nonfunctioning party systems or in ethnically and religiously fragmented societies, divided by political conflict and political interests. First, it poses to political parties and electoral coalitions a huge challenge of party, candidate, and voter discipline and coordination with regard to sophisticated, complex vote allocation strategies depending on the number of votes needed for a candidate to win (likely seat-winning potential) to avoid the danger of vote splitting or high numbers of wasted votes in case of noncompliance. Second, while the SNTV can lead to higher levels of party organization, it has in reality led in countries such as Taiwan and Japan (which changed to a PR system in the mid-1990s) to electoral individualism, party fragmentation, factionalism, clientelistic politics, vote buying, and less-balanced candidate lists, as not a majority of votes is required to win a seat, resulting in controversial and nonaccomodatory campaigns at the electorate's margins (Reynolds, Reilly, and Ellis 2005: 113f; Carey 2005: 9f; Farrell 2001: 47; Hung-Mao 1996: 199; Wang 1996: 96ff). Third, critics outline that SNTV works against newly founded political parties, in particular democratic ones, which lack the necessary resources and capacities for complex vote strategies and discipline. In contrast, traditional and former power brokers who possess arms continue to have access to power and resources through their old jihadi networks, including means for vote buying, proxy voting, and parliamentary representation or intimidation of voters and candidates. Furthermore, the SNTV causes a huge burden on electoral administration, given high production costs for ballot material and logistics, time-consuming vote counting that give rise to fraud allegations, as candidates and their agents have difficulties in understanding and accepting the proceedings (ICG 2005a: i; JEMB 2005a: 22f; EU EOM 2005: 3).

The SNTV was adopted by decision of President Karzai in May 2005 against the advice of (inter)national experts and observers at a late stage of the electoral timeline. The major reasons behind the presidential decision are perceived to be, first, the deep mistrust of members of organized political parties held responsible for the various conflict phases and crimes committed, from the Soviet invasion and procommunist party rule and *mujahideen* rule of Islamic (party) factions to the fundamentalist Taliban (Carey 2005: 10; ICG 2005b: 1). Second, the country lacks a tradition of political parties, even in earlier phases of political liberalization (Goodson 2005: 33). Moreover, a fragmented and hence weak national assembly might be easier to control and might therefore further strengthen the central government and give room for maneuver to President Karzai (ICG 2006: i–ii; ICG 2005b: 6).

The 249 members of parliament (MPs) are elected for a five-year legislative period and the number of MPs depends on the size of the population with provinces serving as basis for the 35 electoral constituencies (including a national constituency for the *Kuchi* nomads) (BBC News 2005). In addition, article 72 (2) of the constitution requires that MPs be highly educated, which substantially narrows the (female) candidacy pool (Shah 2005: 248). The election system currently employed is a hybrid that includes provisions in the constitution and the electoral law for the representation of women and minorities (Kuchi nomads) for both chambers of the parliament as well as the provincial councils. The reserved seats are also directly elected under an SNTV regime.[2] Article 83 of the 2004 constitution stipulates that their number should be at least twice that of provinces existing in Afghanistan, including three for Kuchi nomads. Article 22 of the electoral law codifies that Wolesi Jirga seats should be allocated in accordance with article 83 of the constitution and to the most voted women on the list of candidates, while unfilled seats remain vacant until the next elections in case there are not enough female candidates.[3] "Once the representation requirements are met, the remaining seats shall be awarded according to Art. 21 of this Law," that is, on the basis of the number of votes received per province, with a maximum of one seat per candidate.[4] Potential candidates have to be over 25 years, submit the signatures of 300 registered voters, make a 10,000 Afghani deposit (approximately US$ 200),, and need to step down from government positions before the election campaign starts (ICG 2005a: 14).

Women in the Legislature: Historical Trends

In the words of Wilder (2005: 3), "[A]s Afghanistan has not held legislative elections for the past 35 years, there is little historical information about the nature of electoral politics," even more so with regard to women's political representation and participation. Nevertheless, apart from ethnicity and tribalism, gender remains one of the major structural principals of the Afghan political organization.

It was not before 1959 that women received the right to appear in public without a veil, and it took until 1964 for women to secure their voting rights (Kreile 2005: 109), so that a nearly impermeable gender-segregated public-private divide prevailed for decades. "According to UNIFEM [United Nations Development Fund for Women], although women made up 15% of the *Loya Jirga* [traditionally held, male-dominated or male-only grand councils] in

1977, until 2002 none had actually participated" (Nordlund 2004: 7). In contrast, since the overthrow of the Taliban in 2001, the transitional period is marked by several steps toward democratization, including the breakup of pervasive glass ceilings and glass walls surrounding Afghan women, slowly changing the face of Afghan politics.

Reserved-seats provisions have been the chosen means of paving the way for gender-inclusive public policy making and decision making at different Loya Jirgas. In the 2002 "Emergency Loya Jirga," 10 percent of the 1,600 seats were reserved for women, who participated in higher numbers, increasing their proportional share to 12 percent or some 200 female delegates (HRW 2005: 8).[5] Their number went up to one-third in the Constitutional Loya Jirga convened thereafter to draft the new constitution (Abirafeh 2005: 7). The call for a 25 percent gender quota was met with scepticism of possible window dressing, tokenism, and risk of a conservative backlash in the communities triggered by the strong international pressure "at the expense of laying a foundation for genuine participation" (Abirafeh 2005: 8).

In the following sections we will evaluate which factors are crucial for the proportion of female representation. But, irrespective of the acknowledged fact that "institutions matter," Afghanistan's political history indicates that female representation is highly dependent on women's ability to exercise their active and passive participatory rights in the first place, for example, acquiring knowledge of principal political procedures and exercising one's right of political self-determination (being allowed to vote or stand for political office).

The Impact of the Voting System on the Proportion of Women in the Legislature

The impact of the SNTV on Afghan electoral politics still remains to be seen, also with regard to the proportion of female legislative representation in future elections. Combined with the SNTV system, the quota works principally in favour of women candidates, who could enter parliament even with a comparably small number of votes gathered. However, in the first run, 19 women candidates (approximately 28 percent) managed to win a seat on their own, without having to use the reserved-seat provision to qualify for a mandate (ICG 2006: 7; Wilder 2005: 13).[6]

The crucial question is, *who won how?* under the current election system in the present political context. Some concerns about the disadvantageous effects an SNTV system normally generates have materialized already with the 2005 elections: the parliament is a rather fragmented body with an estimated more than 30 parties—which nevertheless were "electoral kingmakers"—represented and where ethnic identities as well as conservative social agendas have already played a major role for ad hoc coalition building and voting blocs (ICG 2006: I, 8; Wilder 2005: 4, 7–8). Gender continues to be a contested issue and sociopolitical marker, as one former jihad commander and MP from Herat suggests: "Parliament won't divide into many groups— only two: Secularists and Muslims. Secularists support freedom—for example, women not being veiled—whereas Muslims want to live like in the past—where women should wear veils" (Wilder 2005: 7). This cleavage includes women parliamentarians themselves, who do not represent a coherent political group (ibid.).

Under the 2005 SNTV election regime, the majority of women candidates ran as independents. Various power brokers, predominantly opposed to women in politics, captured the quota provision for their own favour, influencing the makeup of the candidacy pool and increasing their own vote share, evident in the configuration of women MPs:

- Few progressive and self-determined women politicians—mostly teachers, activists of nongovernmental organizations (NGOs), officials from the Ministry of Women's Affairs, and other professionals;
- Appendage politicians—many women coming from political families as wives and relatives of prominent commanders, or as wives, sisters, and daughters of Islamist parties members (the best organised);
- Clientelistic tokens of mujahideen factions or other high-ranking influentials—noticeable through expensive campaigns without any visible source of income (interviews conducted; ICG 2006: 7; Johnson 2005; Wieland-Karimi 2006: 2).

How have the voting system and the electoral conditions it created impacted on the proportion of women in the Wolesi Jirga? "Guns, goons, gold and patriarchy" would probably be a catchall slogan for women candidate's experiences under the first SNTV parliamentary elections. As subaltern actors, many of those women tried to champion power brokers owning networks and means of exercising power for decades as well as having access to economic, human, and social capital by legal and illegal means. Women faced a status disadvantage in an extremely gendered election environment that required highly visible individualized province-wide campaigning and that was characterized by the absence of a functioning party system or backing by political parties, a highly insecure, misogynist climate, and a predominantly illiterate electorate uninformed of basic political procedures. In addition, women lacked of the relevant network, particularly among "local influentials who could deliver blocs of votes based on religious or kinship grounds" (Wilder 2005: 17). These actors—village or tribal elders, local mullahs, district officials, and *shura* members—are "influential males" and thus beyond social reach for most women in Afghanistan's highly gender-segregated public space. Professional and workplace networks were more accessible for women since many of them worked as doctors, government officials, or teachers (Wilder 2005: 17f; Tarzi 2005).

Due to the security situation and lacking infrastructure, candidates mainly relied on poster campaigns and/or business cards holding name, symbol, and ballot number and conducted few public or in-house rallies or media campaigns (Wilder 2005: 26–27). Huge public rallies were only held by wealthy candidates and major political party leaders, sometimes in mosques, which women were barred from entering. Others distributed videos and CDs with their campaign speeches to reach secluded women (Wilder 2005: 27). Women candidates encountered themselves at a strategic disadvantage, given cultural constraints on communicating and travelling, and relied mainly on poster or proxy campaigns and indoor rallies at private homes (Esfandiari 2005b). As Rona Tareen, women candidate from Kandahar, explains: "I am under a *burqa;* people cannot recognise me. Men can go to the mosque and talk in public. Women must talk to individuals. You cannot have that same large gathering" (quoted in ICG 2005a: 12).

Many of the women candidates were NGO workers, government employees, and teachers, et cetera, with a comparably lower income that did not allow them to campaign on an equal footing with local commanders or other male rivals (ICG 2005a: 12, 18; EU EOM 2005: 2, 25; HRW 2005: 12; ANFREL 2005: 2). In contrast, powerful and wealthy commanders could manipulate election rules and extend their campaign outreach through both governmental and traditional social structures—they began campaigning before the officially declared start, spent more money than allowed, could afford plenty of candidate agents to "ensure" people's voted,[7] including proxy registration of female voters and subsequent ballot stuffing in several provinces (EU EOM 2005: 2, 25; ICG 2005a: 18; JEMB 2005a: 26; HRW 2005: 22; Wilder 2005: 36).

The Impact of Other Variables on the Proportion of Women in the Legislature

The composition, belief systems, and dynamics of the sociopolitical fabric, underpinning every kind of electoral structures and politics, are perhaps the main conditional factors of women candidates' experiences and performance—despite gender-inclusive quotas—and are rather unaffected by the type of election system in place.

Many Afghan men remain divided on the issues whether (a) it can be considered Islamic behaviour for women to become politicians, (b) women have leadership capacities, and (c) women will follow a balanced agenda that will not discriminate against men (JEMB 2005b).[8] A former minister of women's affairs, Massouda Jalal, stresses that in a male-dominated society, where private and public decision making remains in the hands of men, women cannot enter legislative politics "without support of their husbands or families" (ibid.). This support is paramount in a highly insecure (post-) conflict environment. Women faced difficulties in accessing insecure and badly connected rural areas—serious challenges to their genuine participation in legislative politics vis-à-vis a predominantly rural electorate.[9] Many women candidates felt they did not have access to government assistance and security protection by police and guards because the latter are often heavily influenced by political rivals and warlords (according to a JEMB [Joint Electoral Management Body] official from Kabul, quoted in HRW 2005: 26f). Malalai Shinwari, head of the female candidates' society, explains why few charges have been presented to the authorities:

> A woman is threatened by a car that does not have a license plate. A woman receives a call from "unknown" number telling her to quit. Isn't that a threat? But that woman doesn't have anything to show as proof. For that reason, when she goes to the [complaint] commission, she gets discouraged. Until women have physical proof they're being threatened, nobody cares.
>
> (Esfandiari 2005b)

Women candidates received threats by Islamic militant groups, local power brokers and ordinary people who rebuff any kind of public involvement and political agency by women or perceive them as political rivals (Esfandiari 2005b; Jalalzai and Synovitz 2005). Like the prominent cases of armed attack against Safiya Sidiqi, Shaheeda Hossein, Zohra Sahel (these are women politicians who were running for a mandate in the last legislative elections), or former news presenter Hawa Alam highlight, many of the 328 women candidates were subjected to death threats by gunmen, beaten up, shot at, or had their property set on fire in various countrywide incidents (see Amnesty International 2005; Baldauf 2005; Esfandiari 2005b; Irin News 2005; Jalalzai and Synovitz 2005).

It is generally understood that women's political participation is dependent on their access to education, own income generated, and other aspects of social infrastructure (e.g., health and child care), apart from the political institutions, structures, and the gender culture in place (cf. Zimmermann 1994: 4–10).

Socioeconomic Opportunities

As far as data are available, socioeconomic indicators are highly unfavourable for Afghan women's participation in public and political life. As table 4.1 indicates, current human development levels evidence the impact of socioeconomic conflict legacies and destruction of human, social, and economic

Table 4.1 Human development indicators, Afghanistan, 2004

	2002	*2003*
Human Development Index	0.346	n.a.
● Urban population (%)	—	23.3
● Purchasing power parity (PPP)/ capita (U.S. dollar)	822	—
Gender-Related Development Index	0.300	n.a.
● Life expectancy (men/women, years)	45.0 / 44.0	46.0 / 46.4
● Literacy rate (men/women, %)	43.2 / 14.1	—
● Gross enrolment ratio (men/women, %)	59.34 / 29.57	51 / 27
● PPP/capita (men/women, U.S. dollar)	1.182 / 402	—
● Total fertility rate (birth/woman)	—	7.5
● Female economic activity rate (%, 15 years of age and above)	—	48.2
● Female economic activity rate	—	57
● (% of male rate, 15 years of age and above)		
Gender empowerment measure	n.a.	n.a.

Source: UNDP 2004: 19–23; http://hdr.undp.org/statistics/data/countries.cfm?c=AFG (July 2006).

capital and demonstrate a significant gender bias, hence a status- and capacities-related disadvantage for and deprivation of Afghan girls and women.

Gender Culture

Regardless of social status and ethnicity, Afghan women entering the political arena challenge social taboos and face threats to their physical integrity in a society where Afghan women who enter politics serve as markers of male honour and identity. This notion is equally embraced by influential traditional and current societal power brokers and contenders of the central government, such as warlords, Taliban, and other insurgent groups (cf. Ghufran 2006: 86; Wieland-Karimi 2006: 2).

"A dilemma for women is they often do not know how far they can push social norms and their political freedoms without incurring retaliation" (HRW 2005: 16). Any interaction of women with unrelated men is highly censured and thus their mobility and autonomy as people's representatives are restricted.[10] This cultural notion presents female political aspirants with obstacles—when conducting an election campaign or gaining access to election- and politics-related information beforehand (e.g., civic/voter education). Hitherto they needed the help of male relatives and their families as well as community/tribal influentials to garner votes on a larger scale and to serve as proxies in campaign environments inaccessible to them.[11] Women's perceived dependence on men makes it more difficult for them to gain recognition and acceptance as genuine political leaders in their own right and merit, which is necessary to win a seat and represent people in a province-wide constituency.[12] Consequently, Elaha Surosh from the Committee for Defence of Afghan Women Rights emphasizes that gender is not enough to perform in politics and to represent constituencies. Education and training are vital—especially for society, because the mindset of men should be changed first, since political participation of women depends on it.[13]

Politics, an Exclusively Male-Sanctioned Domain

Barriers and conditionalities to women's legislative representation exist within the political system, its gendered hierarchies and structures, and in the context parameters. A gender-political divide within the state apparatus creates an ambivalent, contradictory environment in which women politicians and political aspirants have to orientate themselves, negotiate, and operate: the constitution prescribes the equality of both sexes and foresees reserved seats for women in the national legislature; the Convention on the Elimination of All Forms of Discrimination against Women was signed in 2003 without reservation, while at the same time article 3 of the constitution determines the supremacy of Islam over any kind of legislation, subject to interpretation by the Supreme Court headed by the conservative Islamist Fazel Hadi Shinwari, in a move to appease and co-opt the religious clergy for governmental approval (Kreile 2005: 115; Gall 2006a; Shah 2005: 239). The allegations of window dressing and tokenism through *malleable women* originated in the present political opportunity structures, under which political parties either neglected to recruit women or used them as proxy voters and proxy representatives for their own political purposes, capturing additional seats via the quota provision (HRW 2005: 13). The ongoing insurgency and violence by Taliban, strongly opposed to women's political participation, constitute a continuous problem and deterrent to female political aspirants in present and future (cf. Gall 2006b; Ghufran 2006: 88). The provinces are predominantly governed by former warlords who keep private militias and remain outside of central government control; moreover, the electoral victory of former warlords and commanders as Wolesi Jirga candidates "will institutionalize their role in the country" despite general public resentment of their political status, given their war crimes record and current involvement in organized crime (Ghufran 2006: 89f; see also Goodson 2005: 34). In such a gender and political environment, many women did not (and probably will not) contest elections owing to travel-related security concerns, conservative family norms, limited financial resources, and intimidation by warlords and their subordinates (HRW 2005: 3).

Conclusion

In the case of Afghanistan, it is not the election system that is the main determining variable of the proportion and effectiveness of female political representation and participation but Afghan-style *classic patriarchy* and its *patriarchal bargains* (Kandiyoti 2005). The gender composition of the sociopolitical environment—the idiosyncrasies of a still male-dominated and misogynist political system and its power brokers, the prevalent gender ideology, and the depriving level of gender-related socioeconomic development—amounts to an androcentric public and political domain whose glass walls and glass ceilings are nearly impermeable.

However, even if the election system constitutes a secondary determining variable of the proportion of women in the Wolesi Jirga, several activists and political analysts alike continue to appeal for a PR list system. In fact, criticism has been raised by the JEMB and nearly all international and national analysts and women and human rights activists, who call for a party-based, preferably PR, system (cf. Carey 2005; EU EOM 2005; ICG 2005a, 2005b; JEMB 2005a; Wieland-Karimi 2005, 2006; Wilder 2005). In interviews conducted, there was consensus that under a PR list system, women would have more opportunity to join candidacy and quota lists or voluntarily withdraw in favour of other women candidates. A PR system would avoid a lot of the gender biases generated under the SNTV in the given sociopolitical environment as described earlier. On the other hand, some were skeptical of the benefits, because a PR system could further strengthen stronger fundamentalist parties and weaken the nascent democratic ones as well as less diversity among contesting candidates. Those critics questioned whether a different election system would make political parties support women candidates with their networks and resources. Some suggested the need for higher quotas proportional to women's population share.[14]

Women in politics still appear to be exceptions to the rule in Afghanistan, thanks, to an extent, to international intervention and pressure, which has provoked allergic reactions of the androcentric sociopolitical establishment. Nevertheless, women politicians make (fragile) inroads, sometimes meandering ones on the incremental track,[15] into gender-inclusive democracy. But there are rifts in the patriarchy.[16] Two indicators are the number of men who voted for women candidates and the increasing number of political women's networks in Kabul and provincial capitals (Wieland-Karimi 2006: 9). In addition, given the strong performance of women in some constituencies, a debate arose whether the 68 reserved seats are a minimum or a maximum constitutional requirement for female legislative representation. For women's rights activists and international observers, the electoral law is unclear and requires modification (cf. interviews conducted; EU EOM 2005: 26).

The Women's Political Participation Committee, an informal NGO and politicians' network and platform, sent a petition letter to the JEMB pleading for an increased proportion of female mandates, which was then forwarded to the president. Both the president and the supreme court refused to grant any additional seats, given the constitutional provision that, in their view, defines the reserved seats quota as a maximum rather than a minimum number of women legislatures.[17] Committee member Najia Haneefi explains that the lobbying for a change in the electoral law will continue so that the two women candidates with fewer votes (compared with men) fill the reserved seats, and the women candidates with enough votes to win directly do not fall under the quota provision.[18]

One-and-a-half years after the parliamentary elections, women parliamentarians have nevertheless made inroads into policy-making and are slowly becoming accepted in politics. One major challenge appears no longer to be the election system that disfavoured women's entry into the assembly, but the overall political setup with a strong presidency and the fragmentation and polarization within the parliament, in particular among the women parliamentarians themselves, who have not been able to caucus on crucial issues for their own constituencies—the Afghan women. It remains to be seen whether the election system will be upheld in the coming elections or whether steps toward a proportional system are taken—as suggested by some civil society activists. In the upcoming revision of the Afghan Constitution, the second major challenge appears to be to keep the quota provision in place and to ensure that in the coming elections, the "right women," that is, qualified, independent women activists and party workers, will be given a chance to contest succesfully.[19]

Notes

1. This analysis draws on relevant secondary sources, including election observer and human rights watchdog reports, newspaper articles, and own interviews conducted in 2006 in February (Colombo, Sri Lanka) and in April (Berlin, Germany) during international conferences.
2. Surprisingly, there was no serious public resistance to the quota system, which can be partly explained by the fact that major mujahideen factions used the provision to place a large number of handpicked women in the new assembly. These women have no prowomen agenda and are dependent on their faction (interview with Niamatullah Ibrahimi, April 2006).
3. See www.anfrel.org/en/pics/current/Election%20Law.pdf (July 2006).
4. Ibid.
5. "Many women participants felt they were prevented from giving any substantive input. Only a few women were able to speak, and some reported their microphones were cut off after five minutes. In contrast, powerful mujahidin leaders (...) were given half-hour-long speaking slots" (HRW 2005: 8). More freedom was reported

from the *Constitutional Loya Jirga,* but "many female delegates still faced threats and harassment during the proceedings, or censored themselves due to fear of retaliation upon return to their home communities"—with some facing later social reprisal, job dismissals, and transfer to less desirable positions as their right of participation was principally contested and resented (ibid.).

6. "One unintended consequence of the provision to have a quota of 68 women's seats in the WJ [Wolesi Jirga] was that it provided an avenue through which not only women, but also some of the more recently established small liberal and left-oriented parties, could enter the NA [National Assembly]. Of the 13 seats won by candidates affiliated with these parties, eight were won by women" (Wilder 2005: 6).

7. Some female candidates have withdrawn after experiencing intimidation by powerful political rivals before even registering or have feared electoral manipulation: "In the provinces, all the commanders have collected votes … Every Friday they kill lots of animals, and feed people, they offer this much money, and land to build a house—even if it is government land" (quoted in HRW 2004).

8. A survey conducted by Asia Foundation in 2004 revealed that 87 percent of Afghans believe that women need male permission to vote and that 18 percent of men will not allow them to do so while 35 percent of interviewed women were not sure whether they would receive permission by male elders or husbands (Asia Foundation 2004: 7, 11).

9. "I have problems travelling to remote areas. I can't take guards with myself, because I don't have enough money to give them. Men don't need guards for themselves. It is a problem for women independent candidates" (Wolesi Jirga women candidate, former teacher, from Mazar-e-Sharif, quoted in HRW 2005: 24).

10. Safiya Sidiqi was one of two female women parliamentarians travelling to London for a major donor conference without being accompanied by her husband, which was understood by several male colleagues as a breach of Islamic Sharia law. (It forbids women from going on long journeys without a *mahram* [close male relative] accompanying). The allegedly un-Islamic behaviour triggered a parliamentary debate (Baldauf 2006).

11. This restriction appears to be a shared experience of women candidates, irrespective of social status and prominence, in front of mosques and other male-only public places and conventions (shuras). In 2004, the only female presidential candidate, Massouda Jalal, was barred from speaking "at the central shrine in Mazar-e-Sharif, the Rowza Hazrat Ali, although government officials and other potential political candidates spoke (…)" (HRW 2004).

12. Opinion gathered from interviews conducted in Colombo and Berlin.

13. Interview conducted in Colombo.

14. Opinion gathered from interviews conducted in Colombo and Berlin.

15. Term borrowed from Drude Dahlerup (conference communication in Halmstad, June 2003).

16. Term borrowed from Judith Huber (quoted in Kreile 2005: 118).

17. Opinion gathered from interviews conducted in Colombo.

18. Interview conducted on April 21, 2006, Berlin.

19. Interviews conducted in Kabul, April 2007.

Subpart II

Majority

5 France

The Single-Member District System: The Hidden Bonus for Notables

Mariette Sineau

Introduction

It was not until the mid-twentieth century that women in France finally earned the right both to vote and to run for office (Ordinance of April 21,1944), while men had enjoyed such rights for nearly a century (since 1848). Although women had no trouble learning to slip a ballot paper into the ballot box, exercising their right to elected office has proven problematic. In France, more than elsewhere, the parliamentary representation of women has been filtered through political parties. Social selection, an inherent effect of election contests, has acted to their detriment, as it does for young politicians and members of the working class.

Over 60 years after their legal entry into the polis, French women still have difficulty crossing the threshold into parliament. As a result of the 2002 legislative elections, only 12 percent of them have seats among the nation's representatives, ranking France eighty-sixth for the parliamentary representation of women internationally (www.ipu.org/wmn-e/classif.htm; April 2007). A symbolic locus of power in the French republic, the National Assembly remains a masculine political space.

France is an ideal country to study the effects of electoral systems on female representation in elected assemblies. For one thing, it has an extremely wide range of voting systems in its various assemblies:[1] this fact provides the opportunity to observe that women have almost always been better represented in assemblies elected by the party list system than those elected according to a single-member district (SMD) system. Second, when France replaced the Fourth with the Fifth Republic, it changed its legislative electoral system: the proportional party-list system used under the Fourth Republic (1946–1958) was replaced in the Fifth Republic by the two-round SMD majority voting system, which itself was temporarily replaced for one election with a proportional system in the 1986 legislative elections. This alternation in voting rules over a short historical period and for the same assembly offers ideal conditions in which to compare the effects of the two systems on the statistical chances of women being elected.

After first describing the workings of the French electoral system and analyzing women's faltering entrance into the National Assembly, I will demonstrate how the logic behind the two-round SMD voting system discriminates against the "second sex." Last, I will expose how other constraints of a political, cultural, and religious nature also help to explain why women in France have always remained on the sidelines of the lawmaking process.

The Voting System

In June 1958, the Fourth Republic crumbled under the weight of the Algerian crisis. This returned General de Gaulle to power and was cause for a new constitution, which was finally adopted by referendum on September 28, 1958. The constitution of the Fifth Republic continues to govern French politics today. The lower house, formerly called the Chambre des députés (Chamber of deputies), took the name Assemblée nationale (National Assembly). Accompanying the change in regime was a change in the electoral system for the election of deputies. The new system, the two-round plurality/majority SMD, is considered to be more modern and efficient, as it is likely to clearly identify majorities for government. But for de Gaulle, the choice of an electoral system was a question of circumstances, and he refused to name the electoral system for the National Assembly in the constitution.

The system is called "single-member district," because there is only one seat in power per electoral district. In the 2002 election, there were 577 such districts in all of France. It is a two-round majority/plurality system: to be elected in the first round, the candidate must obtain the absolute majority of votes. A second round takes place if this absolute majority does not occur. Higher and higher qualification thresholds have been instituted for candidates to be included in the second round: 5 percent of votes in 1958, 10 percent of those registered in 1966 and, since 1975, 12.5 percent of voters registered. In most cases, only two candidates compete in the second round. But in recent times, the ground gained by the radical right party, the Front National, has increased the number of "triangular" elections.

Though in theory the two-round French system leads more frequently to multipartism than a one-round system would, in practice it remains favourable to large parties, given the strong majority leaning it brings about. In France, the bipolar quadrille (two parties to the Left and two parties to the Right) shares almost all the hemicycle, even when a strong proportion of the electorate votes in the first round for nonparliamentarian parties.

The SMD system was suspended for a short period of time: the law of June 26, 1985, passed when the Left was in power, instituted the list-based proportional representation system at the departmental (the equivalent of the county in the United Kingdom or the United States) level. It was under this rule that the 1986 legislative elections were held. The Right, having returned to power, passed the law of July 11, 1986, which reestablished the prior SMD voting system and which remains in effect today.

Women in the Legislature: Historical Trends

To describe female representation in a few words using the figures in table 5.1, it could be said to have started high in 1945–1946, only to shrink during the period of the brief Fourth Republic. Then, with the birth of the Fifth

Table 5.1   Women candidates and elected members to the Chamber of Deputies (Fourth Republic) and the National Assembly (Fifth Republic)

*Chamber of Deputies: Fourth Republic**					
Elections	*Women candidates*	*Total candidates*	*Female candidates (%)*	*Women elected*	*Total seats*	*Elected (%)*
Nov 10, 1946	382	2,801	13.6	35	619	5.6
June 17, 1951	384	3,962	9.7	22	626	3.5
Jan 2, 1956	495	5,372	9.2	19	595	3.2

*National Assembly: Fifth Republic***					
Elections	*Women candidates*	*Total candidates*	*Female candidates (%)*	*Women elected*	*Total seats*	*Elected (%)*
Nov 23–30, 1958	68	2,809	2.4	9	552	1.6
Nov 18–25, 1962	55	2,172	2.5	8	482	1.6
March 5–12, 1967	70	2,190	3.2	10	487	2.0
June 23–30, 1968	75	2,265	3.3	8	487	1.6
March 4–11, 1973	200	3,023	6.6	8	490	1.6
March 12–19, 1978	706	4,266	16.5	18	491	3.7
June 14–21, 1981	323	2,715	11.9	26	491	5.3
March 16, 1986	1,680	6,804	24.7	34	577	5.9
June 5–12, 1988	336	2,896	11.6	33	577	5.7
March 21–28, 1993	1,003	5,139	19.5	34	577	5.9
May 25–June 2, 1997	1,464	6,360	23.0	63	577	10.9
June 9 and 16, 2002	3,288	8,456	38.9	71	577	12,3

*Proportional party-list vote.
**SMD voting system (except in 1986).
Source: Interior Ministry (all of France).

Republic, the access of women to elected office virtually screeched to a halt. I now review the salient features of this history in an attempt to explain it.

In 1945–1946 women drew their legitimacy in politics from the Résistance, symbolizing both the struggle against the occupying forces and a renewal of elites, those of the Third Republic being partly disqualified (Guéraiche 1997). The major parties (Communist Party, Socialist Party, and the Mouvement Républicain Populaire) were well aware of this and made it a point of honor to place women candidates, preferably Résistance fighters or widows of Résistance fighters, close to the top of their lists. However, as the memory of the Résistance gradually faded, their share of the candidates and elected officials gradually dwindled. The first Chamber of Deputies under the Fourth Republic, elected in 1946 using the list system at the departmental level, was made up of 619 representatives. Thirty-five women obtained seats, including 26 Communists, which comprised 5.6 percent of members. This was a promising score, which ranked France at that time with the Scandinavian countries, but this was not to last. In the following two legislatures, the proportion of women members of parliament fell to 3.5 percent in 1951, then to 3.2 percent in 1956.

When the Fifth Republic was born, the list system was replaced by the SMD system right from the first legislative elections, held in November 1958. There was a notable drop in the number of women candidates fielded by the political parties (2.4 percent compared with 9.2 percent in 1956). This resulted in their being sidelined among the newly elected members of the National Assembly, the name given to the former Chamber of Deputies: there were only nine women among the 550 members of parliament, or 1.6 percent. Thus, the 1958 legislative elections was the first stage for French women in their long eviction from the parliamentary scene. For five legislatures, they never achieved more than 2 percent of the seats. After 20 years of the Fifth Republic, the 1978 legislative elections, in which the Left made considerable headway, scarcely elected 4 percent women among the nation's representatives.

In 1981, the United Left (Gauche unie), bringing together Socialists, Left Radicals (radicaux de gauche) and Communists, finally gained power after 23 years of a Gaullist majority and raised considerable hope among women. Yet this power changeover did not result in feminizing the Assemblée nationale (although the Socialist Party had promised French women an expansion of their rights as citizens): the proportion of women in the assembly did not rise above the 5 percent mark. Five years later, during the 1986 legislative elections, which the Left lost, female activists of all political colors regained hope. They were counting on the new voting system, proportional representation by list, to bring a wave of feminization in the assembly. It had a mechanical effect of multiplying the proportion of female candidates by two (which went from 11.9 percent to 24.7 percent), but it did not entail any correlative rise in the number of female elected officials (5.9 percent). This resulted in a record number of women being "beaten." For instance, the Socialist Party, which fielded an exceptional rate of 18.9 percent female candidates, only got 9.9 percent of them elected in the end. The 1988 legislative elections, which had the dual characteristic of once again being fought on the SMD system and being won by the Left, resulted in the same number of female members of parliament as in the previous legislature, a proportion of 6 percent. Given these figures, it would be tempting to conclude at this stage of the analysis that neither the switchover in power from Left to Right nor the voting system had any impact on women's faltering entrance into the parliamentary arena.

Finally, it was not until the 1997 legislative elections, won by the so-called Plural Left (Gauche plurielle) bringing together Socialists, Communists, and Verts members, that the National Assembly was to be made up of more than 10 percent women, and this for the first time in the history of the Republic. The voluntaristic policy decided in 1996 by the Socialist Party helps to explain this great leap forward.

Last, although the 2002 legislative elections were a landmark in the history of successful female election in France, they hardly produced the outcome many had hoped. In this election, the law of June 6, 2000, known as the parity law, induced political parties to reach parity but was not an obligation.[2] Those who did not field equal numbers of female and male candidates, give or take 2 percent, were to be penalized by receiving less than their entitlement to public funds.[3]

The results of the vote by gender show the full measure of the resounding failure of the law: the proportion of women in the assembly rose from 10.9 percent to only 12.3 percent. On the Left, the Socialist Party and the Communist Party only fielded 36.3 percent and 44 percent women candidates, respectively—and only 16.3 percent and 19 percent were elected. On the Right, the two major parties, the Union pour la Majorité Présidentielle (UMP) and the Union pour la Démocratie Française, took even greater liberty with the parity rule, fielding only 20.6 percent and 18.9 percent female candidates, respectively. The result was that only 10.4 percent and 6.8 percent of women, respectively, won seats.

The Impact of the Voting System on the Proportion of Women in the Legislature

I have pointed out the correlation between the reestablishment of the SMD voting system in 1958 and the sudden and lasting halt brought to parliamentary representation of French women. I will now look beyond this phenomenon to examine what discriminating effects the voting system has had on outcomes. At the same time, I will argue that political parties have made an extremely sexist use of electoral rules.

The French SMD system instituted in 1958 has three characteristics, all of which encourage political parties to select a certain type of candidate. And it is this very logic, as we will see, that indirectly discriminates against women.

The first feature is a "local" type of voting system that takes place in small voting districts (France has 577 of them). Such a narrow geographic framework fosters the creation of direct links between elected officials and voters, accentuating the phenomenon of personality voting. A candidate's social or political prominence and his/her qualities as a speaker or a communicator are seen as being decisive factors in winning an election. When candidates are selected, parties therefore have a tendency to choose the candidate who is the most highly visible in the voting district: an incumbent or notable, well-known socially (a lawyer, doctor, or business person) or politically (for instance a mayor, a general councilor[4]).

The second characteristic of the system is that it encourages individual strategies of multiple office holding by which parliamentary representatives constitute electoral fiefdoms, so to speak, for in France it is legal to hold several different elected offices. There was no limitation to this rule until 1985, since when there has been two reforms (in 1985 and 2000). However, it still remains legal to hold two major elective offices simultaneously, notably, parliamentary representative and mayor and parliamentary representative and general councilor. Multiple office holding has become an almost inescapable practice under the Fifth Republic, constituting a powerful obstacle against the entrance of outsiders in the selection process and hence reinforcing the weight of notables.

The third parameter of the system is that it has a runoff round, for which only candidates who received the votes of at least 12.5 percent of the registered electorate at the first round are allowed to run for the second. This implies advantages for candidates from the major parties (who field the fewest women) and disadvantages for the candidates coming from the smaller political groups who tend to field more women. The second round also reinforces the personal aspect of the election: in this decisive round, the candidates fight a sort of duel, a real jousting match, to use a familiar metaphor. Lacking political experience and having little training in the art of oratory, women are perceived by political parties as being less competitive than men, which in turn explains the latter's reluctance to allow women to compete for the voters' favor, especially at the time, the late 1950s, when misogyny was rampant.

The 1958 legislative elections will be taken as a telling example of the gender effects that the SMD voting system has on national representation. Starting with the first election to use the SMD system, parties tailored their selection process to the change in rules. Whereas a proportional representation system by list had enabled parties to diversify and feminize their candidacies at no electoral risk, the SMD voting system requires them to focus selection of candidates on the best-known competitors in order to win the competition. For this reason, they primarily draw their candidates from the pool of local officials, especially among the general councilors, 800 of whom were in the running, with 200 elected. Following the election, 64 percent of the representatives elected in 1958 also held the office of general or municipal councilor. The priority thus given in the selection criteria to elected officials over party activists has inevitably led to the marginalization of women. At the close of the 1950s, women who had the cultural, social, and political resources to make a "good" notable were rare. Only a fraction of them held mayorships and the office of general councilor.[5] Once the party picked them, moreover, they were assigned voting districts that were difficult, if not impossible, to win, which partly explains the gap observed between the proportion of female candidates and the number of women elected (2.4 percent compared with 1.6 percent).

The SMD system has thus worked to women's detriment as an implacable two-step elimination mechanism: rarely selected as candidates, they have even more seldom been those chosen to represent those voting districts in which they were likely to win (Sineau and Tremblay 2007: 163). As a result, only a handful of women successfully reached the second round. Women have thus indirectly suffered from the new system, owing to the new political balance that it generated. The parliamentary strength of the Communist Party did not survive the disappearance of the proportional representation. At the outcome of the 1958 legislative elections, it was virtually wiped out, being left with only 10 seats, whereas it had had 150 in the outgoing assembly. It had been the Communists who, under the Fourth Republic, got nearly three-quarters of women elected. In the outgoing assembly, there were 15 female Communist deputies but only two in 1958.

Women were long to pay the price for the notable rationale underlying the SMD voting system. In other words, a hidden bonus goes to notables and multiple officeholders in the process of choosing parliamentary representatives. This hidden bonus has penalized women throughout the Fifth Republic in both the candidate selection procedure and the election process, as shown in table 5.1. The only way for political parties to alleviate the discriminating effects of the system would be to implement a quota policy so that the selection process does not penalize women as political outsiders. But we know that, unlike the list system, the SMD system makes it technically difficult to implement such positive measures.

If it is admitted that the SMD voting system has resulted in discrimination against women, it remains to be explained why the return to the proportional system for the 1986 legislative elections did not enable them to catch up. The causes are threefold. The first has to do with the means of implementation. The small size of voting districts continues to favor incumbents and local notables in the selection criteria. It must be kept in mind that over half of the French departments have only four seats or less (the minimum is two). On such short lists, the most desirable places were necessarily competitive! The second reason is political in nature: parliamentary parties demonstrated no particular desire to use the proportional system to the benefit of women. This is true of the Socialist Party, which had a number of incumbents it wished to see reelected. Last, female activists, perhaps overconfident in the feminizing virtues of the proportional system, did not exert enough pressure on their leaders at the strategic moment that lists were drawn up (Jenson and Sineau 1995: 314).

The Impact of Other Variables on the Proportion of Women in the Legislature

The French SMD system, coupled with multiple office holding, has indeed been an instrument in the hands of the political parties and it filters women's entry into parliament. Yet, the electoral system should not be the tree that hides the forest, as it is only one element in an institutional whole that cannot be ignored. Furthermore, there are deep-seated and long-standing reasons for the parliamentary underrepresentation of women in France.

It should first be recalled that in addition to the electoral system, other rules instituted by the Fifth Republic to modernize politics pushed women off the political playing field (Sineau 2001: 33–42). First, male domination in politics has its roots in the election of the head of state by universal suffrage. This reform, which makes the president of the Republic the nation's chosen one (its father?), reinforced the symbolic aspect of the strong man, especially under the presidency of de Gaulle. Over time, parliamentary parties have turned into platforms for presidential potentials, recruiting candidates first among men, who are seen to be the best endowed in the race for the supreme office of the state. This general principle of masculine preference has spread through all electoral races, from the municipal to the national level, imposing a virile model of leadership.

The rule that prevents ministers sitting in parliament, introduced by the Fifth Republic, has also influenced the profile of elected officials. The new regime calls extensively on the administrative elite, most often from the École Nationale d'Administration (ENA), to exercise executive functions as well as parliamentary ones. This has been another factor penalizing women. The ENA, although coeducational since its inception, long remained a school for men, who until the 1970s made up more than 90 percent of each graduating class.

Sidelined by the institutions created in 1958, women have also been marginalized by political parties. Under the Fifth Republic, parties have experienced a considerable drop in membership. They less resemble the mass parties they had been under the Fourth Republic than a club of elected officials, reluctant to open up to the lifeblood of society, including women. In such oligarchic structures, women have been perceived by activists as undesirable rivals, without the legitimacy necessary to occupy positions of power. Thus, they are not selected in voting districts where they are likely to win. This is the more true since they have never been authorized to organize independently. Caught up in this dynamic of unfavorable circumstances and rules, women in turn gave into the temptation to reject activism through political parties. The women's liberation movement (Mouvement de Libération des Femmes [MLF]) in the 1970s, marked by its leftist origins, itself eschewed political parties, elections, and the parliament (Jenson and Sineau 1994: 250).[6]

The resistance of political parties to women's entry into politics can also be measured by the lack of enthusiasm for implementing affirmative measures. In the past, the Communist Party was the only one of all the major parties to put into practice an informal quota system and reserve candidacies for women (as well as for young people and workers).[7] The result of this policy was visible and lasting, until the Communist Party's electoral decline. For six legislatures (from 1962 to 1981), it was the Communist Party, with fewer members in parliament, that showed the highest proportion of female deputies.

The Socialist Party, created in 1971, which became the leading left-wing party in the mid-1970s, has not been much more attentive than right-wing parties to feminizing its recruitment. From the legislative elections of 1973 to those of 1993, the proportion of women it fielded, always lower than the Communist Party's (PC), only once passed the threshold of 10 percent. This was in 1986. It waited until 1996 to vote in favor of a 30 percent quota of women candidates in legislative elections,[8] thereby trailing behind its Scandinavian and German counterparts, which much earlier implemented affirmative policies (Caul 1999). This quota, moreover, was not followed to the letter in the 1997 legislative elections: the Socialist Party fielded 27.8 percent female candidates, obtaining 17.2 percent seats for women out of a group of 250 deputies. This quota-fixing policy, initiated by First Secretary Lionel Jospin, was facilitated by the fact that socialists had fewer incumbents to take into consideration, owing to their severe defeat in 1993.

Paradoxically, the Socialist quota was more effective in feminizing the assembly than the parity law of June 6, 2000, had been. Poorly designed, this law did little to help women fight against the hidden bonus given to notables and incumbents. However, it had the effect of feminizing candidacies without feminizing parliament. There were two reasons for this outcome.

First, only small parties (with no hope of winning seats) respected the parity of candidacies, whereas parliamentary parties (except the Verts) neglected to do so. Furthermore, when the major parties fielded women, many of them were virtually stand-ins, assigned to politically marginal voting districts (Murray 2004; Scott 2005; Sineau 2005a).

Why, despite the parity law, do women still seem to be the eternal victims of the same two-step elimination mechanism? The reckoning performed by parliamentary parties may help to answer this question. They base their strategy on the following principle: "'better to pay a fine than field a female candidate," assuming that they stood to gain more in terms of seats (on the basis of which the second fraction of public funding is computed) than what the financial penalties would cost.[9] For this reason, they once again chose to select incumbent officeholders who hold multiple posts, mostly men, more likely in their eyes to win the election. It thus comes as no surprise that among the deputies elected in 2002, over half (52.3 percent) held both offices of deputies and mayors and over a third of them (36.2 percent) were both deputies and general councilors (Sineau and Tiberj 2007: 182–183).

The male domination of parliamentary representation also has far-reaching historical reasons that, in the male conscience, have constructed women as unfit to represent the nation (Sineau 2005b: 50). At the basis of virile traditions in French politics lies the Salic law, unearthed by the absolute monarchy in the fourteenth century. This law precludes women from succeeding to the throne. One of the first acts of the revolutionaries was to pursue this tradition, by a decree proclaimed on October 1, 1789. The aristocracy's privileges were abolished, but those of men were not.

Not content to preserve the French crown for males, the French Revolution also posited the political incapacity of all women as an absolute (which was not the case under the ancient régime), thus establishing in republican con-sciences the idea of female incompetence as regards public affairs.

Last but not least, the Catholic Church, so powerful in France, contributed doubly to perpetuating this traditional division of roles by gender. It did so, first, by denying women access to the priesthood, and therefore to power, and, second, by teaching a twofold moral standard that orders men to command and take care of public affairs and women to procreate and keep house.

Conclusion

Throughout the entire Fifth Republic, political parties have used the SMD voting system and multiple office holding to perpetuate male dominance on democratic politics. Everything leads us to conclude that women would not have been eliminated from the contest for so long under a system of proportional representation by list. This system lends itself better to organizing open and diversified recruitment, through mechanisms such as the implementation of quotas. The counterexample of the 1986 legislative elections does not invalidate this reasoning, because the return to the proportional system was too brief.

If the use made of the two-round SMD voting system has followed such a sexist trend, the fault lies mainly with political parties which, the Communist Party excepted, demonstrated no resolve whatsoever to introduce measures that might offset the discriminating effects of the voting rules. The Verts, an emergent party that incorporated parity in its statutes, might have been willing to feminize the electoral game. However, its divisions have stunted its growth, preventing it from becoming a major party capable of competing with the Socialist Party in the introduction of women friendly practices, a scenario that occurred in Germany (Achin 2005).

Political parties under the Fifth Republic were long able to preserve—with little protest—the model of a masculine brotherhood—so great was the social tolerance with regard to the invisibility of women in politics. Today, things have changed radically in this regard. Indeed, the acuity of the crisis of representation in France has contributed to making the masculine monopoly of the res publica unpopular. Public opinion currently has lost confidence in elites and expressed a hope that women will be able to bring about change at all levels of political activity. In this context, Ségolène Royal, quite popular in the 2006 surveys, was able to win the primary of the Socialist Party, and then to run the 2007 presidential election, challenging Nicolas Sarkozy, the UMP's candidate.

For the 2007 legislative elections (taking place after the presidential elections), political parties understood the urgency of putting forward parity among the sexes, for the sidelining of women has become "politically incorrect" in the eyes of the electorate. But for each party, we can observe a major mismatch between the proportion of female candidates and that of elected female officials. On the left, the Socialist Party, which presented 46.5 percent women, only succeeded in having 25.9 percent of these candidates elected, while on the right, the UMP, had 26.6 percent female candidates, and only 14.3 percent were elected. An attentive examination of nominations allows us to see that the parties tended to designate candidates in the least winnable ridings in the goal of investing or reinvesting men in the safest seats. These partisan strategies explain why women represent only 18.5 percent of the members of the National Assembly following the 2007 elections. The victory of the right—which took the most liberty with parity norms—only accentuated the defeat of women.

Notes

1. Two-round majority single-member district voting system for the National Assembly and for departmental assemblies; one-round proportional party list vote

for French members of European Parliament; mixed two-round party list vote (proportional system with majority bonus) for regional councils and municipal councils in cities of 3,500 or more inhabitants; two-round majority list vote for municipal councils in small towns; and dual electoral system for the Senate (two-round majority single [or multiple] member vote in small departments, one-round proportional list vote for large departments).

2. Whereas for all votes by list, the law imposed on the contrary an obligation of parity of candidacies, alternating male and female candidates.

3. Subsidies were cut by a percentage equal to half the difference in the number of candidates of each sex compared with the total number of candidates. (If a party fielded for instance 40 percent women for 60 percent men, the difference is 20 percentage points, so its funding would be reduced by 10 percent).

4. General councilors are the elected officials in departmental assemblies.

5. After the April 1958 departmental elections, only 11 women were elected general councilor for 1,512 seats up for election (0.7 percent).

6. Except for two groups: Choisir la Cause des Femmes and La Ligue du Droit des Femmes.

7. The Communists were all the less reluctant to field women candidates since, by party rules, the power of elected officials is subordinate to that of the party.

8. Whereas, since European elections are held by proportional representation, the Socialist Party had voted in favor of a 30 percent quota as of 1979.

9. Fines are deducted from the first segment of public funding, calculated in proportion to the number of votes captured in the first ballot.

Early Promise Unfulfilled: The Electoral Representation of Women in Australia

Ian McAllister

Introduction

Although Australia was one of the first countries to grant women the right to vote, it was not until much later that women began to gain election to parliament in any significant numbers. The right to vote on the same basis as men was granted to women as early as 1895 in South Australia, with Western Australia following suit in 1900. With the federation of the colonies in 1902, women gained the right to vote in Commonwealth elections, and in the next few years all of the new states followed, the last being Victoria in 1909.[1] However, this early promise was largely unfulfilled and as table 6.1 indicates, it was not until 1943 that the first woman was elected to the national parliament; indeed, South Australia and Tasmania did not have a woman representative in their state lower houses until the 1950s.

One explanation for this discrepancy between granting women the vote and their gaining representation is the electoral system and the strong elements of compulsion embedded within it. These elements of compulsion has led to a system of strongly disciplined parties where dissent is virtually unknown and legislative recruitment is dependent upon party service and loyalty. But ironically, once the parties took the decision to increase the numbers of women candidates, strong party discipline has been a positive influence on women's representation, particularly within the Labor Party when it eventually decided to adopt a quota system. Other explanations for the discrepancy include the egalitarian settler tradition, changes in public opinion,

Table 6.1   The extension of women's political rights in national and state lower houses in Australia

	Votes for women*	First election eligible	Right to stand*	First woman elected
Commonwealth	1902	1903	1902	1943
New South Wales	1902	1904	1918	1925
Victoria	1909	1911	1924	1933
South Australia	1895	1896	1895	1959
Western Australia	1900	1901	1920	1921
Queensland	1907	1907	1915	1929
Tasmania	1904	1906	1922	1955

* Date of bill gaining assent.

and the role of advocacy groups. The confluence of these factors has helped to increase the electoral representation of women, but in general Australia has not fulfilled its early potential when it granted women the right to vote.[2]

This chapter examines patterns of women's representation in Australia, focusing on the national lower house, the House of Representatives. The first section outlines the operation of the electoral system, while the second section examines the evolution of women's representation in the national parliament. The remainder of the chapter analyses the major explanations for why women took so long to gain parliamentary representation in Australia, following the early extension of the franchise.

The Voting System

In the late nineteenth and early twentieth centuries, Australia was at the forefront of electoral experimentation (for an account, see Farrell and McAllister 2005; Sawer 2001). As early as 1859 all the Australian colonies had established systems of parliamentary government with adult male suffrage. The secret ballot (still known internationally as the "Australian ballot") was also an Australian invention and was first used in South Australia and Victoria in the mid-1850s. But Australia is also of international significance as the home of two prominent forms of the preferential electoral system—the majority preferential vote (MPV) and the single transferable vote (STV). It was the first country to use these systems,[3] and today it is the largest of only three established democracies—the others being Malta (since 1921) and Ireland (1922)—to use these electoral systems widely for all levels of elections.

The reasons for the adoption of preferential voting lie in nineteenth British debates about electoral reform that heavily influenced the early electoral system designers at the turn of the twentieth century. The system that has

Table 6.2   House of Representatives electoral systems since 1901

	State	*Electoral system*
1901	NSW, Vic, WA	Single-member plurality (SMP)
	Qld	MPV; using contingent vote
	SA	Block vote
	Tasmania	STV
1903	All states	SMP
1918	All states	MPV

emerged is quintessentially Australian, and apart from its use in Ireland and Malta, the only significant sign of this system taking root outside of Australia has been in fledgling democracies in the Oceania region (Reilly 1997; Reynolds and Reilly 1997). Table 6.2 shows that the use of a plurality electoral system for House of Representatives elections continued until 1918, when preferential voting was finally adopted; it has remained in place ever since.

MPV is a majoritarian electoral system operating with single-seat constituencies in which, to be elected, a candidate has to win at least 50 percent of the vote. If, on the basis of counting the first preferences on the ballot papers, no candidate achieves an overall majority, the candidate with the least votes is excluded, and her ballot papers are distributed among the remaining candidates based on the next preferences indicated on the ballot papers. The process continues until one candidate emerges with an overall majority. MPV is a nonproportional system, with a poor match between vote proportions and seat proportions (Farrell and McAllister 2005: 78ff). What distinguishes it from plurality electoral systems is the expectation that a candidate should have an overall majority of the vote to be elected (Farrell 2001).

The electoral system is characterized by a strong element of compulsion, most obviously in the system of compulsory voting, but also in the requirement that the voter complete all preferences on the ballot paper. Compulsory voting was introduced in Commonwealth elections in 1924 and by 1941 had been extended to all of the states and territories. Although it is an offence not to vote without a valid reason, strong public support for the system means that there are few nonvoters. Another reason for the low level of noncompliance is the design of the system to be as user-friendly as possible. There are few restrictions on acquiring an absentee or postal ballot, voters may cast a ballot outside the constituency in which they are registered, and extensive steps are taken to assist voters with poor English language skills.

In addition to compulsory attendance at the polling place, in order for a vote to count as valid, a voter must complete all preferences on the ballot paper.[4] This peculiarly Australian practice reflects at one level a general political culture that promotes regulation and efficiency and an emphasis on citizens' duty (McAllister 2002). At another level, it reflects the legislators' view that the compulsory expression of preferences reinforces the system of compulsory turnout, for "if it were to be conceded that voters have the right to be indifferent in regard to a subset of candidates, it would seem to follow that voters have the right to be indifferent in regard to all candidates" (Reilly and Maley 2000: 44).

Compulsory voting and the compulsory listing of preferences have important consequences for the party system and for the conduct of national politics. The first is the dominance of the two-party system, with Labor opposing a conservative coalition of the Liberal and National parties.[5] Frequent, compulsory attendance at the polls and the associated strong public profile enjoyed by the major parties have generated a high level of party identification. While there has been some degree of partisan dealignment in Australia, it has not been nearly as extensive as that in Britain or the United States (Dalton 2000). Minor parties and independents thus find it very difficult to break into national politics. In turn, the compulsory expression of preferences virtually institutionalizes the Liberal-National coalition, avoiding the dangers (for them) of vote splitting, allowing them to field candidates in the same constituency and increasing the likelihood that one or other of them will succeed in having a candidate elected.

For the political parties, the complexity and compulsory elements of the electoral system have resulted in a high level of party discipline and cohesion. The strength of the parties translates into strong party cohesion in parliament, with parliamentary dissent being almost unknown. To the extent that differing opinions on policy issues exist within the parties, they are expressed in factionalism, most notably within the Labor Party (McAllister 1991). At the same time, aspiring candidates for major office must display strong party credentials, so that having worked full-time for a minister or an elected representative has become virtually a precondition for selection for a winnable seat. The net effect is that each party's elected representatives are strongly partisan and, at least in their parliamentary behaviour, highly disciplined.

Women in the Legislature: Historical Trends

Although Australia's first female parliamentarian was Edith Cowan, who was elected to the Western Australian Legislative Assembly in 1921, just one year after the right to stand was granted, a woman did not gain election to the lower house of the national parliament until 1943—with the election of Enid Lyons representing the seat of Darwin in Tasmania[6] in the House of Representatives.[7] Enid Lyons, who was the widow of Joe Lyons, the prime minister between 1932 and 1939, won the seat for the United Australia Party

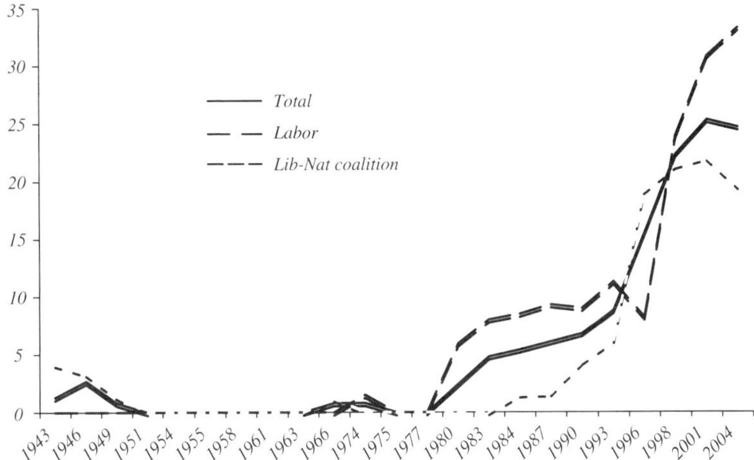

Figure 6.1   Proportion of women members of the House of Representatives since 1943

(the forerunner of the Liberals) and was the only new member of that party to gain election.[8]

The patterns of parliamentary representation among women in the lower house since 1943 are shown in figure 6.1. The trends show the almost total lack of progress in women's representation at each election through the 1950s and 1960s. In the six elections between 1951 and 1963, for example, no women were elected to the lower house. Even in the 1970s there was a dearth of women elected representatives, a period when the other established democracies were significantly increasing their proportion of women elected representatives. Between 1969 and 1977 there was just one woman elected—Joan Child—in 1974, but she lost her seat in 1975, to be elected again in 1980. She remained in parliament until retiring in 1990, serving as Speaker between 1986 and 1989.

From 1980 onward there is a significant increase in the proportion of women representatives—what is sometimes referred to as a "critical mass" (see, for example, Davis 1997; Studlar and McAllister 2002)—by which increased representation in itself accelerates the likelihood that other women will stand and gain election. In 1990, 10 women members were elected for the first time, and that figure has increased steadily ever since, exceeding 20 for the first time in 1996. The 2001 parliament represents the peak representation for women in the lower house, when 38 were elected out of a total of 150. The 2004 election represents a slight decrease from 2001, when 37 members were elected, again from a total house membership of 150.

For most of the period, there were few differences between the parties in terms of women's representation, albeit from a very low base. However, from the 1980 election onward, Labor has consistently surpassed the Liberal-National coalition in the numbers of women elected representatives in its ranks. Indeed, in every federal election since then, there have been proportionately more Labor women elected than coalition women. The sole exception to this pattern is the 1996 election, when the coalition significantly outnumbered Labor as a result of its winning office after 13 years in opposition. In that election, there were just 4 women out of the 49 members that Labor returned, compared with 18 women out of the total 94 coalition members who were returned.

These patterns suggest that there is a broadly similar pattern in women's lower house parliamentary representation between the parties, with a large rise in representation after 1980—somewhat later than its occurrence in many other countries. That having been said, women have been more likely to gain lower house election for Labor than for the Liberal or National party. These patterns are the result of a complex interaction between electoral system rules, the strategies adopted by the political parties to increase women's representation, and the role of external agencies such as public opinion and the lobbying activities of the women's movement. The role of each of these factors is examined in detail below.

The Impact of the Voting System on the Proportion of Women in the Legislature

One of the most consistent and robust findings in studies of women's representation is the importance of the electoral system, especially the favourable impact of party list (Norris and Franklin 1997; Matland 1998a). Other factors that relate to the operation of the electoral system include the degree of competition in a constituency. Women have more success in gaining election if the competition for seats is less at the preselection or nomination stage (Darcy, Welch, and Clark 1994), but once nominated, a more competitive party system provides more incentives for parties to search for new voters (Matland and Studlar 1996; Curtin and Sexton 2004). Reduced turnout lowers women's representation (Norris 2001) but of course does not apply to Australia because of the system of compulsory voting.

Australia has used a variety of electoral systems for the House of Representatives during the course of the twentieth century, as outlined earlier. This experimentation owes much to the political debates in Britain around the turn of the nineteenth century, where impending mass suffrage stimulated discussion about electoral reform. Another influence on Australian experimentation was the role of electoral system activists, such as Catherine

Helen Spence, Inglis Clark, and Edward Nanson, all of whom had a significant influence on the arguments for and against the various systems then under consideration. And a third influence was the experiences of the states, all of which had experimented at various times with electoral system design. Indeed, the first Commonwealth elections in 1901 were conducted using the electoral systems then existing in the states, in the absence of an agreed uniform system (see Uhr 2000).

The role of the electoral system as an influence on women's representation has largely been in the context of promoting strong parties. Compulsory voting and the compulsory ordering of preferences have ensured that the major parties gain strong voter support. In turn, the parties exercise strong discipline among their elected representatives. This has had both positive and negative effects on women's representation. On the positive side, as discussed later, it means that when the parties have decided to adopt quotas for the selection of women candidates (as in the case of Labor), they have been able to enforce the decision across the party membership. On the negative side, when the parties have not regarded women's representation as important (which was clearly the case in the 1950s through to the early 1970s), it has been difficult for advocates to get their message heard.

The Impact of Other Variables on the Proportion of Women in the Legislature

Egalitarianism

Australia's origins as a settler society and the consequent effects on the development of democracy have had a major influence on women's representation. The legacy of the settler society has been a strong emphasis on egalitarianism, which is sometimes identified as encapsulating the distinctive Australian ethos. The notion of equality in Australian society has its origins in the frontier tradition that emerged in the early years of white settlement and in the reliance of the settlers on their friends and neighbours for support—what became known as "mateship" (Ward 1958). This frontier spirit fostered a degree of egalitarianism far beyond that found in the other colonial societies. The result was the creation of a more open, less privileged, and meritocratic society than the one that the settlers had left behind.

Once egalitarianism was firmly established in social relations, demands grew for it to be applied to political institutions as well. Throughout the 1850s, a range of political reforms were introduced in the colonies: by 1859 most of the colonies had introduced universal manhood suffrage; the secret ballot was introduced in all but one of the colonies by 1859; plural voting was abolished in the colonies around the turn of the century; and the principle of payment for elected representatives was also established in most of the colonies by 1890. All of these reforms were many decades in advance of their introduction in the other established democracies.

Egalitarianism had a direct influence in fostering women's political rights. The absence of an inherited political culture and inherited privilege meant that women were accepted for what they could contribute, and in the context of a settler society women were regarded as having at least as much to contribute as men. The granting of political rights to women was seen as a logical extension of their social role. In turn, once the principle of gender equality in political rights had been established, implementing it was relatively easy since the change depended simply on the passage of the appropriate legislation. Even then, of course, there was opposition, but not at the level found, say, in Britain or Europe during the same period. The result was, as noted earlier, the granting of universal suffrage to women years ahead of any other country, with the sole exception of New Zealand.

Changing Public Opinion

Public opinion has played a significant role in shaping women's electoral representation. As opinion has become more favorable to women in the public sphere, advocates have found it easier to press their case with the major political parties. Identifying detailed changes in public opinion toward women is problematic, since few survey questions have been asked over an extended period, and even fewer where the question wordings are consistent.

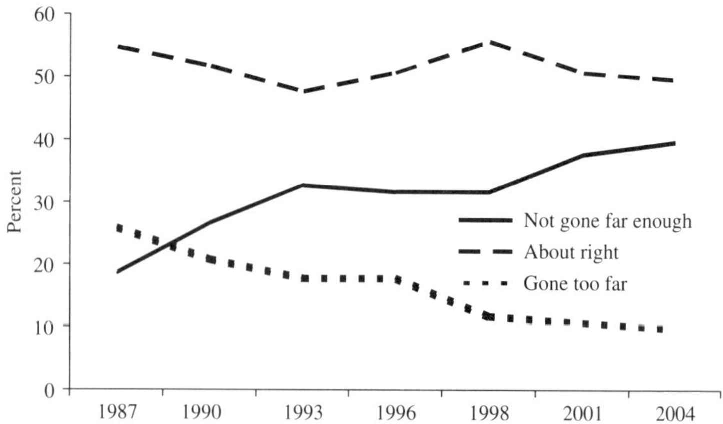

Figure 6.2   Public opinion toward equal opportunities for women, 1987–2004 (percent)

We do, however, have the responses to a question about women's job opportunities, which has been asked consistently in the Australian Election Study from 1987 onward. The question asks whether the respondents felt that the changes in women's job opportunities that had taken place had gone too far, not far enough, or were about right (figure 6.2).

The results suggest a consistent and important shift in opinions on the issue over the 17-year period of the surveys. In 1987 those who thought equal opportunities for women had gone too far exceeded those who thought that they had not gone far enough, although the majority felt the current situation was about right. By 2004, the majority—40 percent—thought that they had not gone far enough, more than double the 1987 figure. Similarly, those opposed to the changes comprised just 10 percent in 2004, compared with more than a quarter of the electorate in 1987. These are very substantial changes in opinions over what is, in public opinion terms, a relatively short period of time and demonstrate the depth to which popular attitudes toward the role of women have changed.

Advocacy Groups

Since the early 1970s, Australia has had a highly effective lobby group campaigning on behalf of greater women's representation and on public issues affecting women more generally. Most prominent among these has been the Women's Electoral Lobby (WEL), established in 1972. WEL was very much part of second-wave feminism, and was composed of mostly professional women born in the 1950s who held clear views about promoting the role of women in the private and public sectors. The goal of WEL is to ensure greater participation by women in all aspects of society, and the movement's platform is based on the demands of second-wave feminism: equal pay, equal employment, equal opportunity, free contraception, abortion on demand, and free childcare (Sawer and Simms 1993: 244–245).

Has advocacy by WEL and similar women's groups played a role both in recruiting women for parliament and in changing the opinions of those who are elected? Evidence from the Australian Candidate Study (ACS), conducted among candidates at each federal election, suggests that it has had a major impact. Each of the studies has asked about prior activity in women's organizations and the support that was provided by such organizations during the course of the election campaign. In the 2004 ACS, 78 percent of Labor women candidates but only 29 percent of Liberal-National women candidates said that they had been "'very active" in women's organizations in their community. It would appear, then, that Labor women candidates had stronger links to women's groups than their Liberal-National competitors, as we would expect.

Quotas

Numerous studies have identified the candidate selection process within political parties as representing the major barrier to the equal political representation of women (Matland and Studlar 1996; Welch and Studlar 1996). Even where political parties were prepared to nominate significant numbers of women candidates, they were often selected for unwinnable seats, and since incumbency is the major attribute determining future election, this creates a vicious circle accounting for future lack of success among women (McAllister and Studlar 1992; Studlar and McAllister 1991). Across a range of countries, the solution to this problem has taken the form of quotas for women candidates, with a certain number of winnable seats being allocated solely for nomination of women (for a review, see Caul 2001).

The Labor Party was the first major Australian party to raise the issue of quotas and to follow it up with concrete policies. Following an internal inquiry in the late 1970s into women's electoral representation in general, a variety of affirmative action measures were considered, including women-only shortlists. The 1981 Labor conference set a target of 30 percent women within the parliamentary party to be achieved by 1990, but did not establish processes to ensure that this target was met, or to monitor progress toward its achievement (Sawer 2000). In the absence of an agreed process, progress was slow. In 1994 a further target of 35 percent of women in winnable seats by 2002 was set, but this time various sanctions were put in place against the state branches if they did not meet the target.

In 2002 the target of 35 percent was further increased to 40 percent, to be achieved by 2012 (Curtin and Sexton 2004). The evidence suggests that quotas—particularly the 1994 quota that, for the first time, identified winnable seats—have been a major factor in increasing Labor representation in the House of Representatives. By contrast, the Liberal Party has historically rejected quotas as a matter of principle, and in the 1980s and early 1990s, their representation of women in the lower house has lagged behind Labor.

Conclusion

Although Australia was the second democracy to grant women the vote, and one of the first to permit them to stand for national elected office, this early promise was unfulfilled for many years. The first woman was not elected to the national legislature until 1943, and it was not until the 1980s that women's electoral representation began to make any significant headway. No single explanation accounts for this discrepancy between the granting of electoral rights and their implementation, but clearly the electoral system was one factor, and more specifically the elements of compulsion within it that have fostered strong, highly disciplined political parties. This was a negative factor early in the century, but as the social and cultural milieu has changed, it has been a positive factor in the 1980s and 1990s, enabling the Labor Party to implement a quota system without the major conflicts that have surrounded the issue in other center-left parties, notably the British Labour Party.

Other factors in addition to the electoral system have undoubtedly been important. The strong sense of egalitarianism and fairness within the Australian political culture has underpinned the recent successes of women in gaining nomination for winnable seats. A popular belief in equal opportunity and personal success through merit have made it difficult for opponents of change to argue their case, at least publicly. And at the same time, advocacy groups such as the WEL Lobby and changes in public opinion, in turn fostered by political, social, and economic changes in the role of women, have helped to expedite increased women's representation. While the fulfilment of Australia's early promise in the political representation of women has been slow to take hold, future decades look set to accelerate that process.

Notes

* The 1987–2004 Australian Election Studies were funded by the Australian Research Council and are available from the Australian Social Science Data Archive at the Australian National University.

1. The situation with regard to upper houses in the states is more complex, and women's rights were generally granted later, see McAllister (2006) for details.
2. A large part of this chapter is based on previous research conducted by the author (see McAllister 2006; Farrell and McAllister 2005).
3. MPV was introduced in Queensland in 1892; STV in Tasmania in 1896; MPV for House of Representative national elections in 1918–19; and STV for Senate elections in 1949.
4. This is in the case of MPV elections; for Senate elections, there is the option of "ticket-voting," although that is not covered since our interest is in lower house elections (see Farrell and McAllister 2000).
5. The coalition was formed in 1920 and has remained in existence since then, except for two short periods in 1973–74 and 1987.
6. At this time, Darwin was the name of a seat in Tasmania (as well as the capital of the Northern Territory).
7. In the same election, Dorothy Tangney, the first female member of the Senate, was elected to represent Western Australia.
8. Enid Lyons had previously contested a Tasmanian state seat for Labor, unsuccessfully, in 1925.

Part II

Proportional Representation

Subpart I

Closed Lists

Challenging Traditional Thinking on Electoral Systems

Hannah E. Britton

Introduction

In many ways, South Africa is an ideal case for examining the impact of electoral systems on the advancement of women into national office. Following decades of the antiapartheid struggle, women's organizations and women leaders worked in concert to ensure a lasting place for women's voice in decision making. These leaders benefited from the timing of this national transition to democracy. They used lessons from the international women's movement and drew from the experiences of women in other postconflict contexts to prioritize a national gender agenda. Because of their efforts, in 2007, South Africa has 32.8 percent women in the National Assembly (NA), the lower house of parliament, bringing the country to the rank of fourteenth in the world in terms of women in national office (Inter-Parliamentary Union: www.ipu.org; April 2007). The choice of electoral system was one important aspect of this success, but that was only one piece of the country's strategy.

The Voting System

Given the contentious and violent apartheid history, a primary consideration in the constitutional negotiations was to design a political system that would diminish political fragmentation and polarization, especially along racial, ethnic, and ideological lines. The apartheid government had operated on a first-past-the-post (FPTP) system, and in many ways it would have been in the electoral interest of the African National Congress (ANC) to maintain that system. At the time of the negotiations in the early 1990, there were 700 electoral districts, and blacks were in the majority in all but five districts. This system would have certainly benefited the ANC and could potentially have given it a two-thirds majority in parliament necessary to write the new constitution unilaterally (Reynolds 1995). Yet, electoral dominance was not the primary concern of the ANC at that time; rather, it was long-term political and social stability of the country (Reynolds 2006; Francisco 2000).

Within an FPTP system in postapartheid South Africa, Reynolds (2006) asserts that not only would the representation of small parties have been smaller, but the representation of women, Indians, coloreds, and whites would also have been so. He believes that ethnic differences would have likely become more pronounced. This type of fragmentation and polarization would have been a threat to the quest for national unity by the new government. On the contrary, proportional representation held the promise of minority representation (PR) and fostered an inclusion of ideologies, genders, races, and ethnicities.

The NA is selected through a multimember district electoral system with closed party-list PR. The 400 members of the NA are chosen every five years through fixed-term direct elections—200 seats of them drawn from regional lists and 200 from national lists. Parties submit both regional and national lists, which they construct in various ways. Most parties allow for input from regional and local branches; most have the final decisions rest with national party leaders.

The entire country of South Africa is essentially a single nationwide district, and the national vote is converted into seats using the Droop Formula.[1] During the negotiations, there was discussion of a 5 percent threshold for representation in parliament. The two parties that anticipated to win the most seats in 1994, the ANC and the National Party, agreed to remove any formal or mandatory threshold for the interest of including smaller parties (Reynolds 2006). A few of the smaller parties were also some of the most radical, and including them in institutionalized politics would prevent potentially dangerous marginalization from mainstream politics. Today, there is no minimum threshold of votes required of a party to win seats in the NA. According to Lijphart (1995), in most respects, the electoral system was guided first and foremost by a goal of proportionality.

Complaints against the electoral system concern accountability and geographic representation. Since South Africa has a list PR system, voters elect parties, and party leaders control which members fill the parliamentary seats. This means that individual members of parliament (MPs) answer to party leaders directly and to voters indirectly. There are few incentives for MPs to challenge aggressively party leaders or party decisions, and there are few incentives to "nurture their own geographical support base" (Lodge 2004: 2).

While the PR system receives wide cross-party support (Reynolds 2006), many in South Africa are concerned that there is no way to ensure proper accountability of nationally elected officials.

A more recent issue of accountability in South Africa is the debate concerning floor crossing. Twice during the five-year parliamentary term, MPs may leave their parties to join other parties or to create new parties without losing their seats in parliament. At least 10 percent of a political party's MPs must be involved in floor crossing in order for them to defect without losing their seats. This 10 percent provision initially was put in place to prevent individual members from defecting for their personal political advancement.

Floor crossing has been controversial because of the closed-list PR system. Voters are electing parties, not individual MPs, and MPs serve at the pleasure of party leaders. When MPs switch parties, they are in essence changing the vote through the recomposition of seats. The very idea of proportionality is thus threatened. Ederberg, Tjernstrom, and Kennedy (2006) additionally note that the South African floor-crossing system benefits larger parties. It is much easier to get 10 percent of the members to leave a smaller party, and rarely do members move from secure large parties to smaller parties, because small parties have an unpredictable chance of winning seats in the next election. Floor crossing continues to be debated nationally for accountability.

Floor crossing aside, the electoral system adopted by South Africa has been widely lauded as a key ingredient for women's success in office. Gender advocates and women leaders worked together across party lines to support this system as one part of a national plan of action to promote the status of women. In many ways, this cross-party cooperation was the outgrowth of decades of political activism by women working within and against the apartheid system.

Women in the Legislature: Historical Trends

While there is a shared legacy of gender subordination of women in South Africa, this cannot be discussed in isolation from the racial hierarchies created by colonialism and apartheid. The colonial period worked to restrict women's participation in the public sphere and to deepen the importance of women's domestic, familial, and maternal roles. But how gender identity was expressed varied across races.

White women[2] obtained the right to vote and to stand for office in 1930, and the first woman was elected to parliament in 1933. There is scholarly disagreement concerning who was at the forefront of the white women's suffrage movement. Walker (1990) contends urban, elite, and primarily English-speaking white women led the movement, as they had more connections with the national suffrage movements in Europe and the United States. Arguably, most Afrikaner women were primarily subsumed within the highly nationalistic and patriarchal ideology of Afrikaner culture and the Dutch Reform Church. But, Walker (1982) acknowledges that Afrikaner women were increasing joining the suffrage movement as they entered urban areas and waged employment in the 1920s. Vincent (1999: 1–2) disputes this interpretation, arguing specifically that Afrikaner women strategically expanded the traditional notion of Afrikaner motherhood, *volksmoeder,* or mother of the nation, to pressure for their right to vote.

There is, however, no dispute that the women's suffrage movement in the 1920s was increasingly marked by racism. Initially, the movement worked for equal voting rights for men and women, allowing their agenda "to steer fairly clear of the question of black women's suffrage" (Walker 1982: 22). Because of the franchise rules of the time, about 40,000 black and colored men had qualified for the vote in the Cape area. Diminishing black political power in the Cape became a central issue for the National Party leader General Hertzog (Walker 1982). If women pushed for equal voting rights as men, this could have potentially increased the overall number of nonwhite voters (which would not play well among white male party leaders) and would do little to enfranchise white women. Since most women were limited in terms of education, property ownership, and wages, they would still have been excluded from voting rights. Thus, it was in women's interest to push for race-based suffrage—often employing the racist language of a "civilized" standard, which would align their movement with growing nationalistic ideology of the white minority population (Vincent 1999: 3–5). Hertzog focused on race-based white women's suffrage, with the Women's Enfranchisement Bill in 1930, as a vehicle to diminish the limited power of the black vote in the Cape. By enfranchising white women, the act would simultaneously double the power of the white vote. Because of their own nationalistic and racial leanings, most white women were complicit with this position (Walker 1982).

Hassim (2006: 140) asserts that "white women placed their racial and class concerns above any solidarity between women" and thus limited the potential for trust and coalition building among women of different races for some time, except in only a few key women's organizations that had established black leadership, such as the Women's League and the Federation of South African Women. The right to vote was not extended to Indian or colored populations until 1984, which was part of the apartheid government's continued attempt to divide and weaken their opposition within the nonwhite majority. The apartheid leaders banked on creating a class of the "privileged oppressed" among the Indian and colored communities and on enticing their complicity with the promise of limited access to power, albeit as second-class citizens. The racist rhetoric furthered the apartheid ideology, asserting that the colored and Indian populations had been brought into the political process because of their steady assimilation into the "civilized" society.

Many within the colored, Indian, and white communities continued to resist this political dogma and refused to partake in elections until full suffrage was achieved—in 1994. This was the first time that both black women and men were able to vote. Black South African women faced multiple obstacles to political participation during apartheid, but they remained a vital force within community-based organizations, struggle politics, and women's groups (Russell 1989; Hassim 2006). Because of the continued legacy of patriarchy that discouraged women's participation in public life and because of the racism of apartheid that barred the majority population from participating, there were at most only a handful of women in parliament until 1994. The most notable woman in parliament for over thirty years was Helen Suzman, elected in 1953 as an MP[3] (Hassim 2006). She frequently voiced lone opposition to new apartheid legislation, and, while she voiced support for the trade union actions and consumer boycotts, she did not support economic sanctions against South Africa (Gastrow 1987). In general, women who were MPs during apartheid found the climate unwelcoming. Shelia Camera, MP, formerly of the National Party and now with the Democratic Alliance, described parliament under apartheid as "'a quintessential boys club' with few facilities for women, and a male-oriented culture" (Meintjes and Simons 2002b: 16).

The main location of political participation for women during this period happened outside formal politics and outside of parliament, occurring instead within civil society organizations and in struggle politics. There were women's coalitions that cut across racial lines, such as the Federation of South African Women, and there were women's branches of political parties and resistance organizations, such as the ANC's Women's League (Walker 1982). Women's local and regional organizations also became a vital political force in the 1970s and 1980s, such as the United Women's Organisation in Western Cape (Hassim 2006). Women were active in trade unions, where they learned vital skills that would translate well to later roles in parliamentary politics in the 1990s (Britton 2001). Women also received extensive educational, military, and political training while in political exile (Hassim 2006).

As apartheid drew to a close in the 1990s and negotiations were under way between the government and opposition forces, women recognized that this was a unique moment to address women's rights (Ginwala 1992; Seidman 1999). The Women's National Coalition (WNC) was formed through the unity of women returning from exile, women power brokers within political parties, civil society organizations concerned with the status of women, and feminist academics. The WNC brought together over one hundred different organizations in an umbrella movement to create a national gender agenda that pushed for a permanent place for women in decision making (Women's National Coalition 1994). The WNC worked to create a national platform of action, called the Women's Charter, which would outline necessary reforms and programs ranging from educational priorities, health care, social welfare, and economic empowerment. It was also able to use its coalition strength as a leveraging tool to pressure the male leaders of political parties to create space for women at the constitutional negotiations (Britton 2002; Hassim 2006). This in part was the first crack in the door that women needed to begin to implement their national gender agenda.

During the constitutional negotiations, women worked to secure a multi-member district electoral system with closed party-list PR—a voting system used by several countries with high proportions of women in parliament. But more importantly, women within their parties worked to foster the advancement of women onto party lists through quotas, selective recruitment, and mentorship.

The Impact of the Voting System on the Proportion of Women in the Legislature

At first glance, the electoral system adopted by South Africa in 1994 appears to have had a remarkable impact on the representation of women in national office. In 1990, at the end of the apartheid era, women held only 3 percent of the seats in the lower house of parliament.[4] Dramatically, women in South Africa gained over 26 percent of the seats in the NA in the first democratic election in 1994. This percentage has continued to grow gradually but steadily, to reach 29 percent in 1999 and 32.8 percent in 2004.

Not only has the overall percentage of women in office increased, so too have the numbers of women on each parties' election list for the NA (see table 7.1).

It is clear that political parties have increased the number of women on their party lists. On the surface, this data would seem to indicate that the closed party-list PR system fosters more women candidates over time. Unlike single-member district (SMD) system where voters in individual districts are looking at individual candidates, in the PR system parties must demonstrate to voters that their lists are representative—ideologically and oftentimes demographically. In the closed party-list PR system, voters are voting for the entire slate of candidates, so demographic representation is often more visible, although it is not always an overt campaign strategy.

Table 7.1   Women on pre-election party lists, South Africa, 1994–2004

Party	1994 Women on national list (%)	1994 Women on regional lists (%)	1999 Women on national list (%)	1999 Women on regional lists (%)	2004* Women on national list (%)
African Christian Democratic Party	12.9	9.6	29.0	24.0	31.8
African National Congress	32.2	32.6	39.0	34.0	35.4
Afrikaner EenheidsBeweging	–	–	14.5	18.5	–
Azanian People's Organisation	–	–	18.0	15.6	37
Democratic Party	31	19	NA	21	31.59
Federal Alliance	–	–	13.0	13.6	–
Freedom Front/ Freedom Front Plus	12	7.8	16.0	17.7	23.39
Independent Democrats	–	–	–	–	30.33
Inkatha Freedom Party	10.4	15.9	22.0	28.6	31.82
Minority Front*	–	–	14	1.6	NA
National Party/ New National Party	NA	11.4	NA	18.4	25.21
Pan-Africanist Congress	11.8	12	22	19	33.64
United Christian Democratic Party	–	–	26.0	24.7	–
United Democratic Movement	–	–	23.0	19.0	24.94

*Regional lists were unavailable for 2004.

– Indicates a year when the party did not win seats in parliament.

NA indicates data not available or not applicable.

Sources: Ballington 1999; and GenderLinks: http://www.genderlinks.org.za/article.php?a_id=290. Accessed April 2007.

As Amanda Gouws (2004: 2) asserts, gender representation has not been a key electoral issue for any political party platform in South Africa.

Looking at the overall percentage of women in the National Assembly, combined with the ever-increasing percentage of women on the preelection party lists, it would be easy to assume that each party is increasing the number of women in office. However, the results also show that even though many parties have more women on their party lists, they are not always being elected into office. This is because many parties often place women in lower positions on the party list. Parties can claim a representative list of candidates, yet they will often place men at the top of the list. There was also a proliferation of opposition parties in 1999. This meant that more and more parties were vying for fewer and fewer seats. The result was that several parties took a low number of seats—and filled those seats with male candidates.

Some parties, such as the ANC and the Minority Front, often place women in winning positions on their party lists. In the case of the ANC, this has a major impact on the overall composition of parliament because of their overwhelming electoral success. As the ANC continues to gain seats in office, this ensures more and more women will be elected into parliament. This is due to the voluntary party quota they adopted in 1994 and their later decision to have a woman in every third slot on the party list. Thus, the reason that the overall percentage of women in parliament has grown is, primarily, the ANC policies and not the measures taken by other parties or the electoral system in isolation (see table 7.2).

Thus, to assume that the high percentage of women is due solely to the form of the electoral system would be a mistake. It is certainly a contributing factor, but it is only one in a larger set of factors. In the South African case, the electoral system is most likely not the essential mechanism. Rather, the election results show that the success of women in office is due primarily to the policies of the ANC, specifically its 30 percent quota.

The Impact of Other Variables on the Proportion of Women in the Legislature

There are several key factors that have contributed to the recent success of women in office, including the postconflict climate, the timing of the transition, and the various affirmative action measures of political parties. First, women in South Africa were poised to demand formal recognition within the transition period because of their roles during the antiapartheid conflict. Within South Africa, women were active as underground soldiers, community activists, and union leaders (Cock 1991; Meintjes 2001). They worked alongside the visible male leadership in the antiapartheid struggle and had been the driving force behind consumer boycotts and mass action, such as the Pass Law protests (Wells 1993). The conflict period disrupted static gender roles that had previously restricted women to the domestic sphere. The period gave them access to experiences and training that would be useful for demonstrating their future political legitimacy as decision makers. Women who had been in exile also had exposure to an international network of women activists, other former freedom fighters, feminist scholars, and leaders of nongovernmental organizations (NGOs). This international network provided lessons that they would use in the postconflict setting (Meintjes 2001).

Table 7.2   Women elected, South Africa, 1994–2004*

Party	1994 Women per party's total seats (%)	1994 Number of women/ total seats	1999 Women per party's total seats (%)	1999 Number of Women/ total seats	2004 Women per party's total seats (%)	2004 Number of Women/ total seats
African Christian Democratic Party	0	0/2	33.3	2/6	16.6	1/7
African National Congress	35.7	90/252	36.1	96/266	38.4	107/279
Afrikaner Eenheids-Beweging	–	–	0	0/1	–	–
Azanian People's Organisation	–	–	0	0/1	0	0/1
Democratic Party/ Democratic Alliance	14.3	1/7	18.4	7/38	20.0	10/50
Federal Alliance	–	–	0	0/2	–	–
Freedom Front/ Freedom Front Plus	0	0/9	0	0/3	0	0/4
Independent Democrats	–	–	–	–	28.6	2/7
Inkatha Freedom Party	23.3	10/43	20.6	7/34	21.4	6/28
Minority Front*	–	–	100	1/1	50	1/2
National Party/ New National Party	11.0	9/82	10.7	3/28	14.3	1/7
Pan-Africanist Congress	20	1/5	33.3	1/3	0	0/3
United Christian Democratic Party	–	–	0	0/3	33.3	1/3
United Democratic Movement	–	–	14.3	2/14	33.3	3/9
TOTAL	27.8	111/400	29.8	119/400	32.8	131/400

*Does not include subsequent floor crossing.

– Indicates a year when the party did not win any seats.

Sources: Ballington 1999; www.ipu.org (May 2006); Electoral Institute of South Africa (http://www.eisa.org.za/ WEP/sou1999results3.htm; April 2006); Gouws (2004); List of Women MPs, South African Parliament website: http://www.parliament.gov.za/pls/portal/web_app.app_people_search_list?p_gender=Female&p_order_by= surname,political_party_id&p_operator=and&p_page_name=PARLIAMENT_MP&p_title=Women%20Members (June 2006).

Second, the timing of the transition is remarkably important. By the early 1990s, there had been decades of experience with postconflict transitions in Africa and Latin America, experiences of quotas in Europe and Latin America, and examples of women's movements across the globe. The timing of the South African transition, as with many recent African transitions, seems essential to its progress and choice of strategies (Bauer and Britton 2006b). Women activists who had been in exile had the opportunity to learn from these other situations (Hassim 2006), and feminist academics and gender advocates were well aware of the international scholarship on electoral systems and quotas (Britton 2002). Had the transition happened much before the early 1990s, it is likely that some of these lessons and connections may not have been visible.

Third, several parties have adopted some form of affirmative action measure to promote women within their party ranks and ultimately onto their election lists. In the 1994 elections, the ANC adopted a voluntary party quota to have at least 30 percent of the seats on its preelection party list for women (Britton 2005). As tables 7.1 and 7.2 show, 30 percent was a minimum and not a ceiling for the party, as the ANC has consistently had greater than 30 percent women on both its lists and in office. For the 1999 elections, the ANC moved to a policy of having every third seat on its party list filled by a woman candidate, thus ensuring that women candidates are not clumped in unelectable seats. In the preparation for the 2004 elections, NGOs and women's groups joined forces to push for a universal 50 percent quota for all parties. While this goal was unfulfilled, several parties have continued to increase the number of women on their party lists. Therefore, the primary reason South Africa has had such a consistently high percentage of women in office is primarily the ANC quota. The South African case may also lend credibility to the argument that quota adoption is easier in a PR system than in an SMD system. So, the electoral system may be a crucial but not sufficient condition for the advancement of women in office.

What is also important about the South African case is the contagion effect.[5] Since the ANC adopted a quota, other parties have been influenced to increase the number of women on their party lists. Many of the opposition parties eschew quotas as problematic or undemocratic, and their leaders argue that they only have candidates based "on merit." They then ironically find themselves in the awkward position of not having enough women "of merit" in their own parties. Thus, a vast majority of parties since the 1994 elections have utilized other forms of affirmative action to advance women candidates, such as targeted recruitment, mentorship, and rapid promotion through lower levels of government (Britton 2005). Additionally, by the 2004 elections, many women had served in local and provincial governments and were experienced public servants. Thus, there was a new pipeline of women eligible for advancement.

It is also important to note what the South African case disconfirms in terms of traditional thinking of women and office holding. Some theories would advance the idea that a high level of socioeconomic development is a prerequisite for women's empowerment. The Nordic countries historically have led in the rankings for women in office, and they have also scored high on their socioeconomic development indicators. Given the slow but steady progress of women in the Nordic countries, many believed that women's electoral success was part of an evolutionary process linked to socioeconomic development. This is no longer the case. In July 2006, Rwanda, Costa Rica, Cuba, Argentina, Mozambique, South Africa, Guyana, Burundi, Tanzania, and Seychelles were all ranked in the top twenty countries in terms of the number of women in national office.[6] It is clear that many countries have found ways to rapidly propel women into national office rather than waiting decades for socioeconomic development to afford the educational, occupational, and economic status previously assumed necessary (Bauer and Britton 2006b).

South Africa is part of an established trend in Africa that demonstrates women's progress can and often does outpace socioeconomic development. South Africa is ranked fourteenth in the world in terms of the number of women in national office, but its Human Development Index rank is 120. There is additional evidence that South Africa's socioeconomic status disconfirms direct correlation with the status of women in office. The total fertility rate is 2.8 for 2000–2005. The public expenditure on health care is 3.5 percent of the GDP and on education 5.3 percent of the GDP. The female economic activity rate for ages fifteen and above is 47.3 percent. There is income inequality for men and women, as the estimated earned income (purchasing power parity, PPP US$) for women is 6,505 and for men 14,326. South Africa's urban population is 56.9 percent of the total population. The GDP (US$ billions) is 159.0 or 474.1 (PPP US$); the GDP per capita is $3,489 (US$) or $10,346 (PPP US$).[7] Because of the history of apartheid in South Africa, wealth is still held in the hands of the few, and socioeconomic development is not widespread. South Africa is a case that demonstrates that socioeconomic development is not essential for democracy and also one that will hopefully show that democracy can be used to advance socioeconomic development.

Conclusion

South Africa indeed provides an innovative case in what is becoming the new pattern in empirical research about the impact of electoral systems on women's representation. Formerly, women made it into legislatures through a slow and steady progress that often kept pace with the socioeconomic development of the country. South Africa and several other African countries have started to challenge these old lessons. They have shown that socioeconomic development is not a prerequisite for women's electoral success. South Africa also demonstrates that the choice of the electoral system is an important but not sufficient condition for women's progress into office. Other variables have been the main factors for women's success in South Africa, including the affirmative action measures of political parties, the timing of the transition, the strength of women's groups, and the disruption of traditional gender roles. The South African case is perhaps most important, therefore, for the theories it disconfirms, and it clearly provides a new framework for future research and activism.

Notes

1. For a full explanation of the Droop Formula as applied in South Africa, see the South African Electoral Laws Amendment Act, 2003 (www.info.gov.za/gazette/ acts/2003/a40-03.pdf; April 2007).
2. Racial categories were created by the apartheid government as part of the divide-and-rule strategy to maintain dominance over the majority population. The designations were supported by and fed into a racist ideology that created a hierarchy placing the white minority at the pinnacle of political, economic, and social power. While there were multiple categories, there many categories that were white (of European descent or heritage), colored (of mixed heritage), Indian (of Indian and broadly Asian descent), and lack (of African heritage). Progressive movements eschewed the categories, and many self-identified as black in order to protest the white minority government. For the purposes of this chapter, I will employ these categories in only a limited sense within the discussion of the apartheid era policies and organizations.
3. Suzman was an MP with the United Party, which later became the Progressive Party, then the Progressive Federal Party, and then the Democratic Party.
4. According to the United Nations Development Programme (UNDP), Human Development Report (HDR), http://hdr.undp.org/statistics/data/countries.cfm?c= ZAF; June 2006.
5. Matland and Studlar (1996) examined the forces of contagion within the SMD and PR system in other countries.
6. www.ipu.org; May 2006.
7. Human development statistics are from the UNDP HDR Report; http://hdr.undp. org/statistics/data/countries.cfm?c=ZAF; June 2006.

8 Spain

Women in Parliament: The Effectiveness of Quotas

Celia Valiente

Introduction

In 2007, Spain ranks eighth among countries in the world as regards the presence of women in the lower chamber of parliament (the Congress of Deputies), with 36 percent female deputies (Inter-Parliamentary Union; www.ipu.org; April 2007). How has Spain reached such a vanguard status regarding the feminization of parliament and passed many other countries economically more developed and with a longer democratic past, such as France, Great Britain, or the United States? The approval and implementation of women's quotas in left-wing political parties is the main causal factor that explains the feminization of the current Spanish parliament. Quotas were adopted owing to the tireless and skillful pressure of party feminists. In the last two or three decades, other factors have created an environment favorable to the increase in the presence of women in the Spanish parliament. One of them was the proportional representation system to elect members of the Congress of Deputies. Other facilitating factors include cultural and socioeconomic variables—since the Spanish society and polity became increasingly secular and conceptions of gender roles more egalitarian, female participation in the labor market increased without interruption and half of the population with university degrees is female.

Previous research on women in the Spanish parliament has usually asked why the proportion of women in the legislative is lower than the proportion of women in the general population (but see Uriarte and Ruiz 1999: 208, among others).[1] I neither deny the underrepresentation of women in parliament nor the interest in studying the causes of such underrepresentation.

However, given the vanguard status of current Spain on female parliamentary presence, in this chapter I focus on the reasons that explain this advancement.

I organize the remainder of this chapter into four sections. First, I describe the voting system used to elect members of the Congress of Deputies. Second, I analyze the evolution of the proportion of women in the lower chamber of parliament since the first democratic elections held in Spain in 1977. Third, I explain how the electoral system has been a facilitating factor for the increase in the presence of women in the Congress of Deputies. Fourth, I analyze other cultural, socioeconomic, and political factors that have affected the proportion of women in the Spanish parliament. The main data for this chapter are secondary sources and four interviews with feminist activists and leaders of the social democratic Spanish Socialist Workers' Party (Partido Socialista Obrero Español, PSOE).

The Voting System

From the mid-1930s to 1975 Spain was governed by a right-wing nondemocratic regime headed by General Francisco Franco. The current Spanish political system was formed during the transition to democracy. It culminated with the public adoption of a democratic constitution in 1978. Parliament is composed of two chambers: the Congress of Deputies and the Senate. Elections are held through universal, free, and secret suffrage. Both women and men aged eighteen or over have voting rights. Members of the Congress of Deputies are elected by proportional representation under the d'Hondt system with closed and blocked lists. The fifty provinces and the two North African territories of Ceuta and Melilla serve as the constituencies. The district magnitude ranges from one in Ceuta and Melilla to thirty-four in Madrid and thirty-one in Barcelona, and almost two-thirds of districts have between four and nine seats. The number of members of parliaments (MPs) in the Congress of Deputies is 350. There is a threshold of 3 percent applicable in each of the fifty-two districts instead of the whole country. It is widely accepted that the Spanish electoral system favors big parties and parties with geographically concentrated support (Magone 2004: 80–81).

Generally speaking, three countrywide parties usually attract the majority of the vote: the social democratic PSOE, the conservative People's Party (Partido Popular, PP), and the United Left (Izquierda Unida, IU).[2] The IU is an electoral coalition to the left of the PSOE. It was formed in 1986 and includes among others the Spanish Communist Party (Partido Comunista de España, PCE). The PSOE formed government between 1982 and 1996 and since 2004. During the whole democratic period, when not in government, the PSOE was the main opposition party. The PP, which formed government between 1996 and 2004, was the main opposition party during PSOE rule. The PCE-IU has been the third electoral force in most elections.

Three regional parties play an important role in forming parliamentary majorities: the Catalan Convergence and Union (Convergència i Unió), the Basque Nationalist Party (Partido Nacionalista Vasco), and the Canary Coalition (Coalición Canaria). During the 1993–1996 and 1996–2000 parliamentary terms, these three regionalist parties supported in parliament minority governments formed by the PSOE and the PP, respectively. In democratic Spain, a process of devolution of powers from the central state to the regions has created a quasi-federal state. The three regional parties have governed their regions for long periods of time.

Women in the Legislature: Historical Trends

As shown in table 8.1, the proportion of women in the Congress of Deputies after the first four democratic elections (1977, 1979, 1982, and 1986) was merely around 6 percent. Suddenly, after the 1989 election, this proportion more than doubled (15 percent). This increase was mainly the result of the adoption in 1988 by the PSOE of a women's quota for party positions and electoral lists. The proportion of female deputies increased continuously in the next four elections (1993, 1996, 2000, and 2004) to reach 36 percent.

These general data mask important differences among parties. In general, and with exceptions, left-wing parties have promoted women's presence in the low chamber of parliament more than conservative parties. As table 8.1 shows, in the first four democratic elections (1977, 1979, 1982, and 1986), only 9 percent or less of PSOE deputies were women. As a result of intense pressure from PSOE feminists, the thirty-first PSOE federal congress in

Table 8.1. Percentage of women in the Congress of Deputies, total and by party, Spain (1977–2004)

Year	Total	PSOE	PP	PCE-IU
1977	6	9	6	15
1979	6	5	11	9
1982	6	9	2	0
1986	7	7	8	0
1989	15	19	10	12
1993	16	18	15	22
1996	22	28	14	33
2000	28	37	25	25
2004	36	46	28	40

Sources: For the 1977–1993 data: Instituto de la Mujer (1994: 79–80); for the 1996–2004 data: Instituto de la Mujer (2006).

January 22–24, 1988, discussed and passed the 25 percent women's quota for party positions and electoral lists. Thereafter, the proportion of female PSOE deputies rose to 19 percent in 1989. It remained almost unchanged in 1993 (18 percent) and increased again in 1996 (28 percent). The mobilization of PSOE feminists within the party to increase the presence of women in high politics did not stop with the adoption of the 1988 quota but continued in the 1990s. As a result of sustained PSOE feminist pressure, delegates at the thirty-fourth PSOE federal congress (June 20–22, 1997) debated and approved the increase of the internal and electoral women's party quota to 40 percent. Subsequently, the proportion of women who became PSOE deputies increased from 28 percent in 1996 to 37 percent in 2000 and to 46 percent in 2004.

As can also be seen in table 8.1, the proportion of women among PCE-IU deputies followed a more discontinuous pattern than that of PSOE deputies. In the first two elections, the proportion of PCE-IU female deputies was 15 percent in 1977 and 9 percent in 1979. After two elections without female deputies (1982 and 1986), the proportion of PCE-IU female deputies increased from 12 percent in 1989 to 22 percent in 1993 and to 33 percent in 1996. Then, it decreased to 25 percent in 2000 and increased to 40 percent in 2004.

Finally, the proportion of women among PP deputies was 11 percent or below in the first five parliamentary terms (1977, 1979, 1982, 1986, and 1989). Afterward, this proportion increased to reach 28 percent in 2004.

The Impact of the Voting System on the Proportion of Women in the Legislature

In general, proportional representation systems are more conducive to women's presence in the legislative than majority systems (Norris 2000; Norris and Inglehart 2005: 249–250; Reynolds 1999: 558–559; Rule 1987: 481, 1994b: 16). This rule seems to be confirmed by the case of current Spain, where more than a third of members of the lower chamber are women (36 percent in 2004). In comparison, the presence of women in the Senate, which is elected by a majority system, has always been lower than that in the Congress of Deputies. The proportional representation system in Spain has some characteristics that are supposed to be particularly favorable to the presence of women in parliament: close lists and a two-to-three party system (outside Catalonia and the Basque country) (Threlfall 2005a: 150).

But the proportional representation system is not the main cause of the current high presence of women in the Spanish lower chamber of parliament. For one thing, Spain had a proportional representation system since the first democratic election, but the presence of women in the Congress of Deputies until the late 1980s was extremely modest: around 6 percent

(Threlfall 2005a: 147, 2005b: 5–6). Some characteristics of the Spanish proportional system are not supposed to be particularly favorable to the presence of women in parliament, such as the small district magnitude (five) (Leyenaar 2004: 25; Rule 1987: 484; but see Valiente, Ramiro, and Morales 2005). Therefore, a factor other than the electoral system is needed to explain the feminization of the lower chamber of the Spanish parliament.

The Impact of Other Variables on the Proportion of Women in the Legislature

Cultural Variables

Cultural variables, such as religion or conceptions of gender roles, have evolved in Spain from 1975 in a sense conducive to a higher presence of women in parliament. In comparison with the period of transition to democracy, Spain is today a more secular society and polity. Conceptions of gender roles are considerably more egalitarian.

As for religion, Catholicism has been identified by part of the literature as a variable detrimental to the presence of women in parliament. Simply speaking, Catholicism has historically defended a traditional view of the role of women in society that excludes them from the realm of politics (Leyenaar 2004: 26; Rule 1987: 481–484). However, more than a decade ago, Rule (1994b: 21) already argued that "the growing proportions of women MPs in such strongly Roman Catholic countries as Spain and Italy illustrate the diminishing negative influence of the church on women's election to parliament" (see also Reynolds 1999).

Spain is a culturally homogenous Catholic country. After the expulsion of Jews in 1492 and of Muslims in 1502, no significant religious community other than the Catholic community has been openly active in Spain in the last four centuries. During Francoism, Catholicism was the official religion of the country, and some Catholic doctrines were reflected in state laws. For instance, divorce was prohibited and abortion was criminalized.

Despite the strong influence of the Catholic church in politics in the past, Spain belongs now to the group of Western countries with secularized politics. The Catholic church runs an important part of the education system and receives state money but does not control the agenda of government.[3] Most gender-equality policies are in line with the policies of other European Union (EU) member states (Valiente 2001). In 1975, the majority of Spaniards were practicing Catholics (almost 60 percent), but three decades later these Catholics were a minority (slightly below 30 percent) (Requena 2005: 377).

In respect of conceptions of gender roles, these influence the presence of women in the legislative (Mateo Diaz 2005: 224). More concretely, Norris and Inglehart (2005) note that egalitarian public attitudes toward women's political leadership favor access of women to parliament. However, these very same authors also propose that "[t]he empowerment of women remains a complex process, and (. . .) favorable attitudes toward women's leadership, by themselves, are not sufficient to produce automatic breakthroughs" (Norris and Inglehart 2005: 261).

Comparatively speaking, the Spanish society was considerably nonegalitarian in 1975 and is markedly egalitarian in current times. In the late 1970s, the view that women (especially married women) belong to the home and not to the public realm was prevalent. For example, in 1975, slightly over two-thirds of adult Spaniards (68 percent) thought that a woman's education should be geared toward raising a family instead of toward professional training. Only less than a third of the adult population (29 percent) believed that a woman should work outside of the home even if it is not essential for supporting her family. Slightly above two-thirds (69 percent) of adult Spaniards thought that unless she receives permission from her husband, a woman should not participate in activities outside of her home, including joining associations and attending meetings or lectures (De Pablo Masa 1976: 372, 377).

Two or three decades later, the situation could not be more different. Using 1995–2001 public opinion data from the World Values Surveys, Norris and Inglehart (2005: 253–254) include Spain and other postindustrial societies such as the Nordic nations, Australia, New Zealand, and the United States in the group of countries with the most positive attitudes toward women's political leadership in the world. In current Spain, the question to be asked in opinion polls is not whether women's place is in the "House" (of parliament), but how big is the majority of Spaniards who support mandatory women's quotas for all political parties (58 percent of adult men and 75 percent of adult women; March 2006 data; Centro de Investigaciones Sociológicas 2006).

Socioeconomic Variables

Socioeconomic variables—such as the proportion of women with university degrees or the presence of women in the labor market—in the last two or three decades have evolved in a sense favorable to the feminization of the parliamentary elite. As regards university enrollment, the higher the number of women with university degrees, the higher the number of female potential candidates to the legislative (Rule 1987: 484; Uriarte and Ruiz 1999: 214–15; Valiente, Ramiro, and Morales 2005: 197). In the twenty-first century, women are 50 percent or over of those Spaniards aged sixteen or over with a university degree (Instituto de la Mujer 2006).

In respect of the presence of women in the labor market, a high proportion of women in paid employment is conducive to a high proportion of women in politics. Employed women may become more interested in politics through participation in the labor market. Paid employment raises the economic autonomy of women and thus their economic resources to run for office (Mateo Diaz 2005: 80–82, 224; Rule 1987: 481).

In the early 1970s, the majority of women of working age did not work for wages. Most Spanish women left the labor market (if ever present there) when they got married or had their first child (De Pablo Masa 1976: 368). This situation has changed significantly in the last three decades. The Spanish female employment rate has constantly increased, and it is now 51 percent.[4] However, it is, together with that of Hungary and Slovakia, the fifth lowest in the EU after that of Malta (34 percent), Italy (45 percent), Greece (46 percent), and Poland (47 percent), and it is five points below the EU average (56 percent) (Jouhette and Romans 2006: 5; 2005 data). Since the percentage of women in the lower chamber of the Spanish parliament (36 percent) is the fifth highest in the EU after that of Sweden (47 percent), Finland (42 percent), and Denmark and the Netherlands (37 percent), factors other than the position of women in the labor market are needed to explain the comparatively high presence of women in the Congress of Deputies.

Political Variables

There is agreement in the literature about the key factor that explains the comparatively high presence of women in the Spanish parliament: the approval and successful implementation of women's quotas in left-wing political parties and especially so in the social democratic PSOE (Astelarra 2005: 272–273; Sánchez Ferriz 2000: 207, 220; Threlfall 2005a: 125, 148–149, 2005b: 8–9; Uriarte and Ruiz 1999: 211).

Feminists were active within the PSOE at least since the beginning of the transition to democracy and sought organizational status within the party. In 1976, a women's caucus, "Woman and Socialism" (Mujer y Socialismo), was formed. It was no more than a study group. In 1981, one of its members was elected to the PSOE Federal Executive Commission and others followed her in successive years. In December 1984, the women's caucus was raised by the party to the status of a Secretariat of Women's Participation at the federal executive level (Astelarra 2005: 133–134; Verge 2005: 4–5).

In the 1970s, and especially in the 1980s, feminists within the PSOE continuously denounced the low presence of women in top political decision-making positions and asked for quotas to remedy this problem. The adoption of the 1988 quota was by no means easy. Most PSOE leaders were much more concerned with class inequalities than with other types of inequalities, for instance, those caused by gender. For many of these leaders, feminist demands were particularistic and bourgeois deviations from the main objective of a socialist party: the improvement of the status of the working class (Valiente 2005: 178–179).

The full account of how in 1988 PSOE feminists achieved their goal of a 25 percent women's quota has not yet been written, since hardly any in-depth research has been conducted on this matter. Various factors facilitated the adoption of the 1988 PSOE quota: international influences, the support to quotas by the majority of PSOE members and the population in general, and the personal connections of PSOE feminists with PSOE male leaders. The Socialist International had recommended that member parties adopt quotas to increase women's presence in political decision-making positions (Threlfall 2005a: 128, 2005b: 9; Verge 2005: 5). According to an opinion poll conducted among PSOE members in 1986, around two-thirds of them (67 percent) were in favor of quotas (Sánchez Hernández 2003: 186). Similar degrees of support were found in opinion polls administered to the adult population of Spaniards (Instituto IDES 1988: 62–63). Some PSOE feminists were not merely unknown rank-and-file members or PSOE activists but the friends, relatives, and even wives of the main PSOE leaders (Threlfall 2005a: 158). For this very personal reason, PSOE feminists were close to the centers of party power and have continuously used these personal connections to advance feminist causes including the quota.[5]

The approval in 1997 of the 40 percent women's quota was again no easy task.[6] Around three-quarters of the 1997 congress delegates were men, and 70 percent of congress delegates held political decision-making positions (Méndez and Santamaría 2001: 49, 60). If the women's quota were not only approved but finally implemented, some of these men would risk losing their very jobs as politicians. The reasons that in 1997 help to explain the success of PSOE feminists' skillful mobilization in favor of the 40 percent women's quota include international factors, the need to partly renew the leadership of the party after the 1996 electoral defeat, and the victory in the 1997 PSOE congress of the internal PSOE branch formed by the so-called renovators (*renovadores*). The Socialist International maintained its recommendation to party members to make relevant efforts to increase women's presence in politics. The Declaration of the United Nations Fourth World Conference on Women held in Beijing, China, in September 1995 described access to political office as crucial for women's well-being and encouraged states to make the necessary provisions for the fulfillment of the aim. In addition, one of the main objectives of the Fourth EU Action Program on Equal Opportunities (1996–2000) was the equal participation of women and men in decision making in all fields (Jenson and Valiente 2003: 87–88; Threlfall 2005a: 151; Verge 2005: 5).

In 1997, the still preponderantly male PSOE leadership approved the 40 percent women's quota in part because the quota was seen as a devise for party renewal. After fourteen years in office, the PSOE lost the 1996 general election in the midst of a wave of political scandals and episodes of corruption. A renewal of the leadership could be perceived by the electorate in positive terms, because the new faces (women and youth) would not be associated with the old guard. Before the 1997 party congress, PSOE feminists convinced general secretary Felipe González to support the 40 percent quota. Although González resigned as general secretary at the congress, his successor, Joaquín Almunia, was in general supportive of feminist causes and particularly of the new quota (interview with Milagros Candela Castillo; Threlfall 2005a: 129, 152–153, 2005b: 10, 14–15; Verge 2005: 8).

Although one could find PSOE feminists in all internal branches of the party, the majority of them belonged to the branch formed by the renovators. Another main internal PSOE branch was that formed by the so-called followers of [Vice President Alfonso] Guerra (*guerristas*). Both renovators and guerristas shared an attitude of indifference and even hostility to feminism. But in general, the renovators have been known to be less opposed to feminist demands. Both Almunia and the majority of congress delegates were renovators, and this was crucial because the conflict between the renovators and the guerristas was very intense at the time of the congress (Almunia 2001: 428; Verge 2005: 8; interview with Patrocinio De las Heras[7]).

Women's quotas were adopted in many Western countries (including Spain) in the 1980s by left-wing parties (Norris 2000: 350). What is especial about Spain is that in general, PSOE quotas have been implemented (however imperfectly at times). Thus, quotas have produced a substantial increase in the presence of women in parliament (Threlfall 2005a, 2005b; Verge 2005: 5, 8–9). More research is needed to fully understand why this partially successful implementation has taken place, given the fact that in numerous countries quotas have been adopted but not implemented (Matland 2006: 278; Reynolds 1999: 561). PSOE feminists mobilized endlessly within the party at the national and subnational level to make sure that quotas were not only approved but also implemented. PSOE feminists organized training sessions for female members, activists, and leaders. These feminists tried to convince female members and activists that they were ready for public office and need to demand their inclusion in electoral lists (Astelarra 2005: 162–163; Verge 2005: 8; interview with Carmen Martínez Ten). In some elections, PSOE feminists were members of the party commissions that approved electoral lists. They convinced the remaining members of the committee to reject lists elaborated by subnational party structures that did not comply with the quota requirement.[8] In their efforts to make sure that the quota was implemented, PSOE feminists found powerful male allies.

For instance, circulars and recommendations signed by the PSOE general secretary supporting the recruitment of women to decision-making positions were sent to the different structures of the party (Astelarra 2005: 162).

Other left-wing parties different from the PSOE also had quotas. This is the case with the PCE-IU. In the late 1980s, an internal party debate on women's political presence finished with the 1989 commitment to a women's quota of 30 percent for internal party positions and on party electoral lists. Two other IU discussions culminated in the adoption of new women's quotas of 35 percent and 40 percent in 1990 and 1997, respectively (Ramiro 2000: 225–226).

The conservative PP has always vehemently opposed quotas. As with many other conservative parties, women and men from these parties think that it is wrong to intervene in the recruitment process in order to elect more women. For instance, Amalia Gómez, general secretary of Social Affairs in the first PP government (1996–2000), dismissed such efforts as "the wonderbra quota" (*la cuota del wonderbra*) (*El País* May 18, 1997: 31). Her more restrained colleagues term quotas a form of discrimination (see Isabel Tocino of PP, minister of the environment, in *Mujeres* 1994). Conservative women argue instead that the recruitment process must be "fair" and "neutral," so that the "best people" (including women) can be elected. Some may accept "soft" measures (such as encouraging women to stand for office) but oppose "hard" ones (such as quotas) (Jenson and Valiente 2003: 86; Verge 2005: 6). However, the increase of the access of women in PP elected positions since the 1990s has been explained by a mimetic effect of the PSOE quotas in a context of intense electoral competition between the PSOE and the PP (Astelarra 2005: 164–166; interview with Martínez Ten; Ruiz Jiménez 2006; Uriarte and Ruiz 1999: 211; Verge 2005: 1).

In the years to come, the access of women to political decision-making positions will be under discussion at the central state level. It is an issue of high priority for feminists within left-wing parties. Organic Act 3/2007 of March 22 on equality between women and men contains, among other measures, a reform of the 1985 General Electoral Act, making a women's quota of 40 percent mandatory for all parties. It is likely that the conservative party would lodge an appeal to the Constitutional Court on the grounds that mandatory quotas are unconstitutional. The PP has already lodged such an appeal regarding similar regional laws (Valiente 2005: 177).

Conclusion

In this chapter, I have shown that Spain ranks eight in a world classification of women in parliament with 36 percent female members in the lower chamber because in the last two decades feminists within left-wing parties succeeded at making their parties adopt and partly implement women's quotas. Spanish women gained presence in high politics in a conducive environment because of the proportional representation electoral system and the increasingly secular and egalitarian society, polity, and economy. It is an open question whether further increases in female parliamentary representation can be obtained with the help of voluntary quotas in left-wing parties or with more radical devices, such as mandatory quotas for all parties that compete in elections.

Notes

1. For a review of the literature on women in the Spanish parliament, see Valiente, Ramiro, and Morales (2005: 193–195).
2. In the past, the PP had other names. Only "PP" is used in this chapter.
3. Approximately a third of pupils of preschool, primary, and secondary education attend private educational centers, the overwhelming majority of which are run by the Catholic church.
4. The female employment rate is the proportion of employed women in each age group (fifteen to sixty-four years in this case).
5. Interview with Carmen Martínez Ten, member of the Federal Executive Commission of the Spanish Socialist Workers' Party, Madrid, May 4, 1999.
6. Interview with Milagros Candela Castillo, president of the Association for Feminist Thought and Action and activist of the Spanish Socialist Workers' Party, Madrid, April 14, 1999.
7. Local councilor in the city of Madrid representing the Spanish Socialist Workers' Party, interview, Madrid, April 20, 1999.
8. Interview with Carmen Martínez Ten. Interview with Micaela Navarro Garzón, secretary of women's participation in the Federal Executive Commission of the Spanish Socialist Workers' Party, Madrid, April 13, 1999.

Preferential (Open) List Systems and Single Transferable Vote

9 Belgium

The Collateral Damage of Electoral System Design

Petra Meier

Introduction

The number of Belgian political institutions and their complexity are inversely proportional to the country's size. Belgium is a parliamentary monarchy with an asymmetric federal structure meant to balance varying power relations between the Dutch-, French-, and German-speaking communities. In the 1990s the number of institutional layers increased owing to the achievement of the federal state structure. To the former House of Representatives, Senate, and provincial and local institutions was added a supplementary level comprising the regions and communities. These institutions are organized along, respectively, territorial and ethnolinguistic lines. The three regions (Flanders, Wallonia, and the Brussels Capital Region) have territorial boundaries, and socioeconomic matters such as employment or mobility fall under their remit. The three communities comprise citizens of a specific ethnolinguistic group (the Dutch-speaking community comprises all Dutch-speaking citizens living in Flanders and Brussels, the French-speaking community all French-speaking citizens from Wallonia and Brussels, and the German-speaking community all German-speaking citizens from Wallonia) and deal with matters such as education or culture.

Belgium has traditionally been a laggard regarding women's position in politics (Woodward 1998). It was one of the last European countries to grant women political rights. In 1948, in the aftermath of World War II and the recognition of women's political rights in France, Belgian women were granted the same political rights as men. Back in 1921 women had got the right to stand for elections, and only for the local elections—passive suffrage. Widows, single mothers of fallen soldiers, or women with an outstanding contribution to the resistance movement were entitled to vote in the other elections as well (Van Molle and Gubin 1998). However, women acquired part of their political rights not on their own account but as the substitute of a heroic man who had died in the war. In case of (a new) marriage they would lose their special passive political rights. Also, the position of women in politics has traditionally been weak. They were few in number and lacked access to top positions. Women's policy agencies were constituted later than elsewhere and did not possess the means necessary to be powerful (Meier 2005; Hondeghem and Nelen 2000).

Notwithstanding this rather negative picture, Belgium is an interesting case to study. First, despite their weak position, feminists within and outside the state institutions made Belgium the first European and the second country worldwide to impose gender quota by law. Second, the number of women rose spectacularly from the second half of the 1990s onward. Third, the progress of Belgian women in electoral politics is, to a large extent, not the achievement of the gender quota. The rest of this chapter will develop this argument, examining in detail the interplay between the electoral system, its reform, the gender quota acts, and other variables influencing the sex ratios in electoral politics.

The Voting System

Since 1899 all elections in Belgium are based on a proportional list system. Political institutions created in the wake of the federalization originating in the nineteenth century, the regional parliaments, adopted the same electoral system. The House of Representatives counts 150 seats, elected in 11 multi-member electoral districts. These districts follow the boundaries of the provinces, except for the districts of Vlaams Brabant and Brussel-Halle-Vilvoorde, which have a peculiar bilingual status. District magnitude ranges from 24 (Antwerpen) to 4 (Luxembourg), owing to large disparities in population density (see table 9.1). Voters can cast multiple preferential votes, but the vote for one or more individual candidates is optional. They can also simply vote for a party. Lists are open but not free—that is, voters can express a preference for individual candidates, they cannot add or eliminate candidates.

The calculation of the seats allocated to the various parties is based on the d'Hondt highest average method. A 5 percent formal provincial threshold is applied, except for Vlaams Brabant and Brussel-Halle-Vilvoorde.

Once the winning seats have been allocated to the various parties, the winning candidates are designed. Preferential votes count for 50 percent in the allocation of seats to candidates. In this perspective, electoral lists are "half-open," the order in which candidates appear on the list does not

Table 9.1   District magnitude in the House of Representatives, Belgium

Electoral district since 2003	Current district size	Regroups the following former districts
Antwerpen	24	Antwerpen (14), Mechelen-Turnhout (10)
Brussel-Halle-Vilvoorde	22	No changes
Oost-Vlaanderen	20	Gent-Eeklo (9), Sint-Niklaas-Dendermonde (6), Aalst-Oudenaarde (6)
Hainaut	19	Mons-Soignies (6), Tournai-Ath-Mouscron (4), Charleroi-Thuin (9)
West-Vlaanderen	16	Brugge (4), Kortrijk-Roeselaere-Tielt (8), Veurne-Diksmuide-Ieper-Oostende (5)
Liège	15	Liège (9), Huy-Waremme (2), Verviers (4)
Limburg	12	No changes
Vlaams Brabant	7	No changes
Namur	6	No changes
Brabant wallon	5	No changes
Luxembourg	4	No changes

completely determine who is elected. But the candidate's position on the list influences his or her chances of getting elected, because those with positions higher on the list can take advantage of the list votes—the votes cast for the party and not for an individual candidate. The total number of votes won by a party is divided by the number of seats allocated to the party increased by one. Candidates having attained or bypassed this quotient are elected, notwithstanding their position on the list. The remaining seats are allocated to candidates in the order in which they appear on the list, adding the necessary number of list votes to their preferential votes so as to make them attain the quotient. Given the fact that list votes count for only 50 percent, the total number of list votes is divided by two. There might still be seats to allocate once the list votes have been distributed, and candidates with the highest number of preferential votes, but not attaining the quotient, are elected. Given the partial impact of the list vote, the candidate-choice option has limited effect.

Several features of the electoral system for the House of Representatives are of a recent nature and were for the first time applied to the 2003 elections. Earlier, the House of Representatives was elected in 20 electoral districts instead of the current 11 ones, and the boundaries mainly followed the administrative divisions of the districts and not that of the provinces. Vote pooling or apparentement was possible across the districts in one province, thereby increasing the chances of winning a leftover seat. There was no formal electoral threshold, which meant bigger effective thresholds in small districts. Last but not least, the impact of the list vote was stronger since the list votes did fully count (Swyngedouw and Vander Weyden 2006).

The political motivation for the reform on the eve of the 2003 elections was one of electoral system design, initiated by the Liberals and the Socialists and facilitated by the exclusion, after four decades, of the Christian Democrats from power. Back in 1993, the electoral system for the House of Representatives had also undergone a couple of changes. These were a result of the St. Michael's Agreements, enshrining a constitutional reform creating regional parliaments and making the Senate a meeting place for the communities. The changes to the electoral features of the House of Representatives were a consequence of these agreements, meant to avoid an explosion of the number of MPs. There was no intention to revise the electoral system for the House of Representatives. On the whole, the electoral system for the House of Representatives has evolved toward an increase in district and party magnitude as well as toward more open lists, increasing the impact of voters to the disadvantage of party leaders.

The last, but important, feature of the Belgian electoral system is the gender quota imposed by law. The 2002 gender quota acts compel parties to put forward an equal number of female and male candidates. Furthermore, candidates of the same sex may not occupy both the top two positions on a list. Noncompliance will result in rejection of the list by the public authorities. This provision is to be reached by the second election to take place after the acts came into force. In the first election after the acts came into force (in 2003 for the legislative elections for the federal parliament and in 2004 for the regional and European elections), all the first three positions on the electoral lists could not be occupied by candidates of the same sex.

The 2002 gender quota acts replaced the 1994 gender quota act "Smet-Tobback," the first of its sort in Europe and the second worldwide, after the Argentinean "Ley de cupos." The 1994 act stipulated that electoral lists must not comprise more than two-thirds of candidates of either sex. In the event of noncompliance, public authorities would not accept the lists for election. The act had been applied to the 1994 and 2000 local and provincial elections (on the occasion of the former, with the temporary measure that lists needed to comprise at least 25 percent women candidates) as well as to the 1999 European, federal, and regional ones. The act had constantly been criticized because it did not insist on an equal number of women and men or impose a "placement mandate" to guarantee women eligible positions.

Women in the Legislature: Historical Trends

Back in 1929, the first women were elected to the House of Representatives. While they were not allowed to vote, they could stand for elections. Until the end of World War II, not even 1 percent of MPs were women. As table 9.2

Table 9.2 Women in the Belgian House of Representatives since World War II

Year of election	Women MPs %					Men MPs %
	0–5%	*5–10%*	*10–20%*	*20–30%*	*30–40%*	
1946	1.4					98.6
1949	2.8					97.2
1950	3.3					96.7
1954	4.2					95.8
1958	4.2					95.8
1961		5.1				94.9
1965	3.3					96.7
1968	3.7					96.3
1971	2.8					97.2
1974		6.6				93.4
1977		7.0				93.0
1978		7.5				92.5
1981		5.6				94.4
1985		7.5				92.5
1987		8.4				91.6
1991		9.4				90.6
1995			12.0			88.0
1999				23.3		76.7
2003					34.7	65.0

Source: Celis and Meier 2006: 22.

shows, from then until the mid-1970s women accounted for no more than 5 percent of MPs, and from the mid-1970s until the mid 1990s for between 5 and 10 percent. At the 1995 federal elections, 12 percent of the MPs elected were women, but the first real breakthrough came in 1999 when women accounted for 23 percent of those elected. A second breakthrough was achieved at the subsequent 2003 elections, where no less than 35 percent of women got elected.

While it took women more than six decades to account for 10 percent of MPs in the House of Representatives, their number tripled in less than one decade, or over the course of two elections. Another interesting feature is the spectacular big jumps of the increase in the seat share of women in a short period of time, while the previous decades were characterized by fluctuating numbers. In 1981 fewer women were elected than at the previous elections, and in the second half of the 1960s no fewer than four elections were necessary for the number of women elected to catch up with that in 1961. Finally, the recent substantial increase of women MPs in the House of Representatives helped the traditional laggard join the top 20 countries with the highest number of women in national parliaments.

The Impact of the Voting System on the Proportion
of Women in the Legislature

The electoral system for the House of Representatives, as for all elected assemblies in Belgium, is highly proportional and hence "women friendly". But proportionality in itself is apparently not a sufficient condition for ensuring an equitable presence of women in the legislature. While the Belgian electoral system has been highly proportional throughout the last century, the number of women in the legislature has been very low for most of that period. Furthermore, the degree of proportionality did not alter profoundly, while the number of women rose considerably over the last decade. The extensive proportionality of the electoral system seems to have facilitated a higher number of women in the legislature once other features have been modified or processes have been launched.

A feature of the electoral system that seems to have influenced the share of women MPs is district, and, more precisely, party magnitude. While it is difficult to assess the exact impact of party magnitude, since it is nearly impossible to account for all other independent variables, there are strong indications that the rise of the number of women in politics is at least partly owing to an increase in party magnitude. While the 1993 changes in the wake of the constitutional reform did not profoundly alter party magnitude, this was the case with the introduction of provincial districts on the eve of the 2003 elections. In 1993 the number of seats decreased from 212 to 150, but the number of districts diminished, too, whereby party magnitude did not alter. The introduction of electoral districts along the boundaries of the provinces eliminated a couple of very small former districts (see table 9.1). This involved a considerable rise in party magnitude since the number of parties remained stable (Deschouwer and Meier 2002).

Parallel to this increase in party magnitude we can find a considerable rise in the number of women elected, namely from just above 23 to 35 percent. Similar leaps forward in the number of women elected can be found in other Belgian assemblies whenever party magnitude increased. An increase in party magnitude has always been accompanied by an exceptional rise in the number of women elected. This explains the phenomenal increase in the number of women elected to the Senate in 1995, to the House of Representatives in 2003, and in Brussels (from 36 to 45 percent) and Flanders (from 20 to 31 percent) in 2004, due to the introduction of electoral districts along provincial boundaries. Also, the largest number of women with legislative power is found in those assemblies with sizeable electoral districts. The parliament of Brussels traditionally has the highest party magnitude and also the highest number of women elected. The parliament of the German-speaking community is also characterized by a relatively high party magnitude and has had a higher share of women MPs than its counterparts.

High party magnitude involves having more winning candidates on a list. Legislative competition has traditionally been important at elections to the House of Representatives, a mandate being highly valued in a (political) career. The House of Representatives is a powerful institution, and being an MP used to be a good preparation for becoming a member of the executive. It not only allows for having the necessary exposure and gathering important experience, but ministers also tend to be chosen from among elected candidates. Politicians with an important local mandate (mayor and, to a lesser extent, aldermen) also value the mandate of an MP in the House of Representatives, allowing them to be a career politician (a local mandate is insufficient to earn a decent living). Owing to high legislative competition and small party magnitude, the few "safe" seats tended to be earmarked. And the low parliamentary turnover, with extensive political careers as a consequence, left but few openings. The increase of party magnitude involved an important opening of safe seats. There are more safe seats, and since parties feel the need to present lists containing a "healthy mix of candidates"—a major aspiration of the last decade, and a synonym for a list reflecting diversity in terms of sex (women), age (initially younger but recently also senior candidates), ethnicity (candidates with roots in mainly Northern and sub-Saharan Africa or Turkey), sexuality (gay and lesbian candidates) and disabled candidates—women are on the winning side.

However, an increase in party magnitude does not seem to be a necessary condition for an increase in the number of women elected as show the 1999 elections to the House of Representatives. The first leap forward of the number of women MPs in the House of Representatives had already taken place in 1999, before the introduction of provincial electoral districts. Similarly, at the 2004 regional elections, the percentage of women elected to the Walloon Parliament rose from 11 to 19, although this legislature had not increased the size of its electoral districts. In both cases the increase of the number of women elected should rather be attributed to the gender quota acts, which will be discussed in the next section.

Finally, the rules for the allocation of seats to winning candidates also seem to have an impact on the number of women elected. Traditionally, seats were mainly awarded to candidates in the order in which they appeared on the list. This was because candidates needed a large number of preferential votes in order to modify the order of the list. Additionally, voters tend to make little use of their more recent right to cast a vote for several candidates on the same list. Rather, they vote for the top candidate, thereby reinforcing the list order (Smits and Thomas 1998; Smits and Wauters 2000). Throughout the last century not even 1 percent of candidates for the House of Representatives (or Senate) managed to breach the list order (Craeghs and Dewachter 1998).

This system tended to be disadvantageous for women. The difficulty in breaching the list order made it nearly impossible for women to get elected if the party gatekeepers had not decided to position them on a safe seat. The few winning positions at the top of electoral lists have traditionally been earmarked for those designed to have a political career and women used not to be among them. Also, well-known politicians, often members of the executive, so as to attract voters and help their parties take maximum advantage of their fame, position themselves on the top of lists. This tendency has been reinforced over time, given the decreasing pillarization of the Belgian society and the subsequent rise in voter volatility as well as the growing mediatization of elections. Given the underrepresentation of women in politics, party leaders were not keen to leave top positions to not-so-well-known women.

The halving of the impact of the list vote to the advantage of preferential votes cast for individual candidates strengthens the open character of electoral lists. In the 2003 elections, 14 percent of candidates for the House of Representatives breached the list order thanks to a good personal score. The elections show that the halving of the list order was slightly to the disadvantage of women: 43 percent of those breaching the list order were women compared with 57 percent men. In the earlier elections nearly no candidates managed to breach the list order, and women with a high number of preferential votes but a low position on the list were not able to translate these into a mandate because the higher impact of the list order counterbalanced their good personal score. In this respect the increased impact of personal scores facilitates the election of women. However, both the elections to the House of Representatives and the other elections of 2003 and 2004 show that more men than women take advantage of the increased openness of electoral lists. While both women and men manage to breach the list order, more men tend to do so and they also tend to jump over women candidates who would have been elected in case of a more closed list (Meier 2003). However, the increased impact of personal scores might further facilitate the election of women in the future. The increased impact of personal scores is favorable for well-known candidates, and here women have a disadvantage, given their historic underrepresentation in politics. The recent increase in the number of women elected will, in the long run, lead to a better balance between well-known male and female candidates and thereby diminish the historical advantage of men when it comes to translating a personal score into a mandate.

In sum, the major changes in the electoral system of the House of Representatives, both the increased party magnitude and openness of electoral lists, facilitated the election of women MPs. None of these changes in the design of the electoral system were initially meant to balance sex ratios among MPs. Furthermore, the spectacular rise of women MPs over the last two elections also resides in other factors, which will be discussed in the next section.

The Impact of Other Variables on the Proportion of Women in the Legislature

Belgian women caught up with men regarding a couple of variables generally thought to influence their position in electoral politics. In the disciplines, from among which political candidates are recruited (law, social sciences, languages, economics, pedagogy), the percentage of women with a university degree equals that of men. However, their position on the labor market is less strong. Belgian women tend to participate less than men in paid work, work fewer hours, and have shorter and less stable careers. However, this variable seems to be neither a necessary nor a sufficient condition as illustrates the higher proportion of Dutch women MPs, whose participation in the labor market is lower than that of their Belgian sisters.

Nonetheless, two variables seem to be to the disadvantage of women with political ambitions. The persisting gender wage gap is in men's favor. A political career costs money, and recent research underlined that women have difficulties in spending the necessary budgets (Fiers et al. 2006). Similarly, a traditional division of labor characterizes the gender roles. Belgian women on average spend eight hours per week more than men on reproductive tasks. Given their lower participation in the labor market, they might not have a double working day, but reproductive and domestic tasks, and especially the care for children and other dependants, do not allow for a flexible agenda. Finally, the existing gender roles partly seem to be a self-fulfilling prophecy. Part of the (male) political elite believes that women are less interested in and have less time for, a political mandate, which inhibits them from approaching women candidates (Deschouwer and Meier 2004; Erzeel et al. 2006).

The latter stands in sharp contrast to the prevailing conception that political correctness requires a certain balance between men and women in politics. When the number of women MPs caught up with the results at the 1974 and 1985 elections, this was partly due to the women's movement's success in turning the weak position of women in politics into an electoral stake. In 1974, the new feminist party Verenigde Feministische Partij–Parti Unifié Féministe stood for elections. It did not hope to win a seat, for it was too small, but it wanted to force parties to position women candidates on safe seats so as not to lose (women) voters. In 1985, the women's movement had been actively lobbying for not only a minister of equal opportunities but also an increase of the number of women MPs. In both cases, the topic was an issue of the electoral agenda, and parties tended to respond to it. From then onward, the women's movement and the political women's groups also lobbied for quota. And the contribution of the latter to the rise of the number of women MPs resides to a certain extent in the groups' capacity to put the issue on the electoral agenda rather than to exploit the features of the electoral system to the advantage of women as does, for instance, the Argentinean quota legislation. The 1999 elections were the first to really apply the gender quota act and this at a large scale, since European, federal, and regional elections took place simultaneously. But the 1994 gender quota act was already heavily criticized for its limited interpretation of gender equality. While the gender quota act had no intrinsic power whatsoever (it defined a minimum of 30 percent of women candidates without any placement mandates while the list order was preponderant), it stimulated a process whereby political parties sought to "outbid" one another in terms of commitment to gender sensitivity. It is this contagion effect, rather than the legal dispositions of the act, that made the number of women MPs rise. A similar dynamic can be observed in 2004 in the case of the election to the Walloon Parliament. Given its very weak position compared with all other parliaments in 1999 (with not even 11 percent female MPs), it was simply not done to have another historically low score of women.

As a legal instrument, however, the 1994 gender quota has not had an effect, and the same can be said of the 2002 gender quota acts. The halving of the impact of the list vote combined with the strategic placing of well-known candidates toward the bottom of the lists increases the likelihood that these candidates will be elected at the expense of candidates figuring at the top of the list. Traditionally safe seats at the top of electoral lists lose their safe character. Well-known candidates at the bottom of the list attract votes, but they have no intention of getting elected or taking up their mandate. But even if they refuse their mandate, someone from the list of substitutes will take up their mandate while the other candidates on the list will not get elected. In this respect the placement mandate of the new gender quota acts has no intrinsic value. Also, the increased size of electoral districts resulted in the new gender quotas losing their impact because the subsequent increase in party magnitude made the new gender quota laws less effective in large constituencies. The only impact the new gender quota acts may have, next to feeding a sentiment of political correctness, is the fact that they increase the number of women candidates to 50 percent. In the long run, this may increase the number of well-known women politicians in elections, which might increase their personal scores and hence their chances of getting (re)elected.

Conclusion

All in all, the number of women MPs has for long been very low. The spectacular rise over the last two elections has been strongly facilitated by a new design of the proportional list system, which has increased party magnitude. Another new feature of the electoral system, the increased voter impact, might in the longer run have a beneficial effect for women. For the moment being, it is rather advantageous to men, who profit from the increased impact of personal scores for the simple reason that there tend to be more well-known male candidates than female ones. It is interesting to observe that adaptations to the electoral system meant to balance sex ratios in politics, the gender quota acts, had, in themselves, less of a positive impact on the number of women elected than those modifications that had not intentionally been introduced to increase the number of women in the legislature. Furthermore, the potential of the gender quotas acts was partly undermined by the parallel modifications of the electoral system, more precisely the increase in party magnitude and voter impact. In the long run, the gender quota might have an indirect favorable impact on the number of women elected, by increasing the number of women candidates to 50 percent. Also, the gender quota acts may feed less traditional conceptions of gender roles, which still operate to the disadvantage of women. All in all, the Belgian electoral system for the House of Representatives and its recent modifications confirm that proportionality and high party magnitude facilitate the selection and election of women. Political variables have an important impact on the position of women in Belgian politics.

STV: A Gender-Proportional System?

Yvonne Galligan

Introduction

In the 2002 parliamentary election, Mary O'Rourke, deputy leader of Fianna Fail[1] and government minister, lost the seat she held for two decades. Nora Owen, former minister and deputy leader of Fine Gael,[2] also lost her long-held seat in that contest. In contrast, Marian Harkin, a nonparty candidate, won a seat on her first attempt in 2002, topping the poll in her constituency. A decade earlier, Eithne Fitzgerald won a seat for the Labour Party[3] on her fifth attempt and in the process won more votes than any other candidate nationwide. These personal political pen-pictures illustrate the uncertainty surrounding the single transferable vote (STV). It suggests that political women, no matter how well established, are in a vulnerable position under this electoral system and that newcomer women can be advantaged given the right circumstances. In this chapter, we explore how much of this uncertainty is linked to the electoral system, and how much can be explained by other factors.

The Voting System

The STV was adopted in Ireland for the 1921 general election. Based on multiple-seat districts, it is designed to provide representation to parties according to their vote share. In this regard, it is different from majoritarian systems where "winner takes all." The larger parties, Fianna Fail and Fine Gael, run multiple candidates in each of the country's 42 constituencies: the smaller parties, such as Labour, Greens, Sinn Fein, and Progressive

Democrats, generally field one candidate each in most constituencies. In addition, a sizeable number of nonparty candidates, known as "independents," are present in elections in many constituencies.[4] Thus, voters in any one district have anywhere between seven and twenty candidates from which to choose a representative, listed alphabetically on one ballot sheet.

To begin with, voters select their candidates in order of preference, giving their most preferred candidate their vote (or "number one"), followed by an indication of their second, third, fourth, and subsequent choices. Voters can decide to vote only for candidates of their preferred party, or they can rank order all candidates. The preferred governing party or coalition, along with local, issue, geographical, and gender considerations, can also influence voter preferences, and this results in extensive cross-party voting. For instance, a voter could choose to give one of the Fianna Fail candidates her "number one," follow this with a second preference for the Progressive Democrat candidate, then indicate another Fianna Fail candidate as a third choice, and an Independent, running on a local issue, as a fourth preference, and so on until all candidates were ranked. Another voter might choose to give her vote to the more senior Fine Gael candidate, followed by the second Fine Gael candidate, then give a third preference to Labour, a fourth to the Green Party, and then not rank the remaining candidates. Thus, from a voter perspective, STV offers considerable choice. It emphasizes individual candidates over parties, and it delivers relatively proportional results (Sinnott 2005: 123).

The technical operation of the STV is rather more complex. Because STV operates in a multiseat district context, each constituency has a "quota"—the minimum votes required in order to win a seat. The quota is calculated on the basis of the valid votes cast in relation to the number of seats to be filled in each constituency. There is a simple formula for calculating the quota:

$$\text{Quota} = \left(\frac{\text{Total number of valid votes}}{\text{Number of seats} + 1} \right) + 1$$

In a three-seat constituency, the quota is one quarter of the valid votes[5] plus one, in a four-seater it is one-fifth plus one, and in a five-seat district the quota is one-sixth the valid ballot plus one.

A second feature of STV is the utilization of voter preferences in determining the result. This is done through a transfer of surplus votes a candidate receives above the quota required to win a seat. Earlier we noted Fitzgerald's remarkable surplus of votes in 1992. If we take this as an example, we see that she obtained 17,256 votes in a five-seat constituency, where the quota was 9,940. In other words, Fitzgerald garnered 7,316 votes more than was required to win a parliamentary seat. Under STV, those extra votes were shared out among the other candidates in proportions that reflected voter preferences—1,078 votes were added to the tally of Liz O'Donnell standing for the Progressive Democrats; 1,250 went to Alan Shatter of Fine Gael; and 1,130 were allocated to Marian White of the Democratic Left. The other nine candidates received varying smaller amounts of votes from this surplus. This illustrates the point that under STV, voter preferences are utilized to the full, and there is minimal vote wastage. A similar process operates for transferring the votes of candidates who have no hope of winning a seat. In these instances, the low-vote candidates are eliminated and their votes transferred to other candidates in accordance with voter rankings. Vote counting, then, proceeds over a number of rounds or "counts," with the surplus of elected candidates distributed, or low-polling candidates eliminated, on each count. It can take up to 12 rounds of counting to fill all the seats in a constituency. The process is manual one, and therefore slow—two days of ballot counting are usually required before the final results are known.[6]

Women in the Legislature: Historical Trends

There have been 17 elections to the Irish parliament, Dáil Éireann, from 1945 to the present. Over this time, women's average seat-holding stood at ten seats, compared with 146 seats for men, giving women an average parliamentary representation of 6 percent. This very low presence over time masks some variations in both increases and decreases in women's parliamentary seat-holding. Women's presence in the legislature reached its nadir in 1961 and again in 1969. On each occasion only three women were returned as members of parliament, constituting 2 percent of TDs (Teachtaí Dálas, or parliamentary representatives). In 1992, women's political seat-holding grew from 13 to 20, with a further modest increase to 22 (13 percent) after the 2002 election (table 10.1). It took until the 1990s for women's proportional share of parliamentary seats to move into low double-digits, earning Ireland the dubious distinction of having one of the lowest levels of women's parliamentary representation in Europe. Six women dominated female representation from 1948 through to the 1970s, accounting for 25 instances of seat-holding between them. All came from established political families, and four were widows of previous seat-holders. The "widows inheritance," the major route to political office for Irish women, was effectively replaced by the "daughter's inheritance" from 1977 onward (Galligan, Knight, and Nic Giolla Choille 2000: 35). Today, the political family connections of individual parliamentarians are about the same for both male and female TDs.

The 1977 election heralded the beginning of an increase in female candidacies, which reached a high of 20 percent of total candidacies in 1997. However, the relationship between women's candidacies and seat-winning is a negative one, with proportionally fewer being elected than selected. The turnover rate at the post-1945 elections overall indicates a similar pattern,

Table 10.1   Female representation in Irish politics, 1948–2002

Year of election	Male TDs (N)	Female TDs (N)	Female TDs (%)
1948	142	5	3
1951	142	5	3
1954	142	5	3
1957	142	5	3
1961	141	3	2
1965	139	5	3
1969	141	3	3
1973	140	4	3
1977	142	6	4
1981	155	11	7
1982 (i)	158	8	5
1982 (ii)	152	14	8
1987	152	14	8
1989	153	13	8
1992	146	20	12
1997	146	20	12
2002	144	22	13

Source: Author calculations from Walker (1993), Nealon (1993, 1997), Kennedy (2002).

with few women among new officeholders. Since 1969, the average number of new parliamentarians returned at each of the 11 elections is 33, among whom are three women. Indeed, the elections of 1969, 1981, and 2002 introduced a combined total of 134 new TDs to the Dail, only 12 of whom were women. Can the electoral system be identified as inhibiting women's political opportunities, or is this problem more a function of voter behaviour and party selection practices? These questions will now be explored.

The Impact of the Voting System on the Proportion of Women in the Legislature

In examining poor levels of female political representation, the extent to which the electoral system facilitates gender presence is one of the first elements to be placed under the spotlight. As we have seen, STV facilitates voters' wishes to an unusually high degree, and so the operation of the voting system and the preferences of the voters are closely linked. In order to compare the fortunes of female party candidates over time, we will focus on the three parties that have been consistently present in the party system since 1945—Fianna Fail, the largest party in the state, which gets an average vote of around 40 percent; Fine Gael, with a vote share of around 25 percent; and Labour, which attracts approximately 10 percent support. Fianna Fail and Fine Gael have their origins in Irish nationalism. Today Fine Gael is regarded as being similar to European conservative parties, and Fianna Fail is seen as a right-of-center party marked by a high level of pragmatism, with Labour being a "conservative" social democratic party. If one also takes into account the positioning of the small neoliberal party, the Progressive Democrats, the ideological orientation of the party system is inclined toward conservatism, with left-leaning parties such as the Green Party and Sinn Fein drawing little support to date and gaining relatively few parliamentary seats.

As noted above, female candidacies have been scarce since 1945 compared with those of males. Fianna Fail has fielded women in a total of 124 constituency contests since the late 1940s. Fine Gael has been slightly more favourably disposed to selecting female candidates and has done so on 129 occasions. The Labour Party has compared well with the two larger parties, putting women forward in 76 constituency contests between 1948 and 2002. A total of 135 individual women have been selected for these contests. One of the major effects of the STV electoral system is that it delivers relatively proportional results and, overall, is in the midrange on the scale of proportionality. In a comparison between STV and other systems with regard to electoral proportionality, Sinnott observes that "Irish elections over the period 1948–89 emerge as much more proportional than those held under first past the post electoral systems, and as more proportional than some held under PR list systems" (Sinnott 2005: 117). According to Gallagher and Mitchell (2005d: 621), the disproportionality of STV is 6.6, as compared with a disproportionality rate of 0.3 for South Africa's electoral system and 9.3 in the case of Canada. Parties in Ireland, however, experience an unequal seat-vote ratio, with Fianna Fail generally receiving a seat bonus of 3 percent, Fine Gael being rewarded with a smaller seat bonus of between 1 and 2 percent, while the Labour party suffers from a minor deficit in seat-vote ratio, at around 0.8 percent (Sinnott 2005: 107–108).

Under the STV system, proportionality is delivered by vote transfers, which play an important role in converting votes into seats. In contrast to plurality systems, this means that multiple candidates from a particular party can win seats if that party's vote is sufficiently high. Given that this vote sharing is an advantage of STV over plurality systems, one might expect the larger parties—Fianna Fail and Fine Gael—to take a "risk" with their candidate tickets and field more women. However, despite the inbuilt mechanism for vote distribution, parties do not utilize this characteristic to encourage women's candidacies.

A related issue to that of female candidacy is that of district size and its impact on women's representation. The general literature suggests that women candidates do better in districts of six seats and over than in smaller seat constituencies on which Ireland's STV system is based. Yet party selection patterns indicate that women are selected to contest in the three-, four-, and five-seat districts, as figure 10.1 illustrates.

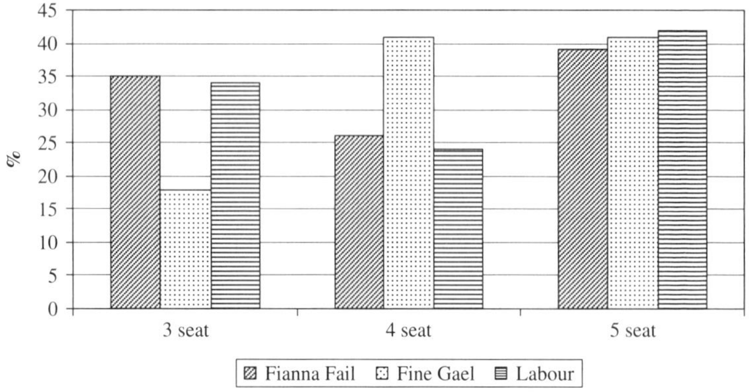

Source: Author calculations from Walker (1993), Nealon (1993, 1997), Kennedy (2002), author's database (2007)

Figure 10.1   Female candidates (%) and constituency size, by party, 1948–2007

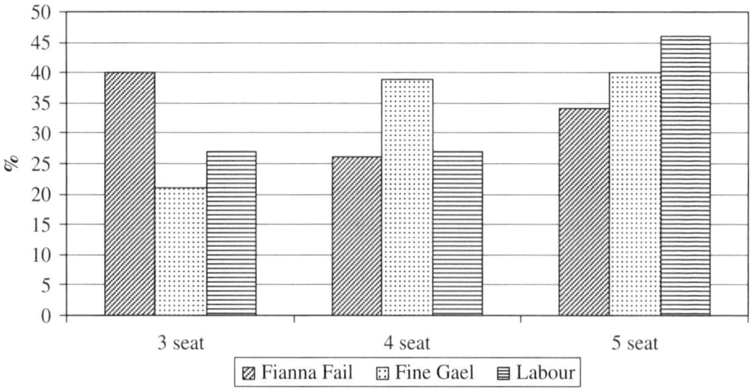

Source: Author calculations from Walker (1993), Nealon (1993, 1997), Kennedy (2002)

Figure 10.2   Female TDs (%) and constituency size, by party, 1948–2002

In figure 10.1, the three parties indicate a tendency toward selecting women in five-seat constituencies, but this trend is moderated by two other patterns. Fine Gael places a similar proportion of its women aspirants in four-seat constituencies. Fianna Fail and Labour favor placing female candidates in three-seat districts. In this regard Fine Gael, as the second largest party, conforms more closely to general expectations in the literature than do the other two parties. If one relates seat contests to seat winning, Fianna Fail female candidates running in three-seat constituencies had a positive advantage over their female colleagues contesting districts of other magnitudes (figure 10.2).

Fine Gael women's electoral successes corresponded very closely to their distribution across constituency size, while Labour female contenders fared best in four-seat districts. Thus, five-seat districts, with a lower quota required for election, do not appear to confer a distinct advantage on female candidates as a whole.

These outcomes suggest, then, that three- and four-seat constituencies are not as negative to women's electoral prospects as the literature would suggest. O'Kelly (2000: 260) confirms this supposition, finding that constituency size does not confer any vote-winning advantage on male candidates over female candidates. Both findings contradict Engstrom's (1987) conclusion that Ireland's relatively small district magnitude hinders female representation.

If district magnitude cannot explain the poor outcomes for female seat-seekers, then we must turn to alternative hypotheses. One factor that is not often examined is the effect of voter change in party preference on women's political representation. In other words, when voters withdraw their support from their previously preferred party, what effect has it on women candidates? The vote swing against Fine Gael was obvious in the 2002 election, when the party dropped its total first preference vote by over 5 percent and its total share of seats by 14 percent. Of male incumbencies, the party lost 19 seats, an attrition rate of 40 percent. Fine Gael's female TDs suffered more severely, with only one of the five female incumbent seats being returned.[7] The voter swing against the party, then, had a more marked effect on the party's female TDs than on male TDs. A similar pattern is evident for the Labour Party in the 1997 election when voters withdrew their support from it. In this instance, the party's vote share decreased by 10 percent and its share of parliamentary seats dropped by 9 percent. Of the five Labour women elected in 1992, only two retained their seats, an attrition rate of 60 percent. Labour's male incumbency decreased by 43 percent—male TDs, clearly suffering less than their female counterparts from voter dissatisfaction.

These findings suggest that vote swings can have a disproportionate effect on female incumbency, which is then accentuated by the absence of women candidates and the unpredictability of vote transfers. Thus, it appears that in specific electoral contexts, women candidates are more vulnerable than men. However, when O'Kelly (2000) examined male and female vote-getting over time (1948–97), he found no overall voter bias against female candidates. Only Fianna Fail party supporters preferred male candidates, while voters for all other parties indicated an equal or slight preference for female candidates. It must be remembered, though, that this analysis was based on first preference votes, and did not take into account the translation of those votes into seats. Nonetheless, it does suggest that overall there is no dramatic voter bias against women candidates. This finding suggests that in any one election, a swing against a party is accentuated in the case of female candidates because there are so few of them in the field. Thus, it is more likely that a combination of low numbers of female candidates and STV transfers (which turns votes into seats) had a heightened effect on the 1997 and 2002 results.

In many electoral systems, incumbency is an important consideration in increasing the opportunities for being returned to parliament. The STV system is no exception, though it does indicate very different incumbency return rates for male and female candidates. An investigation of the 1997 election results emphasized the importance of incumbency in the Irish electoral system, with female incumbents faring much better than male and female nonincumbents (Galligan, Laver, and Carney 1999). An examination of the 2002 results yielded a similar finding, with incumbency conferring a distinct advantage on a candidate's reelection prospects (figure 10.3). Nonetheless, male incumbents still fared better than female incumbents, indicating once again that women's seat-holding in the STV system is more conditional than that of men.

The analysis for 1997 and 2002 also illustrates in stark terms the difficulty confronting new women in gaining entry to the legislature. In 2002, only 7 percent of nonincumbent females succeeded in gaining a parliamentary seat, contrasting with the 47 percent success rate of nonincumbent males (figure 10.3).

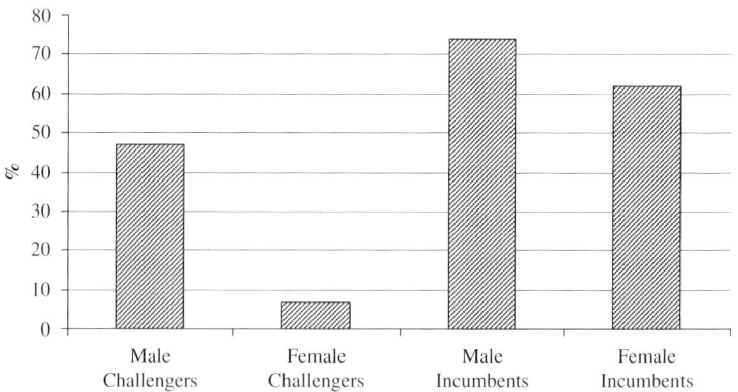

Note: This applies to Fianna Fail and Fine Gael candidates only, as these parties fielded multiple candidates in all constituencies.

Source: Author calculations from Kennedy (2002)

Figure 10.3   Candidate status and electoral success, 2002

The Impact of Other Variables on the Proportion of Women in the Legislature

Women's low seat-holding in Ireland is inextricably bound up with the low proportions of female candidacies. Party selection practices have an obvious bearing on this matter. To begin with, candidate selection is largely decentralized, with local party members having a significant influence on the selection process. Although central party offices have moved in recent years to exert more control over candidate selection, the decision is strongly determined by local party preferences (Galligan 2003). There is some evidence in the United Kingdom to suggest that candidate selection at local level inhibits female nomination and that local selectorates are more conservative than their national officers (Shepherd-Robinson and Lovenduski 2002). In 2002, none of the female candidates for Fianna Fail and Fine Gael were directly chosen by party headquarters, although some were encouraged to put their names forward by senior party figures. The situation was rather different in the lead-in to the 2007 general election, with Fianna Fail adopting a more interventionist approach in candidate selection. National party officers either directly chose or advised local selectorates on certain candidates, among whom were at least four women.

Although attitudes to gender equality among Irish public have become more positive over time, the gap in political interest between men and women is among the largest in the European Union, suggesting that politics is seen as a male preserve (European Commission 1997). The perception of public space as male, and private space as female is reflected in ambiguous views on motherhood, family life, and women's economic independence. On the one hand, support for women's participation in the workplace has increased over time. Women's workforce participation has grown dramatically since the 1970s though, at 56 percent, it lags quite some way behind that of other developed societies. In 2004, three-quarters of women under 34 years employed, but only a third of women over 55 were in work (Cournède 2006: 5), placing Ireland fifty-first in a list of 56 countries in terms of equal economic opportunities for women (NESF 2006: 23–24). At the same time, responsibility for home duties is firmly placed on women's shoulders. Women's child and elder care activities are significantly more time consuming than those of men (McGinnity, Russell, Williams and Blackwell 2005: 54). These facts indicate that there is a persistent cultural bias toward traditional gender roles in modern Ireland, even while younger women remain in, or return to, the workplace. Although some aspects of policy have moved from the male breadwinner model, social policy in general remains strongly influenced by this traditional understanding of gender roles. These underlying value systems make it more difficult for women to seek a party candidacy, and more difficult for their male colleagues to see women as contenders with an equal claim to representation. Thus, it is not surprising that nonincumbent female aspirants face an extremely uphill battle to secure a place on the ballot paper.

The persistence of traditional perspectives on gender roles may also explain the lack of societal interest in the issue of gender equality in political representation. Although Ireland has significant female political role models,[8] their presence has not translated into more gender equality in parliamentary seat-holding. The women's movement has repeatedly raised the issue of equality in decision-making, taking an active role in researching women's political presence, seeking information from parties with regard to their gender equality measures, and presenting a women's manifesto for the 2004 European elections and the 2007 general election, accompanied by countrywide mobilization meetings (National Women's Council of Ireland 2007).[9] However, it does not sustain momentum around this issue, becoming active only in the lead-in to an election, at which stage candidates are already in place.

During the 1990s, Fianna Fail, Fine Gael, and Labour each sought to tackle the issue of women's underrepresentation, in response to pressure from women party members and the need to source additional voter support. Fianna Fail debated the issue from the late 1990s onward, finally adopting a ten-year positive action plan in 2005 incorporating a 33 percent quota for women at all levels of the party up to and including local election candidates (Fianna Fail 2005). In 2003 Fine Gael set a target of increasing its numbers of female TDs from two to between eight and ten and their female senators (upper house) from one to five (Cahill-Kennedy 2004: 14) in the 2007 election. The Labour Party had an informal quota of 25 percent for candidacies in effect since the early 1990s and added to this in 2002 a one-third gender quota for the directly elected seats on the National Executive. Although the party aspired to have women make up one-third of its local election candidates in 2004, only 20 percent of its candidates were female. Although these parties have developed initiatives to stimulate action on gender equality in political representation, the effectiveness of these measures in sensitizing party cultures remains to be seen. Up to this point, party records on gender equality in representation have been shown to be relatively ineffectual, suggesting that the parties are neither committed to, nor concerned by, the democratic deficit indicated by women's absence from decision-making. Given the ambivalent attitudes in society with respect to gender roles, it is not surprising that gender equality in politics is not a priority for parties.

Conclusion

This discussion on women's electoral representation in Ireland's STV system suggests that the electoral system interacts with the low level of female candidacy to produce a small but notable bias against women as political contenders. While voters are in general not gender biased, it appears that female incumbents are less secure in their seat-holding than male incumbents when voter shifts reduce party support. Why this is so does not appear to be connected with district magnitude, especially if one examines the results over an extended period of time. This counterintuitive finding deserves further investigation and may have something to do with conservative party selection patterns: in other words, parties have in the past selected few women, but some of them were fortunate to be selected in winnable seats. This goes some way toward explaining the longevity of some Fianna Fail and Fine Gael women TDs, whose electoral record matches and even exceeds that of their male counterparts.

A very stark finding is the serious obstacles facing nonincumbent women in seat-winning, as compared with female incumbents and males, both challenger and incumbent. Having come through a party selection process, one would consider that female nonincumbents have similar prospects of success as male nonincumbents. That such is not the case is indeed a perplexing point and may be bound up with party strategies for vote-winning—that nonincumbent women in Fianna Fail and Fine Gael are intended to be "sweeper" candidates, garnering votes that then transfer to more senior and better-known incumbent male colleagues. In Labour and the other smaller parties, the challenge facing nonincumbent women is to break into the charmed circle of elected representatives in circumstances where the vote available is already low and fragmented among a number of parties and nonparty candidates.

Results from longitudinal analyses dating from 1948 and studies of individual election results in general indicate that women are not particularly disadvantaged in terms of votes, though this may happen in certain periods of time. It is noticeable, though, that while voters are becoming more open to women legislators over time, Fianna Fail voters take a more conservative view of female candidacies. In contrast, voters from other parties do not discriminate against women, and Progressive Democrat voters positively advantage women candidates.

The overall cultural environment in which Irish politics is embedded cannot be ignored when it comes to understanding women's political representation and the electoral system. The three parties that historically constituted the party system reflect the more widely held conservative views on women's public role. Although each party has made efforts to address the gender deficit in political representation, there is no evidence of a will to accomplish significant change and redress of gender imbalances in political life. For this, the electoral system cannot be held accountable.

Notes

1. Fianna Fail is the largest party in the Irish state. It draws support from all classes and forms a single-party government or is the major partner in a coalition government.
2. Fine Gael is the second largest party in the Republic of Ireland, with about 20 percent of the popular vote, and is the main rival to Fianna Fail. It requires the support of other, smaller, parties to form a coalition government.
3. Labour is traditionally the third party in the Irish political system, averaging around 10 percent support. It has formed a governing coalition with Fianna Fail and Fine Gael on different occasions.
4. Occasionally, nonparty candidates are disaffected members of one of the larger parties and contest the election as independent candidates in order to win a seat at the expense of their former party.
5. Valid votes are those cast correctly: for example if a voter defaces the ballot paper in addition to indicating a voting preference, that vote is deemed invalid, or "spoiled," so is not counted. What makes a vote invalid is defined in the electoral law. Sometimes voters give two candidates a "number one" vote, and because it is not possible to distinguish which one is the preferred candidate, that vote is also deemed to be invalid.
6. A more detailed discussion of the technical operation of STV is provided by Sinnott (2005: 109–117). A computerized voting and counting system was tested in four constituencies at the 2002 election but was highly controversial and subsequently suspended.
7. Of the six female Fine Gael TDs elected in 1997, one died during the interelection period and her seat was won in a by-election by a male party colleague. Another female incumbent retired at the 2002 election and the party ran a male and female candidate for this seat. Four incumbents were available for reelection.
8. The previous and current head of state are women—Mary Robinson and Mary McAleese; the leader of the Progressive Democrats for 13 years was Mary Harney. She vacated this post in September 2006.
9. See www.nwci.ie/highlights/election_2007 (April 2007).

Success under Open List PR: The Election of Women to Congress

Gregory D. Schmidt

Introduction

If a political scientist had to predict where women might enjoy relative electoral success in Latin America, Peru would not be high on the list. Among major Latin American countries, Peru has some of the most glaring socioeconomic inequalities, a notoriously inchoate party system, and one of the weakest recent records of democratic governance and human rights. Like most countries in the region, Peru employs party list proportional representation (PR), the most widely used electoral system in the world, to choose its national legislature. However, whereas the lists in most PR systems in Latin America and the world are closed, Peru uses an open list format. The conventional wisdom holds that open list PR is less propitious for the election of women than closed list PR. Nevertheless, this chapter shows that female candidates have enjoyed a great deal of electoral success under the variant of open list PR used in Peru.

The Voting System

Only in 1956 did literate Peruvian women gain the right to vote and hold elective office at the national level. Following controversial elections in 1962, Peru began to use party list PR with the d'Hondt rule to elect its national legislature.[1] Although this general system remains in effect today, there have since been a number of changes in the conduct of Peruvian congressional

Table 11.1   Key features of Peruvian congressional elections

Type of electoral system	*List PR (d'Hondt) since 1963*
Suffrage	Since 1980 all adults (18 years) with minor exceptions. Obligatory voting
Ballot structure	Open list (double optional preferential vote) since 1985
Structure of Congress	Bicameral (180 + 60) until 1992; unicameral (120) since then
Electoral districts	**Departments:** for Chamber of Deputies until 1990; for Senate before 1980; for unicameral Congress since 2001 **Single national district:** for Senate, 1980–1990; for unicameral Congress, 1992–2000
District magnitude	**Chamber of Deputies (1980–1990):** metro Lima = 40; average for other districts = 5.7 **Senate (1980–1990):** 60 in single national district **Democratic Constituent Congress (1992):** 80 in single national district **Fujimori-era unicameral Congress (1995, 2000):** 120 in single national district **Post-Fujimori unicameral Congress (since 2001):** Department of Lima = 35; average for other districts = 3.4

elections. Variations on five key issues are summarized in table 11.1 and discussed in this section.[2]

First, the 1979 constitution established virtual universal adult suffrage. Prior to the 1980 election—which returned Peru to democracy after a dozen years of military rule—illiterate citizens, primarily of indigenous ancestry, had been denied the franchise. Beginning with the 2006 election, military and police personnel also gained the right to vote. This right is now denied only to Peruvians who have had their political rights suspended, owing to convictions or incapacity (e.g., mental illness). Voting is obligatory if a citizen is younger than 70.

Second, there has been a major change in the ballot structure of Peru's list PR system. The 1963 congressional elections, the first under PR, were conducted with closed lists. After a 17-year gap between congressional elections, Peru also used closed lists in 1980. Under the closed list variant of PR, voters choose only among alternative lists, not among individual candidates. The seats won by each party are filled by candidates according to the order in which they appear on the respective list. Beginning in 1985, however, Peru has used a variant of open list called the "double optional preferential vote" (DOPV).[3] Under this format, citizens vote first for a list by marking the symbol of a party or electoral alliance. In addition, they *may* also cast nonordinal "preferential votes" for one or two candidates on the list that they have chosen by writing the respective number(s) in boxes beside the symbol. Each list is awarded seats in proportion to its share of the valid vote, but preferential votes *alone* determine which candidates fill those seats. Thus, if Candidate A is third on the list of a given party and Candidate B appears in sixth place on the same list, Candidate B is nevertheless more likely to fill one of the party's seats if she has more preferential votes than Candidate A. The DOPV stimulates competition among candidates on the same list, but it also facilitates electoral alliances among different parties because list position does not determine election.

Third, following Alberto Fujimori's presidential coup in 1992, a transitional unicameral legislature, the so-called Democratic Constituent Congress (CCD), replaced Peru's bicameral Congress.[4] The 1993 constitution, still in effect, made unicameralism permanent. Whereas the bicameral Congress of the 1980–1992 period had comprised 180 deputies and 60 senators, since 1995 unicameral legislatures have had only 120 members.

Fourth, electoral districts have varied considerably over time. During the 1950s and 1960s, the country's departments (including the port city of Callao, which has departmental status) served as electoral districts for both houses of Congress. After the restoration of democracy in 1980, Peruvians elected the Chamber of Deputies from the departments and a special district for metropolitan Lima. The Senate, however, was chosen in a single national district from 1980 until 1990, the last election for a bicameral Congress. Under Fujimori, Peruvians voted in the single national district to elect unicameral legislatures in 1992, 1995, and 2000. Since late 2000, when Fujimori fled the country, the unicameral Congress has been elected by departments, without a special district for metropolitan Lima.[5]

Fifth, there have been major variations in district magnitude over time and space.[6] During the 1980–1990 period 40 seats in the Chamber of Deputies were elected from metropolitan Lima, but the average magnitude of the remaining districts was only 5.7. In contrast, all 60 seats of the Senate (1980–1990), all 80 seats of the CCD (1992), and all 120 seats of the unicameral Congress of the Fujimori era (1995 and 2000) were chosen in the single national district. Beginning in 2001, the Department of Lima has had 35 seats in the small unicameral Congress; the remaining districts have had an average magnitude of only 3.4.

Women in the Legislature: Historical Trends

Until the 1990s, progress toward gender equity in electoral politics lagged behind trends toward equality in Peruvian society (see the section "Impact of Other Variables on the Proportion of Women in the Legislature"). Although women were elected to Congress in 1956, the first year of female suffrage, they never filled more than 7.2 percent of the seats in either house of Peru's bicameral legislature (see table 11.2). Moreover, before the 1990s,

Table 11.2   Percentage of women elected to Peruvian national legislatures, 1956–2006

(Female suffrage began in 1956)

	1956	1963	1978*	1980	1985	1990	1992**	1995	2000	2001	2006
Chamber of deputies	4.4	1.4	–	7.2	5.6	6.1	–	–	–	–	–
Senate	1.9	0	–	3.3	5.0	6.7	–	–	–	–	–
Unicameral	–	–	2.0	–	–	–	8.8	10.8	21.7	18.3	29.2

* Constitutional Assembly.
** CCD.
Note: The 1962 elections were annulled by a military coup.
Sources: Blondet and Montero (1994: 20, 119, 128), JNE (2006), Schmidt (2006: 154), and Tuesta Soldevilla (2001: 101–103, 107–110).

female legislators played only nominal and largely symbolic roles. They were largely absent from the steering committees of both chambers and, when elected, filled only the more "feminine" positions of secretary and librarian. Similarly, women played only token roles in the leadership of the various political parties and were absent from the cabinet until 1987 (Blondet and Montero 1994: 131–132, 147–148).

Several factors converged to produce a breakthrough for women in electoral politics in the 1990s:

- the emergence of a cadre of talented female professionals;
- the collapse of the traditional political parties;
- support from President Fujimori; and
- the implementation of gender quotas for congressional lists.

Moreover, this breakthrough was achieved under open list PR, which is widely viewed as being less propitious than closed list PR for the representation of women. These major factors and other relevant variables are analyzed in subsequent sections of this chapter.

Here it is important to highlight the dramatic increase in women's representation in Peru since 1990 (see table 11.2). Women won 8.8 percent of the seats in the CCD in 1992 and 10.8 percent of those at stake in the 1995 election for the first unicameral Congress. After the adoption of gender quotas for congressional candidates, 21.7 percent of the seats in Peru's national legislature were filled by women in 2000. This proportion dipped slightly to 18.3 percent in the 2001 election, but then increased markedly to 29.2 percent in 2006. By way of contrast, in the latter year, women comprised 20.8 percent of the members of the House of Commons in Canada, 19.7 percent of those of the House of Commons in Great Britain, and only 15.2 percent of members of the U.S. House of Representatives (Inter-Parliamentary Union: www.ipu.org; accessed in 2006).

Moreover, Peruvian congresswomen no longer play merely symbolic roles. Three women have served as the president of Congress, the second most important elective office in the country. At the beginning of Fujimori's ill-fated third term, an all-female steering committee ran Congress. Working across party lines, congresswomen have successfully pushed for improved legislation on family violence, rape, and other issues of special concern to women (see Schmidt 2006: 170–171).

The Impact of the Voting System on the Proportion of Women in the Legislature

There is broad consensus in the literature on electoral systems that list PR is more propitious for the election of women than plurality or majority voting (e.g., Matland 2005; Reynolds, Reilly, and Ellis 2005: 60–61, 121). In contrast, very little empirical work has been done on the gendered consequences of ballot structure—that is, closed, open, and flexible lists—in PR systems.[7] Nevertheless, the prevailing view in the literature is that women are more likely to be elected on closed lists than open lists (e.g., see Ballington 2005: 116; Farrell 2001: 167; Htun 2002: 31–33; and Norris 2004: 197).

The Peruvian case, however, proves that women can fare well under an open list format. Since 2000 the percentage of congressional seats filled by women in Peru has been consistently above the slowly increasing world average—16.6 percent in April 2006—and is among the two or three highest for Latin American democracies.[8] After the 2006 election, the proportion of congresswomen (29.2 percent) places Peru among the top six of the world's countries and is well above the overall Latin American average (19.4 percent) and the average for closed lists in the region (21 percent).[9] Within Latin America, the only two countries with higher percentages of female legislators are Costa Rica (38.6 percent), ranked third in the world, and Argentina (35 percent). Both of these countries, however, use placement mandates with their closed lists. This configuration guarantees that high numbers of women will be elected but also deprives voters of any choice among individual candidates.

The success of open lists in Peru does not necessarily mean that open lists are more propitious for the election of women than closed lists. Indeed, the only large-N study on this issue (Schmidt 2005) found no significant difference in female representation. Moreover, available evidence suggests that Peruvian women might well have made similar strides in winning congressional elections had the pre-1985 closed list format been retained. The debut of the DOPV in 1985 was accompanied by a slight decrease in the election of women to the Chamber of Deputies and a slight increase in the female share of Senate seats (see table 11.2). Of even greater significance is the success of female candidates in Peruvian municipal elections, which are held under a closed list majoritarian system. Women filled 27.8 percent of municipal council seats in the 2006 election (Ágora Democrática 2007). Nevertheless, contrary to the prevailing view in the literature, *open lists have not been an obstacle to the electoral success of women.*

Although the percentages of women elected under closed and open list formats are very similar *on average* throughout the world, there is a broad range of variation *within* each category (Schmidt 2005). Thus, rather than merely contrasting general properties of closed and open ballot structures, we need to analyze specific features of the cases within each category. Indeed, several specific features of Peru's open list format have favored the election of women.[10]

First, Peru's DOPV differs from the open list formats used in Brazil and Chile, in which most or all of the voters cast ballots for individual candidates. Many Peruvians do not cast one or both preferential votes. For example, in the 2000 election, the number of preferential votes was slightly less than the number of list votes, even though two preferential votes may be cast for each list vote.

Survey data show that poor voters are less likely to cast preferential votes and that those who do so are more likely to choose only one candidate. In addition, voters from lower socioeconomic strata are more likely to make errors in casting or counting preferential votes, which often leads to the disqualification of individual ballots or entire precincts. In sum, a more affluent and better educated *subelectorate* chooses the individual members of the Peruvian Congress. This subelectorate has more progressive attitudes toward the political participation of women than the overall Peruvian electorate.

A second characteristic of Peruvian open list voting–its duality—also appears to have facilitated the success of women. Rather than campaigning *for* women and *against* men, proponents of female representation can ask Peruvians to split their two preferential votes equitably between the sexes. Many voters have adhered to the slogan of feminist nongovernmental organisations (NGOs), "Of your two preferential votes, cast one for a woman."

More broadly, multiple preferential votes may increase gender equity for reasons similar to the arguments for high district or party magnitude. Whereas the latter help parties to balance their tickets, the former might allow some voters to make a more "balanced choice." For example, a man with traditional values might be reluctant to cast his only preferential ballot for a woman but willing to "risk" voting for a female candidate as one of his choices. According to this logic, Peru and other countries with multiple preferential votes should be, ceteris paribus, more likely to elect women than countries that have only one preferential vote, such as Brazil and Chile. Indeed, in 2006, Peru had a much higher proportion of female legislators than Brazil (8.6 percent). In the same year only 15 percent of the members of Chile's lower house were women, despite the election of Michelle Bachelet and the installation of a cabinet with gender parity (see Inter-Parliamentary Union: www.ipu.org).

A third characteristic of Peruvian congressional elections—constraints on intralist competition—helps to ameliorate one of the chief concerns about gender parity under open lists. Htun and Jones (2002: 39) assert that women will be disadvantaged in open formats because they generally have fewer resources than men for individualized campaigns. Available evidence suggests that this assumption is true in Peru, where there is vigorous competition among candidates running on the same list. Indeed, in 1990, congressional candidates from four different parties running on the list of Mario Vargas Llosa's Democratic Front (FREDEMO) outspent the novelist's presidential campaign by almost two-and-a-half fold. A deluge of tasteless television commercials by FREDEMO congressional candidates drowned out and sometimes contradicted Llosa's message, contributing to his defeat (Schmidt 1996: 337–340).

Since the FREDEMO debacle, however, the leaders of Peruvian parties have usually placed limits on individual campaigns. Typically, the supporters of individual candidates distribute pamphlets, post flyers, and paint names and list numbers on walls. More affluent candidates may also erect billboards and buy print advertising. Individual congressional candidates, however, usually do not buy television commercials, which is the most effective way of reaching the electorate.

Fourth, the single national district that was used in the 1992, 1995, and 2000 elections for a unicameral legislature facilitated the initial electoral breakthrough of women (see table 11.2). The single district allowed professional women—who are overwhelmingly based in Lima-Callao—to run for the entire universe of congressional seats. It also centralized nominations in the hands of national party leaders, who are generally more receptive to female political participation than regional bosses. Moreover, whereas congresswomen drew a majority of their preferential votes from Lima-Callao in 1995 and 2000, congressmen relied on the provinces for most of their support (see Schmidt 2003b: 127–128). The abolition of the single national district was followed by a decrease in the election of women in 2001 (see table 11.2). Women won 12 of 39 seats (31 percent) in Lima and Callao but only 10 of 81 seats (12 percent) in the rest of Peru.

The single national district is not simply a manifestation of high district magnitude, a variable that has been frequently linked to female representation (e.g., Matland 2005; Reynolds, Reilly, and Ellis 2005: 121). Indeed, table 11.3

Table 11.3 District magnitude and the election of women by departments

(Pearson's r)

	Pearson's r	Sig.
Chamber of Deputies		
1985	−.090	.664
1990	.132	.521
Unicameral Congress		
2001	.342	.095
2006	.096	.648

Note: Computed by author from data disaggregated by electoral district.

shows that district magnitude has not been strongly associated with the election of women when the Chamber of Deputies or unicameral Congress was chosen by departments. Only in one year (2001) does the correlation approach the traditional threshold of significance; the associations are weak or even negative in the other years. These findings are noteworthy because the empirical evidence linking high district magnitude to the electoral success of women in list PR systems comes overwhelmingly, if not exclusively, from countries that use closed lists.

The Impact of Other Variables on the Proportion of Women in the Legislature

Among the major Latin American countries with a population of at least 15 million, Peru has the lowest score on the gender-related human development index, which is a powerful predictor of women's political representation (UNDP 2005: 299–302; Reynolds 1999: 567–568). Thus, the electoral success of Peruvian women is all the more remarkable. This section analyzes key social and political factors that have facilitated this success.

The Transformation of Gender Roles and the Feminization of the Professions

The recent political emergence of women in Peru is rooted in lengthy and complex processes of social change that have been reinforced by worldwide trends in favor of greater gender equity. After World War II, the Peruvian educational system expanded rapidly and became accessible to women, while modernization and migration opened up new employment opportunities in an increasingly urban society. These social tends and the growing availability of modern forms of contraception began to transform traditional gender roles, though progress was uneven across the economic and ethnic fault lines of a very stratified society.

Several distinct types of female activists emerged during the late 1970s and 1980s, when women became involved in social movements, feminist groups, political parties, NGOs, self-help organizations, and other associations in civil society. These major advances of women in the public sphere became widely accepted as part of a new "common sense" regarding appropriate gender roles (Blondet and Montero 1994: 17).

During the 1980s a new generation of female university graduates began to make its mark in professions that had been dominated by men. In the public sector, these young female professionals began to work their way up the bureaucratic ladder (Blondet and Montero 1994: 20–21, 133, 149). The feminization of the professions continued in the 1990s. For example, by 1998, a majority (53.6 percent) of accountants and almost a third (31.5 percent) of economists were women (Webb and Fernández Baca 2000: 265).

The Collapse of the Party System and Fujimori

In the 1990s both "supply" and "demand" factors created a "bull market" for women in electoral politics. As we have seen, the feminization of the professions since the early 1980s had created a deep pool of talented women that could be tapped. During the same decade, the failures of democratically elected governments to reverse economic decline and curb increasing political violence produced widespread dissatisfaction with Peru's political institutions. In the late 1980s and early 1990s, the electoral demise of the country's male-dominated traditional parties opened up new opportunities for women, who were widely perceived to be more honest and virtuous than men. Indeed, by wide margins, survey respondents of both genders in the late 1990s said that female political participation should increase and that they were more inclined to vote for a candidate who is a woman. Not surprisingly, attitudes supportive of women in politics were strongest in Lima (Blondet 1999).

Fujimori—Peru's increasingly authoritarian president—was much more adept at adjusting to the "bull market" for women than the opposition (see especially Schmidt 2006). During the 1990s, Fujimori placed women in key government positions, played a decisive role in the adoption of gender quotas, backed other policies benefiting women, and successfully appealed to the female electorate. Nevertheless, the former president is best viewed as an accelerator of greater gender equity rather than its fundamental cause. Had Fujimori not championed quota legislation, it is highly likely that trends in gender relations and feminist political activism would have eventually produced this reform, as in other Latin American countries.

Gender Quotas

The passage of a 25 percent gender quota for political candidates under Fujimori was followed by a doubling of the female presence in Congress in the 2000 election (see table 11.2). Nevertheless, the impact of quotas should not be overstated. Although quotas have assured more women of places on party lists, the election of candidates of either gender is determined by preferential votes under Peru's open list format.

It is important to note that female candidates had become politically competitive *before* the implementation of quotas. In 1992 women running on the pro-Fujimori list were more likely to be elected than men (Schmidt 2006: 154–155). In 1995, female candidates running on all lists that won at least one seat enjoyed a higher rate of electoral success and received a higher average number of preferential votes than male candidates on the same lists (Schmidt 2003b: 128). Indeed, in the latter year, Martha Chávez, a staunch supporter of Fujimori, won the highest number of preferential votes in the single national district. The chief obstacle to the election of women was a paucity of female candidates, who had comprised only about a tenth of party lists in the early 1990s. With the adoption of the 25 percent quota, the female percentage of candidates more than doubled in 2000, and twice as many women were elected.

Moreover, the impact of quotas is affected by interactions with other features of the electoral and political systems. Although the quota was increased to 30 percent prior to the 2001 election, the proportion of women elected actually declined, owing to the elimination of the single national district and the waning fortunes of Fujimori's electoral alliance (see table 11.2). Nevertheless, Anel Townsend, running on the list of Alejandro Toledo—the eventual winner of the presidential race—won the most preferential votes in Lima, which has a third of Peru's electorate.

Region, Class, and Humala

Until recently, female candidates fared much better in Lima-Callao, where the country's middle and upper classes are concentrated, than in the provinces. In 2006, however, a slightly higher proportion of congressional seats was filled by women in the hinterland (29.6 percent) than in the capital and its port (28.2 percent) (JNE 2006). Thus, the spectacular increase in the number of congresswomen elected in 2006 (see table 11.2) is due to the better performance of female candidates in the provinces.

Most of the new congresswomen from the provinces were elected on the list of Ollanta Humala, the populist presidential candidate whose bastion of support lies in southern Peru, the poorest part of the country, which has the highest concentration of indigenous peoples. Humala's party proved to be especially adept at recruiting strong female candidates, who were often leaders of community organizations and social movements. The presidential bid of Lourdes Flores Nano—who finished a close third and almost made the runoff—provided another incentive for all parties to recruit competitive female candidates. Humala lost the runoff, but his party won the largest block in Congress: 45 seats, of which 15 (33.3 percent) are filled by women (JNE 2006). Thus, whereas the initial electoral breakthrough of women had been largely based on support from voters in Lima-Callao and facilitated by the single national district, Humala has played a crucial role in increasing the election of female candidates from the provinces. In Lima, Keiko Fujimori, the daughter of the former president, received more than three times as many preferential votes as any other candidate in the 2006 election.

Conclusion

Since the 1990s, Peruvian elections have shown that women running on open lists can successfully compete with men, contrary to the prevailing view in the literature. Some of this success, however, may be related to particular characteristics of the open list format used in Peru, especially the optional use of dual preferential votes. Future research should focus on how significant variations within open list formats—which have hardly been studied—may affect the election of women. The Peruvian experience also suggests that other variables—such as patterns of campaign finance and advertising—may affect the success of female candidates in open list competition. In contrast, district magnitude—which has been identified as a key variable in closed list formats—has had little impact on the election of women in Peru.

The role of political parties is conspicuously absent in the preceding discussion; indeed, there has been no reason to even mention the major parties by name. Although the traditional parties have made a partial comeback since Fujimori's departure, Peruvian elections remain among the most volatile in the world, and party organizations are generally weak. Moreover, in recent years, two antiestablishment figures—Fujimori and Humala—have played major roles in increasing women's representation. Nevertheless, "contagion" has been rapid. Any differences among the major parties with regard to the election of women are likely short term and far less important than the overall trend toward greater female representation.

Notes

1. The 1956 and 1962 elections had been conducted under a majority list system.
2. For a more comprehensive treatment of the Peruvian electoral system, see Schmidt (2004: esp. 42–45, 48, 50–57, 71, 75–78).
3. Another variation of open list voting had been used in the 1978 election for a constitutional assembly.

4. Although the electoral "playing field" was increasingly unfair under Fujimori, vote fraud was marginal.
5. Under the current system, Peruvians residing abroad vote for Congress in the Department of Lima. During the 1980–1990 period, overseas Peruvians had voted in Senate elections but not for seats in the Chamber of Deputies.
6. This paragraph is based on Schmidt (2001).
7. In flexible formats, list order and votes for individual candidates *both* influence who fill the seats won by a party.
8. This paragraph is based on data from IPU (as of 2006) and JNE (2006). The calculations for Latin America are for lower houses or unicameral legislatures. They do not include Cuba, the region's only nondemocracy, and several countries that have had recent elections (Colombia, El Salvador, and Haiti).
9. The female percentage of Latin American legislatures is also increasing over time. Thus, readers should not compare earlier figures in table 11.2 with the 2006 averages given here.
10. The discussion in the remainder of this section draws on Schmidt (2003b: 126–129).

Part III

Mixed-Member Systems

Subpart I

Proportional

12 Mexico

¿Más Mujeres? Mexico's Mixed-Member Electoral System

Magda Hinojosa

Introduction

The effects of mixed member systems on women's representation have been almost without debate[1]—an oversight that is particularly problematic given that electoral systems "can be, and regularly are, changed" and that the adoption of a mixed member system may be the "electoral reform of the twenty-first century" (Ballington and Matland 2004: 4; Shugart and Wattenberg 2001a: 1). Although no consensus exists on the desirability of mixed member systems, its cheerleaders believe that they merge the most desirable elements of single member district plurality and proportional representation (Shugart and Wattenberg 2001a); however, its critics argue that "[t]he advocates of plurality-PR hybrids believe that they are bringing together the best of two worlds; but they are likely to obtain, instead, a bastard-producing hybrid which combines their defects" (Sartori 1997: 75). Mexico is proof that electoral systems can be altered (even quite frequently) and that mixed member systems are becoming popular, but what can it tell us about how this will affect women's political representation?

This chapter analyzes the forces that shape women's representation in Mexico's Chamber of Deputies. Women's increased political representation is a factor of the use of proportional representation, the passage of an effective gender quota law, and the adaptations made to party candidate selection procedures because of the existence of both single member district and proportional representation seats and because of the recently passed quota.

After an initial explanation of the country's constantly changing voting rules, this chapter then presents data on women's growing representation in the Chamber of Deputies since their initial foray into that body, then analyzes the consequences of a mixed member system on women's presence in the lower house, and finally turns to an examination of the effects of the gender quota law of 2002 and candidate selection procedures on women's representation.

The Voting System

The Mexican political system was defined by the Partido Revolucionario Institucional (PRI) for most of the twentieth century. The PRI formed in 1929 and built its success on its strategic corporatist inclusion of peasants, bureaucrats, and the working classes, but used nondemocratic practices when necessary to maintain its complete political domination. The Partido Acción Nacional (PAN) provided steady opposition to the PRI since the 1940s, while the Partido de la Revolución Democrática (PRD), an amalgamation of PRI splinter groups and small leftist parties from a variety of ideological backgrounds, began actively fighting PRI hegemony in 1989. In an effort to cede seats for power, the government undertook electoral reforms aimed at giving minority parties some representation. These efforts were largely seen as indicative of Mexico's extraordinarily slow transition to democracy (Beer 2003: 13; Mizrahi 2003), which was "finalized" with the presidential victory of an opposition candidate in 2000.

Tinkering with the electoral system began in the 1960s and allowed the PRI to maintain its loyal opposition and the accompanying democratic façade. Mexico's lower house was elected in its entirety using single member district plurality until 1964 when new electoral rules created "party seats," which gave parties receiving at least two and a half percent of the national vote no fewer than five seats in the Chamber of Deputies. Each half percent over that minimum translated into another party seat for a maximum of 20 seats.[2] While these reforms allowed for some proportionality between votes for the parties of the opposition and their representation in the Chamber, "proportionality was not what the drafters of the reform intended to achieve. Party seats were an institutional device designed to provide a 'safety net' for minority parties within the framework of political representation in which officials were elected individually by territorial constituencies" (Nacif 1997: 17).

Party seats were eliminated in 1977 in favor of a true mixed system, combining single member district plurality with proportional representation. The new rules allowed four newly created national districts to elect 100 deputies in the now 400-member body to be filled via proportional representation; these proportional representation seats were granted only to minor parties (i.e., the PRI would receive none of these seats) (Nacif 1997: 21; Weldon 2001). The system was later altered to increase the percentage of proportional representation seats to 200 out of 500 and amended to include a governability clause—the party that won the most single member district plurality seats would be guaranteed an absolute majority in the legislature; if the party failed to garner an absolute majority, it would be given proportional representation seats until it had a majority (Nacif 1997: 23; Klesner 2006). A series of reforms altered the governability clause, increasingly limiting its ability to overrepresent the PRI in the Chamber of Deputies.[3] The governability clause was removed in 1994—but in exchange the PRI was allowed to win proportional representation seats—and in 1996, electoral rules were once again amended so as to prevent any party winning less than 42 percent of the vote from obtaining a majority in the Chamber of Deputies (Nacif 1997; Klesner 2006: 398). The current electoral rules forbid any party from having more than 300 deputies elected either by proportional representation or through the single member districts, thus preventing any one party from having the two-thirds majority required for constitutional changes.[4] The increased electoral importance of the PAN and the PRD will almost certainly result in further changes to the country's electoral rules.

The Chamber of Deputies is currently composed of 500 legislators, who serve three-year terms and are barred from immediate reelection; of them, 300 are elected in single member districts and 200 are chosen using proportional representation. The 300 single member districts are distributed nationally based on population. The 200 legislators chosen through proportional representation are elected from five national districts known as *circuncripciones*.[5] Each of these regions elects 40 deputies on closed lists using the Hare formula and the largest remainder method when necessary. In order to run lists in these regions, a political party must put forward candidates in at least 200 of the 300 single member districts. Up to 60 candidates from each party may be fielded as both single member district plurality candidates and proportional representation candidates. This allows smaller parties to place candidates who could never win in the single member districts on their party lists.[6] Seats are awarded by proportional representation within each of the five regions. For example, if the PRD receives 10 percent of the vote in the first district, it will receive four seats; if in the second district it wins 30 percent of the vote, it will receive twelve seats. The lists are kept separate and vote totals are not pooled (Klesner 2006: 404). To gain representation in the Chamber of Deputies, parties must surpass the 2 percent threshold that exists.

Women in the Legislature: Historical Trends

Women's representation in the Chamber of Deputies has increased substantially since the 1952–1955 session when there was a lone female legislator. Progress had been slow as figure 12.1 demonstrates,[7] with women's share in this legislative body increasing by about 4 percentage points every decade, until the introduction of a quota. The most notable jump in women's representation in the Chamber of Deputies followed the adoption of a stringent new quota law. The quota boosted women's presence in the lower house from 16 percent in the 2000–2003 legislative session to 25.8 percent in the following session. Women's representation dropped slightly following the 2006 election to 23.2 percent.

Women's representation varies not only temporally but also across party lines. As table 12.1 shows, the PRD was initially a trailblazer and consistently

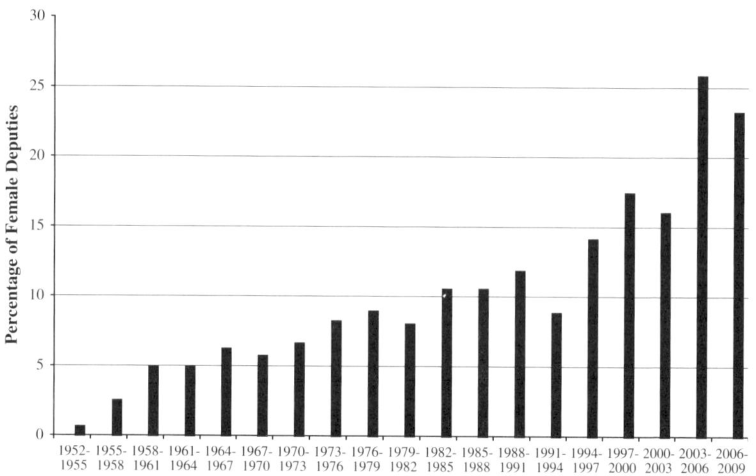

Figure 12.1   Women's representation in Mexico's Chamber of Deputies, 1952–2006

Table 12.1   Women's representation in the Mexican Chamber of Deputies by party, 1994–2006

Party	Female deputies, 1994 (%)	Female deputies, 1997 (%)	Female deputies, 2003 (%)	Female deputies, 2006 (%)
PRI	8.0	15.1	20.5	17.0
PAN	7.8	12.4	34.4	25.2
PRD	11.9	24.0	21.4	21.3

Source: (Stevenson 1999: 76) and data compiled by the author from <www.diputados.gob.mx> (April 2007).

had higher percentages of female representation. In line with its leftist ideology, the PRD actively sought to increase women's participation in politics. It was the first party to adopt a quota law; that quota applied to its proportional representation seats and was initially set at 20 percent, but was increased first to 30 percent and later to 50 percent. Recognizing the need to ensure that women's candidacies would not be clustered at the bottom of its lists, the PRD also set a placement mandate for its quotas. Despite these efforts, the PRD has rarely been able to meet its own goals. Similarly, considering that the PRI has a strongly stated commitment to increasing women's representation and passed a 30 percent quota law in 1996 (which was later raised to 50 percent in 2001), the party's relatively low percentages of female candidacies and female deputies are surprising. On the other hand, the party of the right, the PAN, is ideologically opposed to quotas—the seven legislators who voted against the passage of the 2002 national quota law were all PAN members—and has not adopted internal quotas. Nonetheless, in 1999, the PAN made a conscious effort to increase women's representation: it ruled that each pair of candidates and alternates chosen would include both a man and a woman. The PAN elected a greater percentage of women to office in 2003 than either the PRI or the PRD, by nominating a more gender-equitable slate of candidates, a feat that it was able to repeat in 2006.[8] The PAN not only overcomplied with the new quota law in proportional representation seats but also nominated more women than men to safe seats than either the PRI or the PRD in single member districts (Baldez 2004b). Analyzing these cross-party differences is important in examining the effects of other factors on women's political representation; the substantial differences in the percentage of female deputies across the three main parties documented in table 12.1 highlight the fact that ideology alone cannot explain women's political underrepresentation.

The Impact of the Voting System on the Proportion of Women in the Legislature

Research has demonstrated that women are more likely to be elected in countries using proportional representation systems than in those that use single member district plurality. Considering cross-national findings that proportional representation systems yield more female representation (Rule 1987; Darcy, Welch, and Clark 1994; Rule and Zimmerman 1994; Shugart and Wattenberg 2001a; Ballington and Matland 2004; Htun 2005), we would expect mixed member systems to bring more women into the legislature via the proportional representation seats.

Constantly changing electoral rules in Mexico complicate any analysis of the effects of the electoral system on women's political representation. In particular, the introduction of proportional representation seats coincided with lower fecundity rates, increased educational and professional opportunities for women, and changing public attitudes, making it difficult to discern the impact of the newly created proportional representation seats. The changes that have taken place in women's representation have largely mirrored global trends. Despite these challenges, it is clear that, as expected, women are much more likely to enter the legislature via the proportional representation seats than through the single member district plurality seats.

Female candidates are said to be advantaged by proportional representation systems because parties will balance their tickets by including a more diverse group; when parties must choose a single candidate for a district, they are said to be less likely to nominate a woman (Darcy, Welch, and Clark 1994; Rule and Zimmerman 1994). For example, in the 2006 legislative elections, 39.1 percent of the PAN's deputies elected via proportional representation were women, while only 18 percent of the party's deputies elected from single member districts were women. Substantial differences in the percentages of female deputies elected by proportional representation versus single member districts do exist for all three major parties, as shown in figure 12.2. A study conducted by UNIFEM/CONMUJER (2000) found substantive differences in the percentage of female candidates in single member plurality

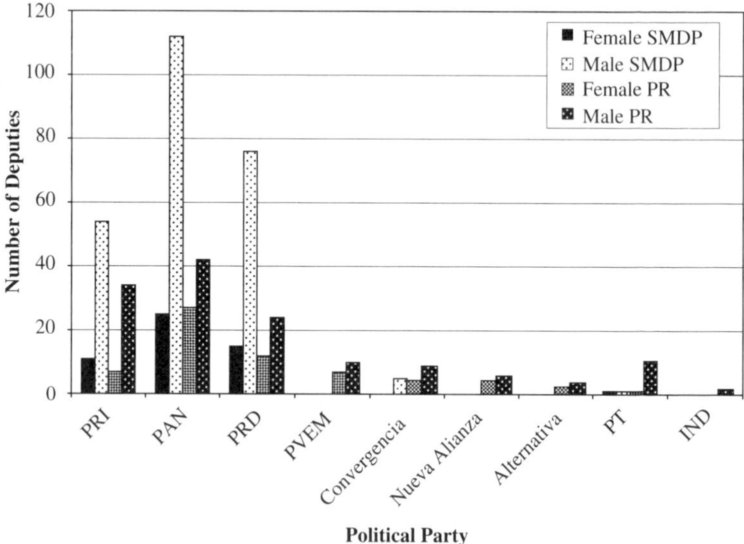

Figure 12.2   Gender composition of the Chamber of Deputies by voting system, 2006

Note: SMDP – single member district plurality.
PR – proportional representation.

seats and in proportional representation seats.[9] More than double the percentage of women were nominated for proportional representation seats than for single member district seats (36.5 percent versus 15.3 percent) in the 2000 elections. Even more overwhelming differences existed in earlier elections; for example, in the 1997 elections, nearly 14 percent of the PRI's deputies elected in single member districts were women, while more than 30 percent of those deputies chosen via proportional representation were female.

Proportional representation has been shown to increase the representation of smaller parties (Nacif 1997: 35). In the 1982–1985 legislative session, the PAN won only four seats through single member district plurality but 39 seats through proportional representation. None of the other minor parties were able to win any single member district plurality seats, though among them they received the remaining 61 seats (Arredondo 1982: 18). The allocation of proportional representation seats allowed minority parties representation in the Chamber of Deputies, which they otherwise would not have had. For example, in 1997, the PRI still dominated single member district plurality seats with 165 of 300 such seats, but the party won only 74 of the proportional representation seats. The PAN won 64 single member seats and 57 of the proportional representation seats, while the PRD was able to win 70 single member seats and 55 proportional representation seats (Molinar Horcasitas and Weldon 2001: 227). Fourteen proportional representation seats went to minor parties.

The effects of this increased representation of minority parties on women are unclear. Ballington and Matland (2004: 6) argue that "[t]he election of a number of smaller parties to parliament can impact negatively on women, as typically parties are headed by males, and party leaders invariably take the first few slots on the list. Women tend to show up further down the list, and being placed midlist will mean they will not win any representation, unless a party wins a landslide victory". Data from 1997 indicate that smaller parties in Mexico, even prior to the adoption of a binding quota law, were not leaving women only the bottom spots on their lists. Smaller parties had greater percentages of female deputies elected from single member districts than the PRI, the PAN, and the PRD and roughly equal proportions of female deputies elected by proportional representation.

The data from 2006, which is presented in figure 12.2, shows that the small leftist party Partido Verde Ecologista de México (PVEM) was promoting women's candidacies: over 40 percent of legislators elected through proportional representation were female. In 2003 neither the small Convergencia party nor the Partido del Trabajo (PT) placed any women in the lower house, despite the fact that the former won five proportional representation seats and the latter received six of these seats; both parties increased female representation in the 2006 elections.

The Impact of Other Variables on the Proportion of
Women in the Legislature

Despite the fact that women's participation in electoral politics has risen substantially over the course of the last 50 years, Mexican women remain severely underrepresented in positions of power. This next section explores other factors that are useful in explaining women's representation in the Chamber of Deputies. The most important forces are interrelated: gender quotas, candidate selection procedures, and the use of proportional representation in Mexico's mixed member system.

Earlier research has demonstrated that women's underrepresentation in Mexican politics is neither a result of a lack of supply of potential candidates nor of a lack of demand for female candidates (Hinojosa 2005). Women are marrying later, postponing childbearing, having fewer children, and continuing to work outside the home after becoming mothers. Mexican women have made tremendous educational and professional gains: currently, they are half of university students in the country and their participation in the labor force has doubled in the last 40 years (though they earn only 75 Mexican cents for every peso earned by a man). Women have been and continue to be politically active and they have held important political positions.[10] Voters do not seem to be preventing women from getting into office. In a poll of Latin American countries by Latinobarómetro, Mexicans had the most progressive attitudes in the region; only 14 percent of those polled agreed with the statement, "Men are better leaders than women." By way of contrast, 26 percent of Chileans agreed with that statement, as did 32 percent of Brazilians, and a startling 50 percent of the population polled in the Dominican Republic (Htun 2005: 114). Electoral data from the 2003 mayoral elections in the state of Mexico indicate no gender bias on the part of voters—44.4 percent of female candidates won their elections, compared with 29.9 percent of male candidates (Hinojosa 2005). And some voters may actually prefer a female candidate, as one Mexican mayor commented, "More than a few times people said to me, *I'm going to vote for you because you're a woman.* They just don't have as much faith in male politicians anymore. People have the idea that male legislators are corrupt" (interview with author, March 25, 2003).

The bottleneck is not at either the supply end or the demand end; instead, women's underrepresentation in Mexican politics occurs at the level of candidate selection. The importance of candidate selection processes to understanding women's underrepresentation has been documented in the general literature on women in politics (Norris and Lovenduski 1995; Niven 1998; Lawless 2003; Fox and Lawless 2004).

The Connection between Candidate Selection and Proportional Representation

Proportional representation systems yield more women representatives because incentives change at the level of candidate selection. Proportional representation systems do not produce more female aspirants nor do they alter the views of voters (and this would be particularly irrelevant in the Mexican system where closed-list proportional representation is used).[11] Proportional representation only affects the political party as it decides the candidates that it will propose and increases the odds that a party becomes "more conscious of balancing its ticket" (Ballington and Matland 2004). The use of either single member district plurality or proportional representation ultimately affects a party's incentives in candidate selection. Similarly, the size of those proportional representation districts also alters the decision-making process for parties as they choose candidates: large districts (in Mexico each elects 40 deputies) make it easier for parties to field women (Rule and Zimmerman 1994); related to district magnitude is the concept of party magnitude: when parties expect to win more seats, they will be more likely to propose female candidates (Matland 1993).

While the effects of proportional representation seats on women's representation are clear, the gender quota law has had even more transparent consequences for getting women into office. Like the choice of voting system, the use of gender quotas is also clearly tied to candidate selection processes, and analyzing this interaction is important to understanding women's representation in the lower house. As one national-level PRI official noted, "It's in the selection processes for candidacies that women are getting left behind" (interview with author, February 13, 2003).

The Connection between Candidate Selection and the Gender Quota

Women's inclusion in the Chamber of Deputies was significantly boosted by the adoption of a national quota law in April 2002, which set a quota of 30 percent. Women's representation in the lower house jumped from 16 percent to 23 percent after the quota was first applied in the midterm elections of 2003. While an earlier quota law had been passed in 1996, it only "recommended" that women constitute 30 percent of candidacies and offered no mechanisms for promoting this suggestion.

The new quota added clear enforcement guidelines and addressed concerns that women's representation suffered because women candidates were placed in alternate positions and in unelectable positions on party lists

(Fernández Poncela 2000; Mujer 2000: 52–53; Rodríguez 2003: 181–182; Tarrés 2006). The existence of alternates who run alongside candidates is conventionally considered to have negative consequences for women who aspire to public office, and all three of the major parties have been accused of relegating women to the alternate spots (Bruhn 2003; Hinojosa 2005). Bruhn (2003: 113) argued that "[t]his pattern functions at its worst as tokenism, but at its best, as apprenticeship. It can even increase the number of women in office, since congressmen resign fairly often." The 2002 quota cannot be met by placing women in alternate positions. Women must also be placed in electable positions on party lists: one of every three seats must be filled by a woman for the first nine spots on each list of forty (Baldez 2004b). A party that fails to meet the quota faces immediate consequences—a party that does not comply will also be ultimately disqualified from running any candidates in that district.[12] As Baldez (2004a: 249) notes, "Fear of being prevented from nominating *any* candidates ensured that the parties filled the quota."

The quota law and candidate selection procedures have interacted in an unexpected way in the Mexican case. Parties are exempt from the quota when they use primaries to choose their legislative candidates. When the quota legislation was being debated, there was little concern that the primary exemption would be of much importance (Baldez 2004a), but the 2003 elections proved otherwise: half of all candidates from the three major parties nominated in single member districts were chosen using primaries.[13] Baldez (2004b: 3) writes that "[t]he interaction between the quota and primary elections reveals the degree to which the process of internal democratization of candidate selection methods has had gendered consequences in Mexico" and effectively argues that the adoption of the quota encouraged parties to abandon earlier candidate selection methods and to begin using primaries to select their candidates. While the parties used primaries to avoid quotas in single member districts, in the proportional representation seats many of the parties nominated more female candidates than were required (Baldez 2004b).

The Effects of Other Institutions on Women's Representation

In addition to the notable effects of voting systems, candidate selection methods, and gender quotas on women's political participation, Mexican rules on reelection as well as the efforts by women to lobby for increased representation have had important effects on women's ability to enter the Chamber of Deputies. Mexico's ban on immediate reelection for legislators should provide a more welcoming environment for female candidates.

Without the incumbency advantage (which proves extremely advantageous to men since they are more likely to be incumbents because of historical patterns of inequitable representation), women should have an easier entry into political positions. While no studies to date have looked at the effects of the reelection ban on women's representation in Mexico, the prohibition on immediate reelection ought to have important consequences in combination with the gender quota law. The quota should be considerably easier to apply in this national setting, since it will never result in kicking a man out of a seat that he was already occupying or expected to have.[14]

Candidate selection processes have been affected not only by gender quotas but also by women's lobbying efforts. While women in the PRD and the PRI have long been vocal about pushing their parties to grant women greater representation, more recently the PAN's women's wing has pushed party leaders to propose more female candidacies (Htun 2005: 115).[15] Women from across the party spectrum have pushed their parties to follow through on their efforts to increase female representation, including in the case of PRI deputy Diva Hadamira Gastélum, who publicly stated that her party would be "playing with fire" if it failed to meet its own internal 50 percent quota (Mora 2006). [16]

Conclusion

Mexico's mixed member system has allowed for *más mujeres* (i.e., more women) in the legislature, though the addition of proportional representation seats to the legislature does not fully explain women's representation. This chapter has presented conclusive evidence that the 200 proportional representation seats in the Chamber of Deputies produce a much larger share of female legislators than the 300 single member districts. Women's representation has received a boost from the addition of proportional representation seats to Mexico's initial single member district system, the adoption of a thorough and enforceable quota law, and changes in candidate selection that have taken place because of both proportional representation seats and gender quotas.

Notes

1. Some notable exceptions include Darcy, Welch, and Clark (1994), Rule and Zimmerman (1994), Matland and Taylor (1997), and notably Barker et al. (2001). The fascinating work presented by Matland and Studlar (1996) provides rich theoretical and empirical data to inform any discussion of the potential effects of a mixed member system.

2. The 20-seat limit included seats won in single member districts. Only minority parties could obtain party seats; these seats were not awarded to the dominant PRI.

3. Refer to Nacif (1997) for a review of the negotiations between the PRI and the PAN that ultimately led to these important changes in the governability clause.

4. The law also prevents any party from having more than an 8 percentage point advantage between its share of the national vote and its representation in the Chamber of Deputies, but makes certain exceptions. See www.ife.gob.mx (April 2007) for details.

5. To avoid confusion, these five national districts will be referred to as regions throughout the rest of the chapter.

6. Weldon (2001: 451) notes that party leaders regularly appeared on both lists to ensure their representation. They would be either elected by a safe district or through a safe spot on the party list.

7. The 1991 elections saw a sizeable decrease in the number of women in the chamber. Stevenson (1999) provides a plausible explanation. The reduction in the percentage of women deputies between 1997 and 2000, while minor, was surprising because the percentage of female candidates in that election actually rose from 25.4 to 33.4 (Mujer 2000).

8. The PRD's initial success was evidently a product of its willingness to place women in more electable positions. Though 24 percent of the PRD's deputies were women, the party proposed a smaller share of female candidates (21.4 percent). For the same elections, 21 percent of the PRI's candidates were female, as were almost 15 percent of the PAN's candidates (SISESIM 2005).

9. The data produced by UNIFEM/CONMUJER disaggregated figures for alternate seats: women were more than half of all candidates in the alternate positions for proportional representation seats and over a third of all candidates for single member district seats.

10. For example, the PRI and the PRD have both been headed by women. María de los Angeles Moreno and Dulce María Sauri have served as PRI party presidents and Amalia García and Rosario Robles have presided over the PRD. Rosario Robles later went on to become mayor of Mexico City. Rosario Green, Beatriz Paredes, and others are well-known politicians.

11. The use of a closed-list system "places the onus of representation on the party gatekeepers—by placing women in large numbers in electable positions, women will be elected to parliament" (Ballington and Matland 2004: 6). In Mexico, the responsibility to place women into electable spots on party lists was legislated by the 2002 gender quota law.

12. Parties that do not comply with the quota law are first given 48 hours to revamp their lists, then issued a reprimand, and given only 24 more hours to alter their lists; they are barred from presenting any candidates in that district if the problem is not fixed.

13. The lack of regulation about what constitutes a primary makes this problematic, as Baldez (2004a) has compellingly argued.

14. Alternatively, the prohibition on reelection may discourage women from running for a seat, since they know that it will be only a three-year position. Nacif argues that the lack of immediate reelection will keep "legislators from pursuing reelection as a long-term career goal" (Nacif 2002: 259).
15. Htun (2005) argues that these efforts ultimately are the reason that the PAN had more female candidates than the PRI or the PRD in the 2003 elections.
16. Neither the PRI nor the PRD have been successful at meeting their own internal party quotas for female representation. Baldez (2004a) explains that the lack of success of those party quotas pushed women to lobby for the adoption of national legislation.

Gendering Parliamentary Representation: A Mixed System Producing Mixed Results

Jennifer Curtin

Introduction

New Zealand is one of a growing number of countries that has adopted, in recent times, a mixed electoral system. New Zealand's Mixed Member Proportional system (MMP) is derived largely from the German model and was first employed in the 1996 national election. However, given that proportional representation is a relatively new development in New Zealand, an analysis of women's parliamentary representation necessarily requires a discussion of the plurality system that preceded the advent of MMP. Focusing on what has happened under two quite contrasting electoral systems provides useful insights into the extent to which electoral systems are mediated by other factors in affecting the representation of women. Moreover, New Zealand's new electoral system has retained a plurality component, meaning proportionality in itself may not ensure gender parity in parliamentary representation. Rather, the structure and culture of political parties and their selection processes remain key indicators of women's chances of success in New Zealand.

The Voting System

For most of its democratic and electoral history, New Zealand has had a first-past-the-post electoral system (FPTP). This democratic history spans more than 150 years, with the first competitive elections held in 1853. So, in 1993, when the New Zealand people voted to change their electoral system to MMP, many interpreted this as a radical step by a country cited previously as the purest of Westminster systems (Lijphart 1984: 16). Certainly, in a comparative sense, the New Zealand case of electoral reform, as a relatively old Westminster system, does look rather unique as it has tended to be the "newer" Westminster democracies that have embraced proportional representation in their lower houses. Moreover, the system adopted by New Zealand did not have British antecedents— it was an adaptation of the German system of MMP.

However, electoral reform in New Zealand, while significant, was not radical if seen as part of a broader constitutional setting (Jackson and McRobie 1998; McLeay 2006). Over the past 150 years there have been regular and often innovative constitutional alterations made to take account of the uniqueness of the New Zealand polity. The establishment of four Maori seats occurred in 1867, universal male suffrage and three year terms were introduced in 1879, and in 1893 New Zealand became the first country to give women the vote (including indigenous women). Over the course of the twentieth century, further changes were made, culminating in a Royal Commission on Electoral Reform in 1986. The commission recommended a change to a proportional electoral system, in particular the adoption of MMP.

In recommending this change, the commission highlighted the need for effective representation of minority and special interest groups and the importance of parliament reflecting other characteristics of the electorate including gender (Catt 1997). While the issue of increasing women's representation did not receive significant attention during the campaign for electoral reform, the Women's Electoral Lobby (WEL) was committed to a proportional system. WEL made a submission to the Royal Commission, and its representatives were active members of the Electoral Reform Coalition, a network that proved critical in the campaign for change between 1986 and 1992 (Jackson and McRobie 1998). By contrast, most high-profile women parliamentarians (from the two major parties) argued against change (McRobie 1993).

More generally, there were mixed reactions in the press by feminists in the lead-up to the 1992 referendum on the preferred model. Mary Varnham, active women's liberationist in the 1970s, noted that "if you are female and less than enamoured with a system which produces an 84 percent boys club on the hill, there's another persuasive reason to vote for a change to proportional representation: it will almost guarantee more women in parliament" (Varnham 1993: 151). Meanwhile ex-National MP Marilyn Waring, who was a supporter of STV, argued that MMP would primarily favour political parties, rather than individual candidates, thereby further entrenching the presence of "a middle-aged white majority regardless of party in office" (Waring 1993: 204).

Despite this being a campaign in which the parliamentarians tended to support the status quo, MMP was voted the preferred model by referendum in 1992 and, in 1993, was followed with another referendum that entrenched MMP as the people's choice. Survey research later found that 68 percent of those who voted for MMP in 1993 wanted to see more women in parliament (Catt 1997).

MMP counts as a mixed system because more than one formula is used to distribute seats in the parliament (Ferrara, Herron, and Nishikawa 2005). In New Zealand's version of MMP, voters cast two votes. One vote is used to elect an individual candidate in a single-member district (electorate) seat, using a plurality formula associated with the original FPTP. The second vote is used to choose a party list, which is closed, meaning that the ranking of list candidates is done by the party not the voter (so voters cannot preference women candidates). The proportional "Sainte-Laguë" formula is used to allocate seats to parties that win at least one electorate seat or 5 percent of the votes cast nationally. This proportional ballot is used to compensate parties for their poor performance in the electorate ballot. In other words, it is the party vote nationwide that determines the overall allocation of parliamentary seats. As such, MMP counts as a fully proportional system.

Women in the Legislature: Historical Trends

New Zealand was the first country to give women the vote in 1893. However, women in New Zealand were unable to stand for parliament until 1919, and the first woman was not elected until 1933. In the period between 1933 and 1946, only five more women were elected; four of the six represented the Labour Party. This trend of Labour proving the party more amenable to women's representation continued throughout the twentieth century. Labour Party women made up the majority of women elected prior to 1981, the exceptions being 1946, 1969, and 1975, when equal numbers of National and Labour party women were elected. At no time since 1946 has the number of National women elected exceeded the number of Labour women politicians.

Prior to 1981 the number of women elected to parliament was tokenistic at best (figure 13.1). Then, in 1981, the trend begins to change, with a significant increase in the percentage of women elected: from 4.3 to 8.7 percent. At the 1981 election three new Labour women were elected to parliament, doubling the Labour women's caucus from three to six. All three were elected to relatively safe Labour seats, thereby providing these women with a possible

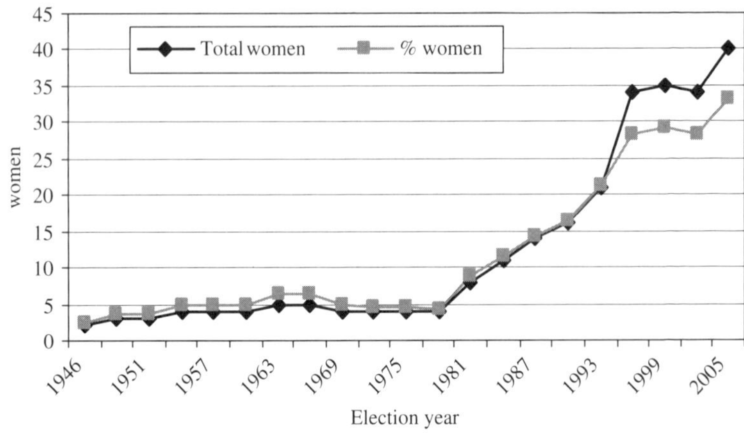

Source: Electoral Commission (2006)

Figure 13.1   Number and percentage of women elected in New Zealand general elections since 1945

Table 13.1   Women candidates and politicians (%) under MMP

Election	Women list candidates	Women list politicians	Women electorate candidates	Women electorate politicians	Total women politicians
1996	28.1	45.5	24.7	15.4	28.3
1999	34.4	39.6	29.3	23.9	29.2
2002	31	29.4	28.2	27.5	28.3
2005	31.8	44.3	27	23.2	33.1

Source: Electoral Commission (2002, 2006).

political career. The election of Labour women was a major factor contributing to the continued increase in women's representation prior to the introduction of MMP in 1996. Also important was the large swing to the conservative National Party in the 1990 election, which enabled a considerable number of National Party women in marginal electorates to win a place in parliament, several of whom kept their seats in the 1993 election. Labour was decimated in the election of 1990, yet the number of Labour women in parliament only decreased by three, highlighting the fact that a solid proportion of Labour women politicians had gained selection to safe Labour seats.

With the implementation of MMP, it is impossible to say whether the incremental increase in women's representation, evident in table 13.1, would have continued under FPTP. What we do know is that the first election under

MMP in 1996 had an immediate effect on women's parliamentary presence. Women constituted 28.3 percent of the new 120-member parliament, with a large number of these women elected from minor parties (14 compared with 13 Labour women and 8 National women). In the 1999 and 2002 elections, there was little overall increase in the proportion of women elected, but the makeup changed, with the number of Labour women increasing from 13 to 18. Then, in 2005, for the first time, the percentage of women parliamentarians surpassed 30 percent(reaching 33.1percent). This outcome has proved the best yet for women in the major parties, with 19 Labour women and 12 National women sitting in parliament, supplemented by 8 women from the minor parties. Indeed, 2005 is the first year since the introduction of MMP that the number of National women elected has exceeded the number of women parliamentarians from the minor parties.

The Impact of the Voting System on the Proportion of Women in the Legislature

In order to better understand how the proportional element of MMP has had an impact on women's representation, it is necessary to look more closely at two interconnected aspects associated with the election of women within mixed proportional systems. The first concerns the changes in women's candidacy rates over time; that is, does the advent of proportional representation lead to an overall increase in the selection of women as candidates? Second, to what extent is the increase in women's representation attributable to the selection of women for party lists?

Looking first at women's candidacy rates overall, it is evident that there was no significant increase in the percentage of women candidates selected for the first election under MMP in 1996. And, in 2005, the percentage of women candidates was only 1 percentage point higher than it had been in 1993 under FPTP. The deviation is in 1999, when there is an upward shift despite a decrease in the proportion of women selected by the major parties, highlighting the impact of several minor parties' propensity to select women. Since 1993, the Labour Party has consistently selected a higher proportion of women than has the National Party.

Several stories emerge when looking at women's candidacy rates in electorate seats compared with party list selection (figure 13.2). First, women are consistently more likely to appear as list candidates, where the district magnitude is large, than as electorate candidates.[1] While there has been some increase in women's candidacy rates for electorates, at no time has it reached over 30 percent. This is despite electorate seats making up the majority of parliamentary seats (69 out of 120 in 2005).

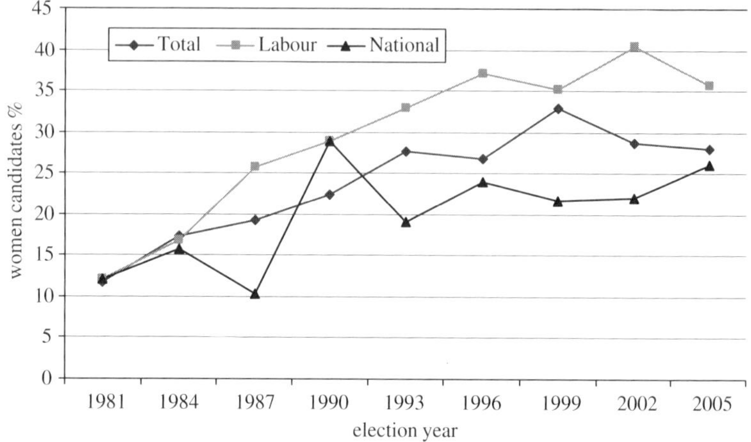

Source: McLeay (1993), Electoral Commission (1999, 2002, 2006)

Figure 13.2   Women's candidacy rates, 1981–2005 (major parties)

However, the election of women from lists compared with that from electorates has been less predictable. In 1996 and 1999, there was a significant difference in the proportion of successful women list candidates compared with the proportion of women who won electorate seats. Then, at the 2002 election, there was little difference between the two; women were 29.4 percent of list politicians and 27.5 percent of electorate politicians. By 2005, women were, once again, more likely to be represented through the party list than through electorate success.

So how might we interpret such fluctuations? Part of the answer lies in the placement of women on party lists. In the campaign for electoral reform, there had been an expectation that the introduction of the party list vote would force political parties to select a balanced list to attract voters (Catt 1997). However, there was no uniform response from parties on this issue. The anatomy of party lists in both 1996 and 2005 (table 13.2) reveals that parties on the Left are significantly more likely to place women in their top ten positions on their lists, although there has been a decrease in the number of women placed in the second ten positions in 2005.

In both 1996 and 2005, the Labour Party was almost as likely to select women as its minor-party counterparts. Looking at the parties on the Right, National has regressed over time in terms of its placement of women in its top ten positions. In 2005, the first National woman on the party list was ranked tenth. The interesting exception amongst the parties on the Right is the market-focused right-wing ACT (Association of Consumers and Taxpayers) party, where four women were placed in the top ten (two of whom were in the top four).

Table 13.2   Position of women on New Zealand party lists, 1996 and 2005

	Alliance*	Prog*	Green*	Maori*	Labour		National		NZ First		United Future		ACT	
	1996	2005	2005	2005	1996	2005	1996	2005	1996	2005	1996	2005	1996	2005
1–10	5	4	5	4	5	4	3	1	3	2	n.a.	2	4	4
11–20	4	4	3	2	7	3	2	3	2	2	n.a.	3	3	1
21–30	3	2	6	4	4	4	3	2	3	1	n.a.	2	2	3
31–40	4	3	5	3	6	4	1	3	1	1	n.a.	4	1	2
41–50	4	5	2	7	6	6	1	4	0	n.a.	n.a.	2	0	3
51–60	1	1	1	1	1	3	2	1	3	n.a.	n.a.	1	0	2

* The Alliance incorporated the Green Party, Mana Motuhake (a Maori party), and New Labour. By 2005 these three groups had broken away from the Alliance.

Sources: Catt (1997), Electoral Commission (2006).

In seeking to explain the divergence between the parties, an important factor is the degree of central party involvement in the selection process. While the introduction of MMP has required parties to implement new rules on selection for party lists, the Labour Party, the Green Party, the Progressives, and ACT have all ensured some element of central influence in the selection and ranking of candidates: and it is these parties that have the more gender-balanced party lists. By contrast, the National Party has a highly decentralized system of selection, with central intervention frowned upon (Salmond 2003). This was highlighted when Jim Bolger, ex-leader of the parliamentary National Party, was unable to use his influence to ensure local branches selected more women (Miller 2005: 11). The exception to the rule is New Zealand First, which has a highly centralized selection system but a poor record in placing women in winnable positions.

However, there is the Maori Party and Jim Anderton's Progressive Party replaced New Labour. Comparing the Alliance in 1996 with the Greens, Maori, and Progressives is not completely satisfactory but does give an indication of the propensity of the minor parties on the Left to select women to winnable positions on their lists.[2]

Where women are positioned on the party list matters differently depending on whether the party is a major or minor party. For example, minor parties are likely to win few, if any, electorate seats because of the plurality element of the system, meaning that gender balance in the ranking of the top ten party list candidates is significant. It also means there will be considerable intraparty competition for the top ten list positions, which may explain the lack of female selection by several of the minor parties on the Right. However, because the major parties are most likely to win the electorate seats, the positioning of women on party lists becomes more complicated. If one major party wins a large number of electorate seats then its allocation of party list seats may decline; the opposite is also true. That is, if the party wins fewer electorate seats but gains a significant proportion of the national party vote, its list allocation may increase, producing a volatility factor (table 13.3).

Table 13.3   Distribution of electorate/list seats won under MMP (number)

Election	Labour electorate seats	Labour list seats	National electorate seats	National list seats
1996	26	11	30	14
1999	41	8	22	17
2002	45	7	21	6
2005	31	19	31	17

Source: Electoral Commission (2002, 2006).

Moreover, there is a tendency for the parties to allow dual candidacy for most of their electorate candidates, meaning there are increasingly few list-only candidates selected by the major parties. In combination, these two factors (volatility and dual candidature) not only enhance the importance of gender parity on party lists but ensure female and male candidate names are alternated *throughout* the list. So, in contrast to the minor parties, gendering the middle-order list positions (25–45) of the major parties becomes as important as gendering the top positions. Returning to the data in table 13.2, we see that Labour is much more likely to select women in large numbers in the middle-order blocs compared with their National counterparts.

In summary then, MMP can only result in equal representation for women if equal numbers of women and men are selected for winnable electorate seats as well as winnable party list positions. Otherwise, theoretically, parity would only result if women were significantly overrepresented in winnable list positions. In other words, women's underrepresentation as electorate candidates would be "compensated" for through the list selection process. There is little chance such a strategy would be considered, especially given that neither National nor Labour has expressed an interest in gender quotas.

Instead, (safe) electorate seats are more likely to produce high incumbency (Matland and Studlar 2004) and are deemed to be a better route to a parliamentary career for women in the major parties than seeking a (safe) position on a party list. While significantly better than the National Party at selecting women, many of Labour's "safe" constituency seats are still held by male incumbents (McLeay 2006). Because there is a tendency to rank incumbents higher on the party list, the gender disparities in representation are compounded. By contrast, for women from the new, smaller political parties, the party list has become the primary route because the plurality system employed in the single-member districts undermines minor-party representation. The representation of women has been enhanced by the election of the minor parties on the Left, which have consistently fielded large numbers of women candidates, but there is a considerable degree of voter volatility in support for minor parties, so the fortunes of women in these parties are less assured over the long term.

The Impact of Other Variables on the Proportion of Women in the Legislature

Although New Zealand was the first country to give women the vote in 1893, the fact that it was to take more than 25 years before women gained the right to stand for parliament, in 1919, and another 14 years before the first woman was elected, indicates that milestones are only part of the story. The first Maori woman MP was elected in 1949, but there were few other milestones prior to the 1980s to suggest that the early advent of the vote represented a political culture more open to women. However, since the 1980s, there have been several aspects of women's representation in New Zealand that warrant attention and may even count as milestones. Reviewing these provides a more nuanced understanding of how other "political" variables have mediated the impact of proportional representation.

The first significant factor is that by 1993, women's representation in the New Zealand parliament had reached 21.2 percent under a pure plurality system, with neither of the major parties having a gender quota in place. This is a feat achieved in no other majoritarian single-member system. So, although the introduction of MMP in New Zealand in 1996 has been important to women's increased parliamentary presence, much of the transformation in women's representation occurred between 1981 and 1993. As indicated earlier, much of this increase was a direct result of the Labour Party more than doubling the number of women elected to parliament during this time.

While the increase in Labour women elected may in part be a consequence of a "contagion effect" from smaller parties on the Left (in particular the Values Party) (Curtin 2006; Matland and Studlar 1996), also important was women's agency within the Labour Party. Prior to the 1970s, the Labour Party was considered elderly, male dominated, and trade-union conservative and in need of rejuvenation (Shields 2001). This need, in combination with the rise of the women's movement, provided political women with a window of opportunity to pursue an agenda for change. While WEL is often accused of politicizing women's representation, the trade union movement, other single-issue movements and women's groups were also important in this process of politicization and in directing women's political activism through the Labour Party (Wilson 1992; McLeay 2006; Shields 2001).

Upon entering the Labour Party, a core group of women pursued a conscious strategy to advance the descriptive and substantive representation of women. They created a number of institutionalized separate spaces within the party, establishing the Labour Women's Council in 1975 and the Women's Policy Council and reintroducing Labour Women's Conferences. Their objectives were to increase the numbers of women in the party hierarchy and the parliamentary party and to develop a coherent women's policy. The pursuit of separate structures by women was not new in the Labour Party but each time had been met with considerable resistance by the party power brokers. Nevertheless, these Labour women were relentless in their demands, unafraid of conflict, to the point of picketing their own party's conference (Wilson 1992: 46). By 1984, the Labour Party looked completely different: the membership, candidates, and elected parliamentarians included significantly more women. By 1995 there had been three women party presidents—Helen Clark became deputy leader in 1989 and took over the party leadership in 1993.

With the introduction of MMP, new rules have been introduced governing the selection and rankings on party lists. The gendering of Labour Party culture has ensured that these new rules incorporate an "equity review," whereby after each bloc of five candidates has been chosen, the selection committee pauses to ensure the list fairly represents Maori, women, men, ethnic groups, the elderly, and the youth (Catt 1997). In practice, this "equity review" has contributed to a second "milestone"; that is, a more diverse Labour caucus overall, which includes several lesbians, two Maori women, one of whom is the first transsexual woman MP in the world. By contrast, there are few, if any, proactive measures taken by National Party selection committees to ensure that its lists adequately reflect New Zealand society. While the National Party has had several women party presidents, it is not evident these women have used what little indirect influence they possessed to increase the proportion of women selected. Here again, the decentralisation of National's party structure impacts in that it largely prohibits intervention around gender equity in candidate selection.

A third "milestone" is the feminization of political leadership that has become a feature in New Zealand from the mid-1990s onward. In 1997, Jenny Shipley of the National Party became the country's first woman Prime Minister. At the 1999 election, the Shipley government was replaced by a Labour-led government headed by Helen Clark. Seven women were given ministerial positions, constituting 35 percent of Clark's first cabinet (this had dropped to 30 percent in 2006, with one ex-cabinet minister taking the role of first woman Speaker of the House). In addition, two of the significant minor parties, the Maori Party and the Green Party, have women leaders, and there have also been two women governors general since 1990.

It is hard to say how this gendering of political leadership has impacted on political culture in New Zealand. In the very least, there is an increasing public expectation that women will be selected to winnable positions. This is evident by the backlash against the leader of New Zealand First in 1999 after he dumped the party's only two women parliamentarians to unwinnable positions on the party list. This incident had the almost immediate effect of reduced support in the opinion polls (Vowles 2000: 147). By contrast, the presence of Clark as party leader in the 1996 election campaign appears to have contributed to winning the women's vote for Labour (Aimer 1997), and evidence suggests Labour continues to attract more of the women's vote than does National (Curtin 2002).

Contagion effects in the gendering of candidate selection are possible between two major parties in their attempt to capture the middle ground, but this does not seem to have occurred in the case of the National Party in

New Zealand. Rather, there have been attempts by National to portray the feminization of political leadership as a form of "feminist" conspiracy, representing a backlash politics of sorts from the major party of the Right (Devere and Graham 2006). While this may be the National Party's attempt to position itself as different to Labour, and appeal to male voters who may feel alienated, it is not clear that this has undermined the legitimacy of women's place in parliament.

Conclusion

In New Zealand, the introduction of MMP has produced mixed results for women. A multiparty system has resulted, with "new" parties emerging on both the Right and the Left of the two major parties, several of which have been proactive in their recruitment of women candidates. It was expected that new system would require the "old" parties to attend to the gendering of representation in order to attract voters. However, while the Labour Party has undergone a process of feminization, the reticence of the National Party to do the same highlights the fact that the increased parliamentary representation of women evident in recent years still largely depends on left-wing parties winning elections or gaining a considerable proportion of the national vote. While the Labour Party in New Zealand has headed minority governments continuously since 1999, there is no guarantee it will continue to do so. In 2005, the National Party nearly doubled its party vote, giving it 48 seats compared with the 2002 figure of 27 (Levine and Roberts 2006). Thus, if the parties of the Right continue to increase their share of the vote without providing more gender balance in candidate selection, the parliamentary presence of women in New Zealand may decline, irrespective of proportionality.

Notes

1. Although the district magnitude factor can be overstated (see Curtin 2006; Schwindt-Bayer 2005).
2. Not all analysts consider the Maori Party leftist.

Subpart II

Majoritarian with Partial Compensation

The Impact of Early Party Consolidation on Female Representation and the Mixed Electoral System

Gabriella Ilonszki

Introduction

In 2006, after the fifth democratic election since 1990, the proportion of female MPs is 10.6 percent in the Hungarian parliament, which gives it the ninety-third position in the world. As a European Union (EU) member state with consolidated political institutions, this is astonishing, even if we acknowledge that postcommunist settings are unfavourable for gender representation due to patriarchal culture that was maintained in the communist period and also due to the general environment of systemic change (Funk and Mueller 1993). But other postcommunist countries tend to produce better results. Out of the EU member eight postcommunist countries, Hungary is placed last in terms of gender representation and the improvement from the first democratic election is the second lowest. Hungary and Lithuania among them apply a mixed electoral system—and they are at the two extremes of the representative continuum (see table 14.1).[1] Has the electoral system been a factor at all in the persistence of the low level?

Academic literature has been inconclusive about the impact of electoral systems in postcommunist countries. While there is an agreement that institutions also matter in this respect (Matland and Montgomery 2003b), still others drew attention with respect to the Hungarian case to the fact that the mixed electoral system worked in the expected direction only in

Table 14.1 Proportion of women in new EU member states in Central and Eastern European countries

Country	Year of first democratic election	Proportion of women in % in lower chamber at the first election	Year of last election	Proportion of women in % in lower chamber at the last election
Lithuania	1990	9.9	2004	22
Estonia	1990	5.7	2007	22
Poland	1991	9.1	2005	20.4
Latvia	1990	15.0	2006	19
Slovak Republic	1990	12.0	2006	16
Czech Republic	1990	10.0	2006	15.5
Slovenia	1990	13.3	2004	12.2
Hungary	1990	7.3	2006	10.6

Source: IPU (www.ipu.org/wmn-f/classif.htm; April 2007).

1990—that is, at the first democratic election when a significant correlation could have been observed between gender and the single member district (SMD) versus the list part of the electoral system (Montgomery and Ilonszki 2003). Since then, however, this correlation has disappeared—women have not been elected in larger proportions in the proportional representation (PR) list part than in SMDs. While earlier discussions could have left questions open with good reason, hinting at the still transitory environment (Moser 2001), more than 15 years after systemic change and in a democratically consolidated political environment, we cannot, and should not, avoid attempting to give answers to some pestering questions. Is it the impact of the electoral system that causes representation deficit or there are other factors that have to be considered in the explanation?

In the following sections, I will systematically analyze the consequences of the mixed electoral system on gender representation with a strong emphasis on the latest, 2006, elections. Already, at first glance, it is obvious that women's positions have not improved in the representative and electoral context. Why is it that the consolidation process does not have a positive impact? Generally, one can assume that democratization and the Europeanization trends in a stable political and economic environment would bring forward positive tendencies. Certainly this is not the case. My argument is that certain aspects of party consolidation and not the electoral system itself can be blamed for the low level of female representation. The role of the party gatekeepers in the level of female representation has been well demonstrated (Caul 1999). This argument will be put in a developmental context here by examining different aspects of party consolidation. The analysis will consist of four major sections: first, the electoral system will be introduced with some basic data over the five consecutive elections and a more detailed analysis of 2006; second, the presence of women in parliament will be described; third, the direct impact of the electoral system on women's parliamentary representation will be assessed; finally, the obstacles in front of women will be presented with party consolidation in the focus.

The Voting System

The most recent occasion when Hungary could create and apply a democratic electoral system only occurred in the process of systemic change among the conditions of a negotiated transition at the end of the 1980s. Since then, the agreement about a mixed-member proportional (MMP) electoral system has not changed. This stability of the electoral system is somewhat exceptional on the regional level. Indeed, the only important change in the original electoral law was the modification of the threshold requirement from 4 to 5 percent in 1994 (Benoit 2005). In the creation of electoral law, the German mixed electoral system was regarded as a model, but the Hungarian system—as we shall see—has majoritarian tendencies to ensure stable governance, a major (although apparently unfounded) concern of the negotiators. Both SMDs and List PR are part of the Hungarian electoral tradition: both were in use in between the two world wars in different parts of the country, while after 1945 a List PR and in the communist period first a List PR then an SMD system prevailed.

The 386-member parliament is elected in three tiers: 176 mandates come from 176 SMDs in two rounds vote, and the other mandates come either from the 20 regional closed PR lists or from the closed compensation national list.

The SMD election is successful if a candidate gets more than 50 percent of the vote, while in the second round, a relative majority suffices among the top three candidates of the first round result. On election day, the citizens also vote for a party list in one of the 20 regions. Only a party with at least two SMD candidates in that region can establish a regional list, which proves to be a strong obstacle in front of small parties. List mandates are counted by the Hagenbach-Bischoff formula. Regions are of different size—district magnitude varies from 4 to 28, but 28 is exceptional: it is the list of the capital city, Budapest, which homes one-fifth of the country's population. On average, the district magnitude is 6.5 when we exclude the Budapest region. The maximum number of overall list mandates is determined by law (at 152).

When the quota for a list seat is not met, fragment votes as well as remaining regional mandates are reallocated among parties whose remainders are at least above two-thirds of the initial quota. These unallocated seats appear in the third tier, in the national compensation list. Thus, there is no vote on the national list, which is merely a compensation list built on the fragment votes both from the regional lists and from SMDs. Parties are entitled to set up a national compensation list only if they could establish at least seven regional lists (that is in at least one third of the regions). Parties would receive mandates from the national list according to the d'Hondt formula. The minimum number of these mandates was set at 58, again by law, but this number has always been higher because of the fragment votes.

Women in the Legislature: Historical Trends

Before the communist period, only a weak tradition in gender representation prevailed. Women had limited voting rights before WWII, various census limitations were in use, and among the conditions of "façade" democracy only a handful of women appeared in parliament. Women suffrage was introduced in 1945. Democratic elections were then held in 1945 and in 1947 under a proportional list system, but at the second occasion serious limitations were put in place. The approaching communist takeover substantially hindered free and fair elections. The number of women representatives was low (16 at both occasions out of 386 MPs) and they mostly came from the Social Democratic and the Communist Party of the time. During the communist period, the number of women in parliament was substantially higher (in the 18 to 30 percent range) than now, but in the absence of free elections this is not part of the representative—not to mention the democratic—tradition.

Table 14.2 demonstrates the low level and relative stability of female representation in the posttransition period. In the first and third parliamentary periods, a conservative majority and conservative government meant somewhat smaller female proportions (7.3 percent and 8.3 percent, respectively) while the second, fourth, and fifth elections concluded in a higher but still low result—in the 9–11 percent range. At these occasions the successor party MSZP (Socialists) and the smaller center left Liberals (SZDSZ) were in government. As we shall see, the Left-Right dimension is not that a strong dividing line between parties as it was originally expected, that is the Left is also reluctant to select many strong female candidates. And as table 14.2 indicates, the proportion of female MPs in socialist party group has not yet reached the level of 1990 when—probably due to the old reflexes and the losing position of the postcommunist party—proportionally more women were around. Since after 1994, when the Left regained and stabilized its political space, the number of female MPs in the MSZP has only minimally increased.

Table 14.2   The number and percentage of female MPs by party, 1990–2006

Party	1990		1994		1998		2002		2006	
	No.	*%*	*No.*	*%*	*No.*	*%*	*No.*	*%*	*No.*	*%*
MDF	8	**4.8**	6	15.8	1	**5.9**	1	4.2	1	9.8
SZDSZ	8	8.5	11	15.7	3	12.5	2	**10.0**	2	10.0
MSZP	5	15.1	22	10.5	14	10.4	23	**12.9**	25	**13.1**
Fidesz	2	9.1	1	5.0	10	**6.7**	9	5.5	11	**7.8**
KDNP	1	4.7	1	4.5	–	–	–	–	2	**8.7**
FKGP	3	6.8	2	7.7	3	6.2	–	–	–	–
MIÉP	–	–	–	–	1	7.1	–	–	–	–
Total	28*	7.3	43	11.1	32	8.3	35	9.1	41	10.6

* The sum is 28 for reason of an additional independent female MP.
Note: Bold: parties in government.
Party names: MDF = Hungarian Democratic Forum; SZDSZ = Alliance of Free Democrats, Liberal Party; MSZP = Hungarian Socialist Party; Fidesz = Alliance of Young Democrats, Hungarian Civic Association; KDNP= Christian Democratic People's Party; FKGP= Independent Smallholders Party; MIÉP= Party of Hungarian Justice and Life.
Source: Ilonszki, Kelemen, and Széles (2003: 14).

Among the conservative parties, female representation is regularly lower. It is worth noting that in the growing and now largest Conservative Party (Fidesz), the proportion of female representatives began to grow only at the 2006 elections but still it has not reached the 1990 level (of course, owing to changing electoral performance the numerical context is different). We must note however that in 1990, the Fidesz did not belong to the conservative party family but was a right liberal party. Both in 2002 and 2006, the smaller conservative parties (MDF and KDNP) managed to get into parliament with the help of an electoral agreement/coalition with the Fidesz.

The Impact of the Voting System on the Proportion of Women in the Legislature

The new MMP electoral system, which was part of the package of laws that was agreed upon between the reform communists and the opposition groups in the summer of 1989 and then enacted by parliament in that autumn (Act XXXIV/1989), did not take into consideration gender or any other minority representation. The major concerns of the negotiating partners were rooted in the communist versus noncommunist dimension and the political majority–political minority dimension. The reform communists sought to maintain the SMD electoral system in the hope that their candidates would be much better known than the new parties' newcomers, while the opposition was keen on having a list system where the party logic and proportionality would ensure them a better chance.

Table 14.3   Mandate distribution of female MPs, 1990–2006

Year	SMD mandates			Territorial list mandates			National list mandates			All female mandates	
	All	Female no.	Female %	All	Female no.	Female %	All	Female no.	Female %	No.	%
1990	176	6	3.4	120	8	6.7	90	14	15.6	28	7.3
1994	176	15	8.5	125	17	12.8	85	11	14.1	43	11.1
1998	176	12	6.9	128	13	10.2	82	7	8.5	32	8.3
2002	176	13	7.4	140	16	11.4	70	6	8.6	35	9.1
2006	176	15	8.5	146	19	13.0	64	7	10.9	41	10.6

Source: Montgomery and Ilonszki (2003) and own counting.

That the new electoral system was not gender sensitive does not imply it had no (positive or negative) impact on women; as for the party distribution above, the mandate distribution of female representation also illustrates how the electoral system affects women's parliamentary representation. Table 14.3 provides the exact picture. After the first—and it seems exceptional—election when the results in the three tiers worked in the expected direction (then, women were underrepresented in SMDs and also a representation difference prevailed between the regional lists and the national list to the advantage of the national list where the district magnitude is largest), the number and proportion of female mandates is pretty stable in SMDs—exactly the same in 2006 as it was in 1994, and numerically more than twice as many female MPs come from SMDs than from the national list. Paradoxically, the number of female candidates in this tier has permanently decreased: in 1994, there was not a single female candidate in 71 SMDs, there was only one female candidate in 63, and there were two or more female candidates in 42 SMDs, while in 2006, the candidate distribution was 87, 69, and 20, respectively. Half of the voters do not meet a female candidate at the constituency level at all! The lower level of female presence is connected to the fact that small parties—which have been disappearing—were more open to run female candidates in SMDs, and at the same time, it also proves that larger parties are still reluctant to place women in directly competitive positions despite the proof that they are able to win these seats.

As to the national list, it happened only at the first election that the national list mandates were significantly overrepresented among the female seats. In 1990, half of the female mandates while in 2006 less than one-sixth of the female mandates came from the national list. In the meantime, the number of national list mandates also decreased—from 90 in 1990 to 64 in 2004—owing to a decrease in the fragment votes, that is a more "straightforward" party system. This one third decline contrasts the number of women elected on the national list that has been halved by 2006 since 1990, that is the disadvantage of women is quite clear here. Lastly, we can observe a somewhat increasing proportion and number of female mandates on the regional lists. Although since 1998 the number and proportion of female mandates tends to be the highest on the regional lists, this reveals only a relative advantage because—as we shall see—the party gatekeepers continue to dominate this tier of the electoral system.

The Impact of Other Variables on the Proportion of Women in the Legislature

Above, we have observed the low level of female representation—with some hints at party system transformation. The negative—or at least controversial—impact of this transformation will be presented in more detail and in three broader themes. Party system change, selection processes, and the concrete placement of female candidates are all "suspect" in maintaining or even increasing female representative disadvantage. Beforehand, two major steps of party consolidation have to be kept in mind. First, in 1994 the victory of the successor party (MSZP) meant that the Left spectrum of the political scene became settled, and by this time, the parties' organizational attributes were also established. Then, by 1998, the two big parties stabilized their positions and the turn towards two-party system became evident.

The Party System Change

From a clear case of multipartism, Hungary has turned towards a two-plus party system, the effective number of parties being 2.69 in 2006 (see table 14.4). Parties dominate the electoral process (see the shrinking number of independent candidates) and the number of parties that are present in the playing ground has decreased—fewer parties run candidates or establish a national list now than before. With one—albeit temporary—exception (MIÉP), only those parties that participated in systemic change were in parliament in the past 16 years. All parliamentary parties in 2006 were around already in 1990 (see table 14.2).

It is generally agreed that the tendency towards bipolarization, and a more confrontational political style as the result, are not favourable for women to enter politics. Table 14.5 on the number and gender distribution of candidates allows some other observations. After the founding elections, the candidate pool peaked in 1994. Since then, the number of candidates has been on the decrease. One reason is the disappearance of the small parties and the other that even the parliamentary parties have fewer candidates

Table 14.4 Some dimensions of party system change in Hungary

	Effective no. of parties	*No. of parties in parliament*	*No. of parties running at least one candidate*	*No. of nonparty candidates*	*No. of parties with a national list*
1990	6.71	6	28	199	12
1994	5.23	6	37	103	15
1998	4.46	5	26	53	12
2002	2.84	4	22	40	8
2006	2.69	5	21	12	10

Sources: www.valasztas.hu/ (April 2007), Benoit (2005), and own counting.

Table 14.5 Gender distribution of candidates, 1990–2006

Year of election	*Male candidates in all parties*		*Female candidates in all parties*	
	No.	*%*	*No.*	*%*
1990	3,191	91	316	9
1994	4,084	88.5	529	11.5
1998	3,657	85.8	605	14.2
2002	2,840	82.2	614	17.8
2006	2,284	83.3	456	16.7

Source: valtor.valasztas.hu/vaaltort/jsp, Farkas and Vajda (1991), and own counting.

because they run them in more than one tier. In the two large parties, the average nomination of one electable candidate increased from 1.5 to 2.3 in Fidesz and from 1.6 to 2.2 in MSZP in the 1990–2002 period (Sebestyén 2003). It means that, on average, candidates run in more than two forms, a combination of SMD, regional list, or national list.

The proportion—and even the number—of female candidates has increased from 1990, however, with some decline in 2006. Are they more established in the nonparliamentary parties? Not at all: in 2006, 312 women and 1,577 men were running in the ranks of (later) parliamentary parties and 144 women and 707 men in the ranks of nonparliamentary parties (including a dozen independents). This shows that almost exactly the same share were women in the two party groups: candidates are available. Bipolarization does not necessarily discourage women. Still, an imbalance in the structure of candidacy can be observed: only every eighth female candidate (312 versus 41) but every "four and half-th" male candidate (1,577 versus 345) gets a mandate in the parliamentary parties. Because parties are responsible for candidate selection, an analysis of the selection itself will identify the sources of inequality.

Selection and Deselection

Thus, the representative linkage was the broadest in 1994 although for women that was not the peak year. The widening female candidate pool did not result in higher female representation. One reason is that—as it has been demonstrated elsewhere (Ilonszki 1999)—party institutionalization went in parallel with centralization and personalization in most parties. Party gatekeepers ensured their central (or even exclusive) role in determining candidate selection and, more concretely, the placement of candidates. The possible exception is the Socialists, where the external party was strong enough to make its interest respected in terms of candidate selection, and where a relatively larger body of embedded female politicians was around partially owing to the former regime.

Depending to how the selection process became established, female positions have become increasingly unsafe. At the first three elections, male and female parliamentary turnover rates were very close (indeed, with some advantage for women). Since then, we can observe the stabilization of the male parliamentary elite and a growing discrepancy between women and men in this respect: women tend to be deselected in large numbers, as table 14.6 shows.

Unsafe positions are more typical for women both on the Left and on the Right. In the conservative parties, the dominance of the male party selectorate is the institutional explanation while on the Left a well-established but not gender-sensitive female group is complemented with a wider but unsettled candidate pool. Not surprisingly, the impact is the same—substantive female representation is missing. Women are highly dependent on their parties either because they do not have their own resources (on the Right) or because they are selected only in view of the fact that they are highly partisan and "similar" to the male group (on the Left). The difference between men and women with party leadership background of MPs is illustrative: after

Table 14.6   Turnover in the parliament by gender, 1990–2006

Election year	Newcomers			
	Female		Male	
	No.	%	No.	%
1990	26	92.9	346	96.6
1994	27	62.8	218	63.6
1998	13	43.3	175	49.2
2002	13	37.1	107	30.9
2006	19	46.3	88	25.5

Source: Own database.

minor differences earlier, the percentage point difference was 10 in 1998, 20 in 2002, and 15 in 2006 to the advantage of women—female MPs have more party leadership functions than male MPs. Interviews and other survey proof also reveal higher level party dependence among female politicians (Ilonszki and Antić 2003: 131ff).

Placement of Candidates

In addition to selection and deselection, the placement of candidates is another instrument that causes female underrepresentation (Matland 1995). Since candidates can run but do not necessarily run in all three tiers, and positions are determined mainly by party gatekeepers, it is particularly important to consider which places would bring an electoral chance, at least a mathematical chance, to win. This includes all the SMD candidates and those list candidates that are placed within the electable mandate numbers— that is, within the district magnitude (on average 6.5 on the regional lists and minimum 58 on the national list, as was described above). Indeed, it is only a mathematical—and not a political—figure, because it does not calculate former electoral performance and relies on an unrealistic assumption, namely, that a party wins all SMD and all list mandates that are available (with the exclusion of the other parties). While political science has been for long discussing a more politically sensitive mandate typology (Niemi and Fuh-sheng Hsieh 2002), in the following the mathematical approach will be applied—which is normally used in the Hungarian academic analysis and, more importantly, it perfectly illustrates male-female differences in terms of opportunities and then in terms of outcomes.

Table 14.7 shows the proportion of strong female candidates (that have a mathematical chance to win) by party: at the first three elections (in 1990,

Table 14.7   The proportions of electable female candidates by party[*]

	1990	1994	1998	2002	2006
MSZP	10.0	10.8	8.9	12.5	14.0
SZDSZ	11.9	12.0	14.1	19.6	15.9
MDF	5.9	8.3	6.1	7.4[+]	14.5
Fidesz	12.3	7.9	9.1		9.0
KDNP	6.4	9.1	19.9	na[++]	

[*] Only for the parties that received a mandate at the given election and are still in parliament in 2006—cf. table 14.2—MIÉP and FKGP dropped out of parliament.

[+] The MDF and Fidesz ran in an electoral coalition in 2002.

[++] The KDNP did not run its own candidates but formed a parliamentary party group, separate from the Fidesz only in the new parliament.

Sources: Sebestyén (2003) and own counting.

1994, and 1998) the proportion of strong (i.e., electable) female candidates was about 10 percent of all strong candidates. The Left-Right division between the two major parties has been on the increase: the MSZP produces an upward trend while the figures of Fidesz stagnate. Again, we must note that in 1990 the Fidesz did not belong to the conservative party family as it does now.

When compared with table 14.2, it becomes clear that for small parties this approach is too generous. Although in 2006 both the liberal SZDSZ and the conservative MDF ran somewhat more electable female candidates than the Socialists, their electoral weakness (they have just managed to exceed the 5 percent threshold) explains this "generosity." But even for the large parties the obvious question remains: is it enough to apply the "'electable" concept to understand their female representative agenda? First, we have seen that in SMDs only few women run and relatively many win. They are the strong, professional female politicians, mainly from the Socialist Party. Second, with the consolidation of the party system (fewer parties) and thus with the increase in party magnitudes, do the parties have the incentive to begin ticket balancing on the lists? With respect to party magnitude, we have to note that by 2006 all territorial lists work as multimember districts for the parties (the exception is Budapest for MDF and Pest County for the MDF and the SZDSZ, where their party magnitude was 1). Indeed, with the afore-mentioned exceptions, only the Fidesz and the MSZP won list mandates in 2006—the MSZP won 71 seats in the 20 lists, and the Fidesz won 69 seats in the 20 lists, their district magnitude ranging between 2 and 10 versus 2 and 13, respectively, and on average it was around 3. (Formerly, particularly in the first elections when more parties won regional mandates, party magnitude was 1 or 2.) Do the big parties care for ticket balancing? Do they place women in the first three places of the regional lists? In 2006, 13 women in the Socialist Party and 4 women in the Fidesz occupied a position among the top three (excluding the Budapest regional list). This reflects the Left-Right difference, but also the reluctance to implement ticket balancing in each party. And thirdly, the Fidesz placed proportionally more women on the national list in winning positions, those that would be the token of symbolic representation. The political resources of these women politicians are obviously fewer than of those on the Left, thus they cannot promote substantive female representation.

Conclusion

Despite a relatively large female candidate pool, we have observed decreasing opportunities for women: lack of safe parliamentary positions, placement strategies, and centrally controlled selection processes have all proved this, and some features of party consolidation are in the background. The elite-driven transition and then early consolidation probably explain these phenomena more than the electoral system itself. The electoral system has been used (or abused) in the wider systemic context.

The timing of party consolidation (too early), its main actors (participants or direct successors of systemic change), and dominant ideals (insensitivity toward minority representation) have been working against the widening of the representative linkage. Party consolidation took place earlier in Hungary than in other postcommunist countries. A comparative analysis could strengthen the hypothesis that early party system consolidation is a major factor in low female proportions: more flexible institutions, a longer learning process of how democratic institutions (including the electoral system) work would produce larger female proportions—despite similar nondemocratic traditions and the communist past.

The concrete features analyzed above are complemented with the "old" traditions, the negative impacts of which cannot be neglected either. Unresponsive constituency, weak civil society, virtually nonexistent women's movement, and patriarchal traditions belong to the explanation of low women's representation in parliament. On the elite level, the professional—mainly Socialist—female politicians can hardly serve as role models, because they are stuck in their professional posts. The conservative side seems to follow not a modern but an old style conservative tradition. Despite the obvious party differences, there is no leading force or fundamental intention to handle this representative deficit of women. Although the MSZP introduced a quota regulation in 2002, this was put in place half-heartedly. It only rules that 25 percent of the candidates should be women, but details are not specified and, as we have seen, in the election context are not properly applied.

Electoral system reform has been on the agenda for some time. The main reason of course is not the vague representative linkage but the intention to decrease the number of MPs, the Hungarian parliament being too large for the country. Party elites largely work against this option however in defence of party sinecures. Maybe it will be mainly the EU with its representative expectations (Ilonszki 2005) that would move both the Left and the Right toward more representation.

Note

1. Lithuania put the mixed electoral system in use in 1992, and there are some differences between the working of the Lithuanian and the Hungarian system.

Subpart III

Majoritarian

Societal, Electoral, and Party Explanations for the Low Representation of Women in the House of Representatives

Raymond Christensen

Introduction

The 2005 elections for Japan's House of Representatives were a milestone for women's representation in the country. For the first time in nearly sixty years, more women were elected to the House than were elected in the 1946 election, the first election in which Japanese women could vote. Much of the credit for Japan reaching this modest milestone is given to Prime Minister Junichiro Koizumi, who has made the elevation of women in the ruling Liberal Democratic Party (LDP) an important part of his reform initiatives for both the party and the country. In the 2005 election he selected women for the top positions of his party's proportional representation lists in six of Japan's eleven regions. He personally recruited eleven women to run as LDP candidates in thirty-two target districts, and eight of the eleven were elected.[1] These eight by themselves account for nearly all of the nine-seat increase in women in the House of Representatives accomplished in the 2005 election.

It would seem, therefore, that much of the recent progress in women's representation in Japan can be credited to a prime minister who is sympathetic to the cause of women's representation. It would be a mistake, however, to believe that Koizumi's efforts on behalf of women's representation have gone beyond dramatic, symbolic gestures designed only to burnish his reputation as a reformer. His efforts have not significantly changed underlying patterns of male domination within the LDP. Though he has placed women in high-profile positions in election campaigns, the underlying dynamics of candidate recruitment, along with their gender imbalances, remain largely unchanged. Specifically, women are disadvantaged in the LDP candidate recruitment process for Japan's district races in contrast to party lists in proportional representation races. This disadvantage for conservative (LDP) women in the district races is changing only slowly, as Japanese society changes, and for reasons largely unrelated to Koizumi's actions.

Thus, the relatively low numbers of women representatives in Japan can be explained by three important factors. First, the electoral system, with its strict campaign regulations, has made it difficult for women to win the LDP nomination for district races. Second, societal factors that impact the number of women in all high-status occupations have restricted the pool of women available as candidates for all elective offices, but especially as candidates for the LDP in district races. Third, despite the paucity of LDP women in district races, the party, even prior to Koizumi, has a strong record of promoting women on party lists in proportional representation races. The LDP itself seems to be supportive of women candidates, but societal and electoral factors intervene to make the candidacies of LDP women in district races difficult. These barriers, thus, restrict the number of women in Japan's House of Representatives to surprisingly low levels.

The Voting System

Japan provides an excellent test case of the impact of electoral systems on the representation of women because the country has used four different electoral systems in the past sixty years of elections for its House of Representatives. The use of these different systems in the same country, sometimes in the same election, makes it possible to control for a host of other explanations of women's representation (for example, societal and cultural factors, electoral regulations, or the status of women) while changing only the type of electoral system used.

The most prominent electoral system that is associated with Japan is its use of multimember districts in which voters cast one vote for their preferred candidate. This system, called the single nontransferable vote (SNTV), was used in the House of Representatives for nearly every seat in every election from 1947 to 1993. Each election district selected three to five representatives, giving rise to the alternative acronym for this electoral system—MMD (multimember districts).[2]

A second electoral system used is single member districts, though this system has never been used, in any election, for the entirety of seats up for election. Since 1994, Japan has used a mixed electoral system, combining single-seat districts with proportional representation lists. Japan's voters now cast two ballots, one in their local election district and a second for a regional party list. Single-seat districts have been used for a majority (300) of the House of Representatives seats in the 1996, 2000, 2003, and 2005 elections.

The third system is proportional representation, which has been used in the House of Representatives for 200 of 500 seats in 1996 and 180 of 480 seats since 2000. Japan's proportional representation system (for its House of Representatives) requires political parties to draw up candidate lists in each of Japan's eleven regions. The votes are aggregated only at the regional level, so the proportionality of the system depends on the number of seats allocated to the region. Japan's regions range in magnitude from six to twenty-nine seats.[3]

The mixed electoral system that Japan has used since the 1996 election has several other features that potentially impact the representation of women. First, the system is not linked; a party's success in electing candidates in the single-seat districts does not affect the number of seats that a party wins in the proportional representation races. Thus, the system is less proportional in its overall results, and the number of winners on a party list is not affected by the number of seats that a party has already won in the district races.

In addition, Japan's version of the mixed electoral system allows for the double listing of candidates. A candidate may run in the district as the party's nominee and also be placed on that same party's list for the corresponding region. In practice most of the party list candidates take advantage of this double listing possibility and simultaneously run in a district race and on the party list. Japan's rules also allow for parties to list candidates in the same position on party lists with ties to be broken by each candidate's ratio of how well she did in her district race against the eventual winner. Most of the parties also use this tie-breaking provision extensively. Thus, though Japanese voters cannot directly alter the ordering of party candidates on the party lists as they would be able to do if Japan had an open-list proportional representation system, the voters can indirectly affect the rank ordering of candidates by voting for that candidate in the district race. As a candidate's vote ratio improves in a district, her ranking on the party list improves relative to other candidates who are also double listed and ranked at the same place on the party list. As most parties use the double listing and tie-breaking provisions extensively, in practice party list races in Japan's House of Representatives are the functional equivalent of an open-list proportional representation system.

A fourth and final system was used for only one election in the House of Representatives. Japan's first election after World War II (1946) was conducted using large magnitude districts. Voters cast either two or three ballots for candidates who ran in districts that elected from four to fourteen representatives per district. This election was noteworthy not only for its one-time use of large-magnitude districts but also for the first time presence of women candidates on the ballot and women voting for the first time in a national election in Japan.

The existing literature on the impact of electoral systems on women's representation makes specific predictions about the relative level of women's representation comparing each of these electoral systems. The proportionality of an electoral system, which is largely determined by the magnitude of the electoral districts, directly affects the number of women elected under that system. If an electoral system is more proportional, it is possible for parties to balance their tickets within a specific district by having multiple candidates with different attributes that would appeal to different sectors of the electorate (Schwindt-Bayer and Mishler 2005; Rule 1987; Matland and Brown 1992). Thus, a party would be more likely to balance its slate of candidates by having at least one woman candidate in a district in which it is running three candidates than if it is running only one candidate in a district. Similarly, if a party is confident of winning twenty seats in a large proportional representation district, it is even more likely that at least several of those twenty seats will go to women candidates. This simple concept leads to expectations that women will be best represented in the proportional representation regions (magnitude six to twenty-nine seats) used from 1996 to 2005, next best represented in the 1946 election (magnitude four to fourteen seats), next best represented in the SNTV system used from 1947 to 1993 (magnitude three to five seats), and worst represented in the single-seat districts used from 1996 to 2005 (magnitude of one seat). Of course, other factors also affect women's representation, but simply looking at the electoral system, predictions can be made from an analysis of only the magnitude of the districts used under a particular electoral system.

Women in the Legislature: Historical Trends

The representation of women in Japan's House of Representatives has one characteristic that follow international trends and two that make Japan stand out as an international anomaly. The first trend that is consistent with international trends is the gradual rise in women's representation over time. From the 1950s until the 1980s, women were only 2 to 3 percent of the Representatives. In the past decade, women's representation has increased to between 5 and 10 percent.

Despite this increase, however, Japan remains an outlier among advanced industrial democracies in the low numbers of women in its House of Representatives. Rule (1994b: 17) found Japan to be the lowest of twenty-seven of countries she surveyed in the late 1980s, and about 20 years later, though the number of women serving in Japan's House of Representatives has more than tripled from 2.3 percent to 9 percent, Japan still has the lowest levels of women's representation of those same twenty-seven countries. In fact, Japan ranks one hundred and second of the 136 countries surveyed by the Inter-Parliamentary Union (2006), far behind every Western European country.

A second anomaly is the first election in which women could vote in Japan. In 1946 women won 8.4 percent of the seats (39 of 464 seats), and it took until 2005, nearly sixty years later, for women candidates to finally beat the historic high set in 1946 by winning nine percent of the seats (43 of 480). In 1946, Japan was comparatively a world leader in women's representation (Darcy and Nixon 1996: 4–5). It quickly fell from that perch in subsequent elections as the number of women representatives declined precipitously.

The Impact of the Voting System on the Proportion of Women in the Legislature

Figure 15.1 gives the results for women elected under each of Japan's electoral systems. Clearly, proportional representation and very large districts enhance the representation of women. The best years for the representation of women are the 1946 election, which used large magnitude districts, and

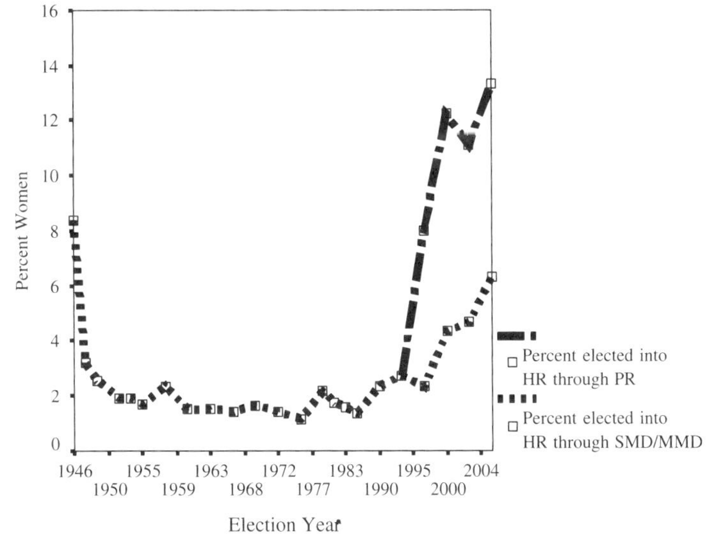

Sources: *Asahi Shimbun* (various issues); *Asahi Senkyo Taikan* (various issues); Japan Jichisho (2000)

Figure 15.1   Women's representation under four electoral systems used in Japan, 1946–2004

the recent proportional representation elections in the House of Representatives. In fact, the level of women's representation is at least twice as high in the House of Representatives proportional representation races than it is in the district races that were held as part of the same election.

A more interesting finding from figure 15.1 is the fact that multimember districts in the House of Representatives (1947–1993) are as inhospitable to women candidates as single-member districts are. In fact, because of increases across time in women's representation, more women are elected from the single-member districts now than were elected from the multimember districts of twenty years ago. This finding runs counter to the prediction that multimember districts should enhance the representation of women. In fact, in Japan, the impact of multimember districts is largely indistinguishable from that of single-member districts.

The Impact of Other Variables on the Proportion of Women in the Legislature

The electoral system is only one factor that affects women's representation. For example, large-magnitude districts enhanced women's representation in the 1946 election, but other factors also help explain the strong performance of women candidates in that election. Women candidates were promoted by the Occupation authorities and they were not tainted with the stigma of being associated with Japan's wartime regime. Many incumbents had been purged by the Occupation, creating a political vacuum, and many voters were confused by the new electoral system and thought that one of their ballots had to be cast for a woman candidate (Ogai 1996). Just as the anomalous results of the 1946 election can be explained by both the use of large magnitude districts and several other factors, I now turn to the three most important factors (other than the electoral system) that seem to have consistently affected the number of women elected to Japan's House of Representatives.

The Impact of Campaign Regulations on Candidate Recruitment

The anomaly of Japan's multimember districts being as hostile to women candidates as single-member districts can be explained, in part, by Japan's stringent campaign regulations. These regulations have made the "precampaign" the most important factor in gaining election to the House of Representatives. Candidates cannot advertise, door-to-door campaigning is illegal, and fliers and posters are stringently regulated to specified numbers, types, and locations. In practice most of the campaigning in Japan occurs before the actual election period and consists of building up lists of prospective supporters through a variety of efforts, none of which may mention campaigns or voting. The importance of these precampaign efforts, however, differs by the type of election district. These efforts are most consequential in rural areas where a candidate's connections to the voters are still strong. In more urban districts, it is harder for a candidate to make such connections, and many voters decide their vote based on media coverage of the official campaign or impressions of the candidates gleaned from the highly regulated campaign efforts.

These rules, especially in the LDP camp, put a premium on a certain type of candidate, one with extensive connections in the district and one who is able to raise large sums of money to finance the extensive precampaign activities that are so important in the more traditional districts. Thus, in more traditional districts, the strongest LDP candidates are local politicians, hereditary politicians, or retired bureaucrats. Local politicians already have a support group that they try to expand in running for the Diet. Hereditary politicians often inherit their father's or other close relative's support group and try to use that same group of supporters to gain their election. Ex-bureaucrats are considered some of the best educated and most well connected of Japanese citizens and are well poised to begin creating their own personal support network. There are very few women who are successful local politicians or former bureaucrats, and traditionally, political support groups were always passed on to male heirs rather than female heirs.

In addition, the LDP exercised little control over the candidates who ran in the districts (in contrast to its party list candidates), eliminating the possibility that the party might have tried to balance its local tickets by having a woman or minority candidate running alongside its male candidates. Rather, each candidate was his or her own political entrepreneur, trying to create a personal support network strong enough for victory, against not only the opposition but also copartisan competitors. As there were disproportionately fewer women in strong local politics positions, inheriting their father's support groups or retiring early from the well-respected national bureaucracy, there were few women that were strong prospective candidates under this system.

This model of candidate selection is less important in more urban, less traditional districts and in the candidate selection process of many of the opposition parties. In less traditional districts, it has been common to elect what the Japanese call "talent" candidates. These are people who have widespread name recognition because of their successful careers in sports, television, writing, or entertainment. These candidates have an advantage in districts in which building a personal support network is difficult. They capitalize on their name recognition and attract votes with their popularity. Women are represented quite well among talent candidates. And even among nontalent candidates, it is easier to attract attention as a reform candidate in an urban district if the candidate is young or is a woman, characteristics that would set the candidate apart from the stereotypical Japanese politician. Thus, in contrast to traditional districts, women should be better represented in districts in which precampaign activities and personal support groups matter less and the fame or image of the candidate matters more.

Similarly, many opposition candidates are selected according to different criteria that are not skewed so heavily against women candidates. Many of the opposition parties are organizationally based (unions, religious groups, and the Communist Party) and these parties choose their district race candidates with less concern about personal support groups and the activities of the precampaign period. Because these opposition parties run a different type of campaign, they draw from a different pool of potential candidates. The organizations that support these parties find it much easier than the LDP to take a woman from their organization and sponsor her as a candidate in a district race. Though many opposition candidates will also try to create personal support organizations and compete actively in the precampaign period, these facets of their campaigns are relatively less important than they are to LDP candidates. Figure 15.2 shows this

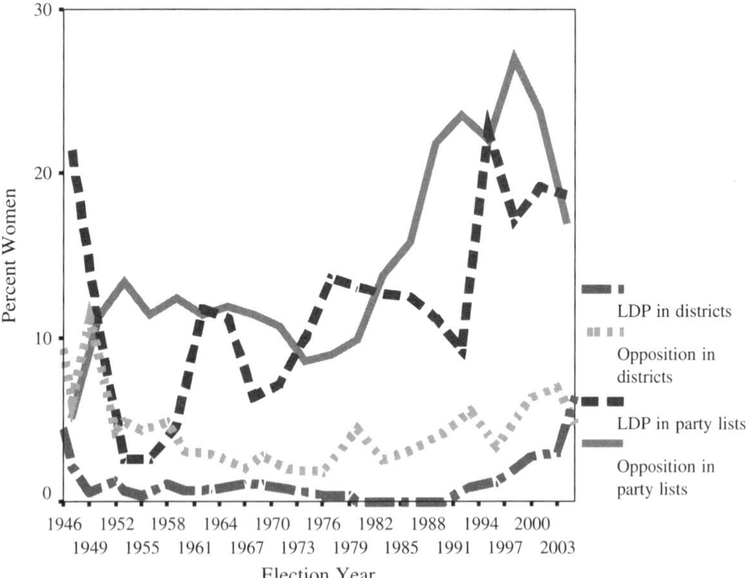

Sources: *Asahi Shimbun* (various issues); *Sanshu Ryoin Meikan* (1990); Japan, Jichisho (2002)

Figure 15.2   The LDP and the opposition, comparing women's representation in districts and party lists

divergence; the opposition parties have consistently elected a significantly higher percent of women from the districts than the LDP has. Only with Koizumi's direct intervention in 2005 in selecting thirty-two LDP district candidates have the numbers of LDP women winners in districts equaled the opposition record in those same district races. Koizumi's efforts also show the different nature of campaigns in these urban districts. He promoted women candidates as a part of his reformist agenda, and he successfully neutralized the advantage that the opposition parties previously had in Japan's urban areas. In 2005, for the first time in decades, the LDP outpolled the opposition in the urban districts that had traditionally been an area of weakness for the LDP.

The Impact of Political Parties

Another possible explanation for fewer LDP candidates in district races is that the LDP is more hostile to women candidates than the opposition parties. This explanation gains support from the fact that Koizumi's initiatives in favor of women candidates have single-handedly erased any difference between the LDP and the opposition in terms of the number of women being elected in district races. Perhaps the LDP's dismal record in promoting women candidates is a result of the biases of that the party's leaders, and Koizumi, in contrast, is the first LDP leader to actively promote the candidacies of women. Alternatively, the opposition parties could be argued to have a long history of supporting women candidates, especially in contrast to the LDP's poor performance in this area.

Though the argument of LDP bias against women candidates seems supported by the evidence, a closer analysis of figure 15.2 actually undercuts the argument that the LDP is a party that is generally hostile to women candidates. Figure 15.2 shows the commitment of parties toward women's representation by contrasting the record of the LDP against the several opposition parties for both proportional representation and district races.[4] The LDP has been nearly as supportive of women candidates in party list races as have been the opposition parties, but only in district races has the LDP lagged significantly behind these same opposition parties. In district races the LDP has elected more women as a percentage of its winners than the opposition in only one election, the 2005 election. In contrast, in about one-third of the party list races, the LDP has had a percent of women winners equal to or surpassing that of the opposition. It would be odd for the LDP as a party to support women candidacies in party list races but to be hostile to women running in district races, especially when most of those district races have been multiseat districts. This difference however is consistent with the alternative explanation, that different types of campaigns, selection mechanisms, and candidate pools create the divergence between an LDP that does as well as its competitors in placing women on party lists but differs significantly from those other parties in supporting women candidates for district races.

That this difference does not stem from the attitudes of party leaders is also shown by an analysis of when various parties began supporting significant numbers of women on their party lists. The conservative parties that later merged into the LDP in 1955 had women as 21 percent of their winners on party lists in a non House of Representatives election as early as 1947. This is hardly the reaction of a party that is hostile to women candidates. In contrast, the Japan Communist Party waited until 1968 to run its first woman candidate on its party list, though now women comprise between 20 and 50 percent of candidates in the party list. Similarly, the now defunct Democratic Socialist Party ran its first woman candidate on a party list in 1983. Koizumi's efforts to put women in prominent positions on the LDP's party lists are a tradition within the LDP and its predecessor parties going back to the 1940s. His sponsorship of large numbers of women for district races is a clean break with LDP tradition and reflects the trumping of his reformist strategy over the candidate pool and candidate selection mechanisms that normally create barriers to the election of women LDP Representatives in the district races.

Societal Factors

Another possible explanation for Japan's relatively low representation of women lies in the few women in other high-status occupations in Japan. Just as the number of women in the House of Representatives has risen from 2 percent to 9 percent from the 1980s to 2006, women's representation in other fields has only recently begun also to rise from abysmally low levels. For example, the number of women in graduate school has risen from 1.6 percent in 1980 to 7.2 percent in 2005. The number of women appointed to the important government consultative bodies (Shingikai) has grown from 2.6 percent in 1975 to 30.9 percent in 2004. The number of women hired in the highest grade of civil service jobs has increased from 2.2 percent in 1976 to 20.6 percent in 2006. The number of women in local politics has similarly advanced from 2 percent women in prefectural (Japan's equivalent of provinces or states) assemblies in 1986 to 6.9 percent in 2004. Women in city assemblies have risen from 3 percent to 11.5 percent over the same period. The number of women doctors has increased from around 10 percent in the 1980s to 16 percent in 2004. The number of women lawyers has increased from 5 percent in the 1980s to 12.5 percent in 2004 (Naikaku 2006).

Each of these indicators shows an increase, often a dramatic increase, in the number of women in high-status occupations, beginning in the 1980s. Similarly, women's representation in the House of Representatives also began its increase at the same time. The low level of women's political representation in Japan, though unrepresentative of the number of women in Japan, is representative of general trends of women's representation in other sectors of Japanese society.

These numbers might seem confusing when other comparative numbers show Japan to be much more similarly situated to other countries that have much higher levels of women's political representation. For example, the number of women attending college has nearly equaled or exceeded the number of men attending college since the late 1980s.[5] The number of women graduating from high school in Japan exceeded the number of men graduating in 1970 and has always been greater since then. The number of women employed in 2004 lagged behind most Western European countries, but not by much—60 percent of Japanese women work compared with 64 percent in France and 65 percent in Germany.

Certain peculiarities about the Japanese employment system help explain the gap between having similar numbers of women working in Japan while having low numbers of women in politics and higher status occupations. The expectations of most high-status employment in Japan make it extremely difficult for a woman to maintain a high-status job while also playing a substantial role in family responsibilities. Indeed, most Japanese women take primary responsibility for family support, a stance that allows their husbands to meet the very high expectation of their employers. Japanese women go to school and work in relatively high numbers, but they choose, and are directed into, lower-status jobs that preclude advancement to high-status jobs or political careers. Only in the past two decades has this been changing as more women are choosing to enter these high-status occupations.

Conclusion

Koizumi has made notable efforts to increase the presence of women in important political positions, but many of his efforts have been undone or limited in their scope. The number of women running under the LDP label in the district races has more than doubled, but the actual numbers of LDP (and opposition party) representatives is still quite low. Thus, many of Koizumi's reforms with respect to women's representation have rung hollow. This tendency is only exacerbated by the Japanese electoral rule that party list candidates can be double listed and run in the districts. Some of Koizumi's women were guaranteed high and protected spots on the party lists, but in future elections, most of these privileged candidates will revert to ordinary status and be forced to run in districts while being double listed in a tied position with all of the other LDP candidates running in that region. Even Koizumi's symbolic efforts will be easily undone by this rule and norms of fairness that will push Koizumi's successors to take away the privileged status of some of these women candidates. The double-listing provision will also make it difficult for the LDP to assign even greater numbers of its party list seats to women because many of those positions have to go to the double-listed candidates, and if there still are few women running as LDP candidates in the single-seat districts, it will become almost impossible for women to take a larger share of the LDP's party list seats.

However, my skepticism of the LDP's new-found support of women should not be interpreted as a claim that the LDP is hostile to the cause of women's representation. The LDP and its predecessors have a commendable record (for Japan) of supporting women candidates on the party lists. The LDP's record is poor only in the districts where campaign imperatives make it difficult to find strong women candidates for those districts. Even this limitation, however, is changing as the role of Japanese women in all aspects of society is changing. There are now more women in high bureaucratic positions and working as lawyers. There are now more women serving in prominent local political positions. In addition, it is now accepted for a woman to inherit her father's personal support network, and several of the LDP's women incumbents in districts are women who inherited a personal support organization. Each of these changes opens the door for more women to be recruited and successfully run in the single-seat district races. Furthermore, Koizumi's efforts have created a class of women incumbents who will not simply disappear when he retires from the prime ministership. These women are well positioned to maintain their offices, even if they are removed from privileged positions on the LDP party list. Finally, the LDP cannot ignore the appeal of women candidates in helping to project an image of an LDP that is reforming and is open to new ideas and new candidates. The campaign tactic of using women candidates to appeal to unaffiliated voters that Koizumi has used so effectively will likely be available and be used by his successor.

Notes

1. These target districts were the districts in which LDP incumbents were expelled from the party after they defected from the party on a crucial legislative vote, prompting the 2005 election. Koizumi personally recruited challengers to run on the LDP label against these renegade members of the party.
2. Reed (2003: 18) explains why different names exist for the same electoral system. In addition, there have been some exceptions to the rule that the districts were of

a three- to five-seat magnitude. In the last years of the SNTV system, some two-and-six seat districts were created, and one single seat district existed from 1954 to 1990.

3. The first elections in the 1990s had regions with slightly larger magnitudes, ranging from seven to thirty-three seats.

4. I have included party list data for Japanese upper house elections (House of Councilors) even though that house is not the focus of this chapter. I do this because, prior to 1996, the only party lists drawn up in elections were those for the House of Councilors and using this data makes it possible to compare LDP and opposition attitudes toward women candidates on party lists.

5. The number of women in four-year university courses is less than the number of men, but when women attending two-year college programs are included, the percentage of women attending postsecondary education is equal to that of men.

Conclusion

Manon Tremblay

The general objective of *Women and Legislative Representation: Electoral Systems, Political Parties and Sex Quotas* was to examine the effects of voting systems on the proportion of women in national parliaments, while also evaluating the role of other variables (cultural, socioeconomic, and political). To do this, 15 countries were studied. These were divided among the following three electoral families: (1) plurality/majority systems: Uganda, United Kingdom and the United States (all First Past the Post [FPTP]); Afghanistan (Single Non-Transferable Vote); France (Two-Round System); and Australia (Alternative Vote); (2) proportional systems: South Africa and Spain (Closed List PR); and Belgium, Ireland and Peru (Preferential [Open] List PR and Single Transferable Vote [STV]); and (3) mixed-member systems: Mexico and New Zealand (proportional [MMP]); Hungary (majoritarian with partial compensation); and Japan (majoritarian [MMM]).

The analytical approach adopted in this work was to look more closely at the influence of voting systems on the proportion of female legislators. The main idea that inspired the work was that voting systems do not automatically determine the proportion of women parliamentarians. Although they are of fundamental importance in influencing the degree of feminization of parliaments, and although some characteristics intrinsic to voting systems may in themselves influence the proportion of women legislators, voting systems are not independent of their contexts. Indeed, voting systems interact with a host of cultural, socioeconomic, and political variables, thus creating an entire dynamic influencing the feminization of parliaments. This approach acknowledges the effects of electoral mechanisms, but assumes dynamic interactions between voting systems and other factors (and notably political parties and sex quotas).

The chapters in this book have not only facilitated an assessment of the heuristic value of this approach in understanding the proportion of women in parliaments but have also served to refine it. This exercise has produced four findings. First, it is clear that voting systems have a major influence on the proportion of women in parliaments. This is to be expected, given that electoral systems have the important task of distributing parliamentary seats among the political parties and among female and male candidates who have courted the electorate and won its support. However, except where the preferential vote is practiced, the prior choice of which individuals are given the chance to contest these seats is exercised by the parties themselves. As Norris (2000: 350) writes, "By itself the electoral system is neither a necessary nor a sufficient condition to guarantee women's representation." In other words, in a strict sense, the voting system is an accessory mechanism in the feminization of parliaments, but a mechanism of primary importance nonetheless.

The second finding, building upon the preceding point, is that it is impossible to understand the effects of voting systems on the feminization of parliaments without taking into account the role played by political parties and sex quotas. Indeed, it is the political parties that truly orchestrate legislative representation, including its degree of feminization. In other words, electoral systems and political parties work in tandem to define the composition of legislative assemblies, the former influencing the strategies, decisions, and actions of the latter. In her contribution to this book, Magda Hinojosa writes, "Proportional representation only affects the political party as it decides the candidates that it will propose and increases the odds that a party becomes 'more conscious of balancing its ticket.'" Indeed, of all the cultural, socioeconomic, and political factors affecting the election of women to legislative assemblies, parties are surely the most influential variable. However, the influence of parties on the feminization of parliaments varies according to electoral rules, parties' ideological orientations, the culture of the society in general, and women's movement mobilizations, among many other elements. Party influence also varies according to another crucial tool: sex quotas. However, sex quotas do not automatically result in a high proportion of female parliamentarians. In fact, as several chapters in this work have shown, sex quotas must possess certain features, such as placement requirements and sanctions for infringement, in order to improve the likelihood that women will be elected. For sex quotas to be effective, it is also essential that parties comply in good faith with the spirit of the measures.

The third finding is that socioeconomic factors have perhaps the least definitive effect on women's access to parliaments. Indeed, it would be reckless to claim the existence of any clear relationship between a high percentage of women parliamentarians and a high level of socioeconomic development. Although the evidence from some Northern European countries is consistent with such a relationship, the case of South Africa suggests a need for caution. France, Japan, the United Kingdom, and the United States of America, which have in common a high level of socioeconomic development and a low proportion of female legislators, provide further evidence that there is no consistent and significant relationship between these two variables.

The fourth and final finding is that cultural factors play a role that is ambiguous and still poorly defined but nevertheless very important in the feminization of parliaments. Of course, like socioeconomic factors, cultural factors do not make up a homogenous whole, with certain cultural and socioeconomic factors having a greater influence in determining the percentage of women parliamentarians than other factors. Notably, a cultural factor that seems to positively contribute to women's access to legislative assemblies is the acceptance within a society of the value of equality between women and men. The following pages are devoted to looking more closely at these findings, beginning with the impact of the electoral system.

The Impact of the Voting System on the Proportion of Women in the Legislature

As mentioned in the Introduction and as several of the contributors to this book also observed, plurality/majority electoral systems are less likely to promote women's legislative representation than list PR systems (see among others Norris 1997a, 2004: 187). Evidence from various countries studied in this volume contradicts this general statistical relationship: Hungary (MMM with partial compensation), Ireland (STV), and Japan (MMM) all have smaller proportions of women parliamentarians than the United Kingdom and the United States (both of which use FPTP). Moreover, in Scotland and Wales, more women were elected under the majoritarian tier of the mixed-member system than under the PR one. For Childs, Campbell, and Lovenduski, the experiences of Scotland and Wales "provide additional evidence against those who contend that there is always a positive relationship between proportional electoral systems and higher levels of women's numerical representation." The case of New Zealand (where the proportion of women parliamentarians was high even before the country adopted a MMP system) also supports the argument of those who caution against equating PR with a high percentage of women in parliament. Hence it is necessary to avoid generalizations and to adopt, instead, a microanalytical perspective more suited to capturing the details that, in the technical design of the plurality/majority, PR, and mixed-member electoral systems, can explain deviations from expected outcomes.

Gallagher and Mitchell (2005a: 5–15) suggest analyzing and comparing the voting systems in light of six dimensions: proportionality, district magnitude, levels of seat allocation, number of votes cast, ballot structure, and finally parties' selection of candidate. The next section will deal with the first five of these dimensions; the last is analyzed in the final section of this concluding chapter.

Proportionality

Proportionality refers to the match between the percentage of valid votes cast by the electorate to each of the various political parties and the percentage of seats in parliament that each party ultimately holds. As mentioned in the Introduction to this book, a high proportionality of seats to votes favours a higher percentage of female legislators (Farrell 2001: 157–159, 166; Norris 1992). Meier's chapter in this book examines this aspect of the impact of voting systems on the feminization of parliament: she finds that the high proportionality of the Belgian regime favours the election of women. Future studies should further explore the role played by disproportionality in determining the proportion of women MPs. As Farrell (2001: 166) reasons, proportionality is intimately linked to the type of voting system (plurality/majority, PR, or mixed). I suspect, therefore, that the level of proportionality per se has less influence on the proportion of women legislators than do the other characteristics inherent in the various types of electoral system. For example, in South Africa, where the disproportionality between votes and seats is very low (0.3 according to Gallagher and Mitchell [2005d: 621]) and where there women make up 32.8 percent of the National Assembly, Hannah E. Britton maintains that this high level of women's representation is due less to the voting system (a Closed List PR) than to the quota policy adopted by the African National Congress (ANC).

District Magnitude

This measure refers to the number of seats per constituency. While the 15 case studies in this volume present no consensus on the factors that shape women's parliamentary representation, very low district magnitude (especially where there is just one representative per electoral riding) emerges as a factor that consistently limits women's access to parliaments (see the chapters on France and the United States). This finding supports the idea that majoritarian systems, which are mostly single seat, impede the election of women. The problem is accentuated by a decentralized process of candidate recruitment (as in France), which favours the selection of either incumbent MPs or of prominent local persons able to accumulate many representative mandates. However, the case study on the United Kingdom shows that the freedom of local riding associations to choose their candidates for a legislative election can be circumscribed; political parties' national executives can make their objectives known when it comes to gender equity representation by developing detailed rules for framing the candidature selection process and by establishing approved lists of nominees from which each association must choose its candidates. National executives can even set aside for women the ridings that are most promising for victory (as in the United Kingdom's all-women short lists). It is sufficient for political parties to have a real desire to make room for women, a desire that, as Mariette Sineau reminds us, was painfully lacking in France. (I will return to this point later.) Reserved seats are another strategy used to sidestep the difficulties that single-seat constituencies cause for the feminization of parliaments. However, the experience of Uganda suggests that this strategy has more negative than positive effects on the parliamentary representation of women, notably in terms of the legitimacy and influence of those women who do enter parliament in this way.

Single-seat constituencies pose another challenge to the feminization of legislative assemblies: this is the low turnover rate of MPs that is common in such electoral districts. However, as Donley T. Studlar notes in his study of the United States, stimulating turnover in parliaments by imposing term limits does not necessarily translate into an increase in the proportion of female legislators.

Since single-seat constituencies involve a form of competition that is unfavourable for the election of women, it is just a small step to concluding that multimember districts promote women's electoral success. This idea is widespread in literature on women and electoral politics. Again, a more nuanced approach to this general rule is required, as shown by the chapters on Japan and Peru. Moreover, the cases of Ireland and Spain show not only that small- and medium-sized districts do not necessarily disadvantage women, but also that women sometimes perform better in such constituencies than in large electoral districts.

This measure of district magnitude is closely paralleled by that of party magnitude. The latter refers to the number of seats a political party can hope to win in any given electoral district. According to Matland (2006), party magnitude has more influence on the election of women to parliament than district magnitude. Indeed, a high party magnitude delivers seats to candidates further down the party's list, reaching the middle or end, where women are frequently listed. Petra Meier proposes the same observation for Belgium, as does Jennifer Curtin for New Zealand. However, Curtin shows that, in the MMP context, the process does not work exactly as predicted by Matland's general reasoning: because it is difficult for small political parties to win seats in the local tier, intraparty competition for the top list positions becomes tougher and such a struggle can disadvantage women. Britton (South Africa) also notes the negative impact of multiplication of small political parties in parliament on the election of women. This observation reminds us that, as Ferrara, Herron, and Nishikawa (2005: 139) conclude, it is inaccurate to conceive of mixed-member systems as just two tiers (one majoritarian and one PR) immune from crossover; in reality each tier is influenced by the other to create an electoral dynamic that belongs uniquely to mixed-member voting systems. More studies are required to better understand this dynamic of interaction inherent in mixed-member systems and its consequences for the election of women to parliaments.

Levels of Seat Allocation

Legislative seats are allocated to districts at various levels: these are the local (as in FPTP systems), regional (such as Mexico), and national (as in New Zealand) tiers. As mentioned previously, in theory, a high district magnitude favours the election of women (though Matland [2006] argues that party magnitude is more important). Consequently, the national tier should offer better chances of electoral success to women than the regional tier, which, in turn, should offer better chances than the local tier. Case studies in this book challenge rather than confirm this reasoning—and, as a result, indirectly support Matland's (2006) point of view. In Hungary, it is in the regional tier rather than the national one that women most successfully access its national legislature. However, the regional tiers of the Japanese and Mexican mixed-member systems yield the opposite results, with fewer women elected to these tiers than the national ones (though Mexico has sex quotas, which is not the case in Japan).

The diversity of findings presented here means we are not able to make a conclusive statement about the impact of levels of seat allocation on the election of women. This reinforces the idea that animates the work as a whole: that voting systems do not automatically determine the proportion of women in parliaments. In other words, national tiers do not automatically give rise to higher percentages of women than regional and local tiers. Again, we must avoid simplistic reasoning that is unable to grasp the complexity of voting systems and their influence on women's parliamentary representation. It remains to be determined precisely why it is not possible to discern a consistent relationship between seat allocation and the percentage of women MPs. This is an excellent subject for further research.

The Number of Votes Cast (One, Two, or More)

In several countries, each voter holds just one vote, which can sometimes create a dilemma: if a voter entrusts her unique vote to a female candidate, she cannot also support a male candidate. This might be interpreted (or manipulated) to mean that "a vote for a woman is a vote lost for a man." Voting systems in which each voter has two votes sidestep this pitfall. Indeed, in his chapter on Peru, Gregory Schmidt explains that when voters have two votes, it is possible to avoid this electoral zero-sum game between women and men by developing a message that promotes an equitable share of these two votes between a female and a male candidates. In Afghanistan, where each voter casts just one vote for the many seats to be filled in each electoral district, Andrea Fleschenberg remarks that the impact of this single vote system on women's representation remains to be seen. In Japan, Raymond Christensen suggests that the double-listing provision may penalize women candidates (notably those running under the hegemonic Liberal Democratic Party ticket).

It is clear that further studies are necessary to better understand the relationship between the number of votes each voter holds and the number of seats to be filled, in terms of the impact this has on women's access to parliaments. Is the electorate more inclined to vote for women if it can simultaneously entrust other votes to men? And does it become more difficult to do so if each voter has only one vote to fill many seats? What influence do variables such as gender/feminist consciousness, party identification, and the cultural and socioeconomic profile of the voter have on voters' decisions about whether to vote for a woman or not when each voter holds more than one vote? Do these variables exercise the same influence when each voter holds only one vote? In mixed-member systems, is the electorate more inclined to vote for a man in the majority representation tier (this type of seat is sometimes seen as being more professional than list seats because the latter are dedicated to the representation of "minority groups" such as women) but to indirectly support a woman in the PR tier by voting for a party that presents a strong contingent of female candidates on its list?

Ballot Structure

Gallagher and Mitchell (2005a: 7–10) distinguish three types of ballot structure: (1) nominal, in which voters choose one candidate (as is the case in FPTP), one list (as in South Africa and Spain), or one or even several candidates on the same list (as in Belgium); (2) rank-ordering, where the voter must rate candidates' names by order of preference (as in Australia and Ireland); and (3) "dividual," which allows voters to allocate their votes to many political formations, whether within one tier or two tiers (as in New Zealand, where voters can entrust their votes to one party in the FPTP tier and to another party in the PR tier). Again, further research is necessary to understand the role of ballot structure in the election of women to parliaments—a task no study has yet tackled in any systematic way. However, a number of the chapters in this volume cast some light on this aspect of the conditions under which women access national parliaments.

One argument widely employed in the literature on women and electoral politics to explain how PR systems give rise to more feminized parliaments than plurality/majority systems is that, under a nominal ballot structure, political parties may constitute sociodemographically diverse lists of candidates. Many of the chapters in this book support this argument. By contrast, the Irish system uses a rank-ordering ballot structure: STV prevails and voters must classify their choices according to first, second, third, etc., preference. Yvonne Galligan observes that, although the electorate does not negatively discriminate against female candidates, their low numbers mean that the negative effects of a swing against a party are accentuated for women. In Australia, where each voter must order her several electoral preferences on an alternative vote ballot, Ian McAllister suggests that these obligations have favoured the rise of strong and disciplined parties, which has in turn promoted women's access to the House of Representatives (at least for the Labor Party).

The question of ballot structure raises the further issue of whether closed or open lists most favour the election of women. It is widely thought that closed lists are most favourable to women because they allow groups of women to more easily and effectively pressure parties to include female candidates on their lists and, as a result, allow the electorate to evaluate more easily the diversity of their lists. Although Matland has previously endorsed the view that closed lists are favorable to women (see Matland 1998b), he has recently changed his mind, arguing that "the use of preferential voting, i.e. open lists, is unlikely to dramatically hurt women in most cases" (Matland 2006: 286; see also Matland 2005: 105–106). In short, the results of studies that have examined this question remain extremely contradictory and inconclusive. This work presents findings that indicate a similar ambivalence. For example, the contributions on South Africa and Spain suggest that closed lists are favourable to women, while the chapter on Peru finds open lists favourable to women in that country.

This section on the impact of the voting system on the proportion of women in the legislature was organized into five dimensions, which may be further aggregated into two groups: on the one hand, we have examined those factors that regulate voters' votes (i.e., the number of votes cast and the ballot structure) and, on the other hand, we have inquired into those factors that govern competition between parties (i.e., proportionality, district magnitude, and levels of seat allocation). The next section deals with the sixth dimension that Gallagher and Mitchell (2005a: 10–11) distinguished in analyzing and comparing voting systems: competition within parties. It is through understanding this aspect that it has become increasingly obvious that the electoral system does not automatically determine the proportion of women in parliaments, but rather that the effects of the voting system are conditioned by cultural, socioeconomic, and political factors. Political parties are the most important of these factors, particularly in terms of the parameters that guide them in distributing candidacies and seats to men and women. Here, sex quotas play an important role, too.

The Impact of Other Variables on the Proportion of Women in Legislature

As mentioned earlier, the analytical approach taken in this book is to suppose that voting systems do not automatically determine the proportion of women in parliaments; this is to assume that they are, in fact, part of a more global dynamic involving the interactions of voting systems with a host of cultural, socioeconomic, and political factors. The case studies gathered here shed light on the importance of political factors—especially voting systems, parties and sex quotas—in the composition of parliamentary assemblies. The impact of these factors is most strongly felt in the selection of candidates, as many studies have already shown (see, notably, Caul Kittilson 2006; Matland 2005; Norris 1997d; Lovenduski and Norris 1993; Norris and Lovenduski 1995). It is the parties that establish the demand for candidates to fill legislatures and it is also the parties that orchestrate the (necessarily limited) supply of candidates among whom voters must choose. Indeed, the pitfalls encountered by women wishing to be selected by a party cast light on a paradox intrinsic to democratic representation: although in practice one of their missions is the management of democracy, political parties are not, themselves, particularly democratic organizations.

In single-seat constituencies (as in Australia, France, the United Kingdom, and the United States), problems arise from the fact that a political party can present just one candidate per electoral district. Consequently, parties select either the person already in place (i.e., the incumbent MP) who, by definition, has proven her or his ability to win elections, or a person aspiring to election who is seen by the party as being likely to win the contest. Norris and Lovenduski (1989) suggest that a political party will conduct this selection according to a model of *homo politicus:* in other words, the ideal type of candidate whose "neutral" characteristics correspond more with men's experiences and attributes than women's (see also Reynolds, Reilly, and Ellis 2005: 37, 61). Sometimes, as Mariette Sineau observes, parties select women but proceed to sacrifice them in lost-cause constituencies. Nonetheless, in their chapter Childs, Campbell, and Lovenduski maintain that we must not conclude that single-seat constituencies are intrinsically hostile to the election of women, especially where political parties have a sincere desire to share their parliamentary representation between women and men. As they argue, "[T]he United Kingdom's system of majoritarian election may be particularly conducive as it is unlikely that voters will choose not to vote for the party of their choice just because its candidate is female."

Conversely, the requirement for a party to present a plurality of candidates is no guarantee that it will select women. Indeed, as Curtin observes about the New Zealand experience, political parties do not always fulfil the expectations others have of them: "In the campaign for electoral reform, there had been an expectation that the introduction of the party list vote would force political parties to select a balanced list to attract voters[. . .]. However, there was no uniform response from the parties on this issue." Of course, parties do select women but too often place them in noncompetitive positions on their lists—in other words, where they cannot be elected. Although many of the chapters in this book highlight political parties' negligence, the case of France is a particularly obvious (and sad) illustration of this: at the 1986 election, this country, the birthplace of human rights, returned to a list-based proportional representation system and the proportion of female candidates increased considerably from the preceding election held under a majoritarian voting system (from 11.9 percent to 24.7 percent). Yet the proportion of women elected increased only slightly (from 5.3 percent to 5.9 percent). It can also happen that parties simply "deselect" women, withdrawing a woman's status as its official legislative candidate, as we learned in the chapter on Hungary.

Childs, Campbell, and Lovenduski are accurate in their assessment that the goodwill required for political parties to open their parliamentary wings to women depends on parties' ideological positions. To begin with, if the representation of minorities (and especially women) is not on the political agenda, it is likely that parties will feel no obligation to open up to women, a fact emphasized by the chapter on Hungary. Moreover, in a general way, right-wing political parties demonstrate resistance to the inclusion of women among their ranks, while this is certainly less so in leftist parties (see the chapters on New Zealand, Spain, and the United Kingdom, among others). As long as the political structure is dominated by right-leaning parties, as is the case in Ireland or the United States, for example, there is little chance of seeing the proportion of women parliamentarians increase.

Several of the case studies presented in this work have referred to women's (or feminist) political parties. But we must acknowledge the negligible and only momentary influence of this strategy on women's access to parliaments. Of course, as Meier recognizes, electoral success is not the objective of these political formations. In reality, women's parties are put in place for other reasons, for example, to foster debate and stimulate the mobilization of women within parties and civil society. In Belgium, the Verenigde Feministische Partij—Parti Unifié Féministe caused political parties to position women in eligible places on their lists. Nonetheless, it remains the case that women's parties rarely overcome certain disadvantages (e.g., the need to divide feminist energies between formal political institutions and mobilizations in civil society), and players in politics and public opinion often marginalize and even ostracize these parties, which, in turn, helps to undermine their credibility and legitimacy.

The degree to which the candidate selection process is centralized must also be taken into account in understanding the role that parties play in the feminization of parliaments. The chapters on New Zealand and the United Kingdom—countries with centralized party systems for candidate selection— provide evidence for the view that such processes favours women. Conversely, the cases of Mexico and the United States—where parties use decentralized primaries that nullify any attempts to impose sex quotas—also support the idea that there is a relationship between centralization of candidate selection and the election of women. Hinojosa explains that, leading up to the Mexican elections of 2003, the three main political parties turned to primary elections to select a large majority of their candidates, an option that freed them of the obligation to respect the law on sex quotas. Moreover, parties form systems; they do not act independently of one another. The chapter on Hungary demonstrates the negative impact that a still-developing and nonconsolidated party system has on women aspiring to be (s)elected.

Because the election of women is not necessarily assisted by political parties playing more passive roles in the selection of legislative candidates, parties' influences on the feminization of parliamentary assemblies must be viewed in more nuanced ways. We must, in fact, admit that other factors also hinder a more balanced division of parliamentary seats between women and men. Indeed, although political parties are an important variable in all analytical models used to explain the proportion of female legislators, they cannot account for everything. How else could we explain, for example, cases where parties play a negligible role in the selection of candidates (as in Japan's majoritarian seats and in the United States) but which nevertheless produce a low proportion of women MPs? Studlar braves likely criticism by suggesting that part of the explanation of the low presence of women in politics may reside in women themselves. It is to these other factors—political, cultural, and socioeconomic—that will now turn our attention.

Two political factors clearly have an impact on the proportion of women parliamentarians: sex quotas and women's movement's mobilizations to increase the number of women in politics. Dahlerup (2006a) recently produced a comprehensive book on sex quotas and their roles in the feminization of parliaments; I will not repeat this material here. It will be sufficient to highlight a few of her points. The first is that sex quotas can be very effective tools in increasing the proportion of women in parliaments. For this to be the case, however, quotas must be used in a context that maximizes their positive results. According to Matland (2006), this requires a voting system that generates high party magnitudes, rules regulating the placement of candidates on lists (although Meier shows that this requirement can sometimes miss its mark), and political parties that prove their goodwill by applying sex quotas. The cases of France and Hungary clearly illustrate that adopting sex quotas is not in itself sufficient to immediately increase the number of female legislators. These case studies also show that without collaboration from the parties (sometimes requiring sanctions for noncompliance), sex quotas may be useless in working toward this goal.

A second lesson is that the efficacy of quotas in feminizing parliaments does not stem from their intrinsic nature—that is, whether they are legal (under constitutional or electoral law) or voluntary party quotas. As Dahlerup (2006c: 304) argues, "Voluntary party quotas can be just as efficient as legal quotas, but rely on constant good faith compliance of the party leadership" (see also Davidson-Schmich 2006). As the cases of South Africa, Spain and the United Kingdom show, a party quota adopted by a major political party can translate into a substantial improvement in the proportion of women parliamentarians. In New Zealand, there is an informal quota measure (called a "soft quota" by Krook, Lovenduski, and Squires [2006]) according to which the selection committee must "pause for thought" after each block of five candidatures to make sure the candidate list fairly reflects the composition of society and its various groups. This measure has had positive results in the feminization of the House of Representatives. On the other hand, the case of France reminds us that a legal quota (i.e., a binding quota under constitutional or electoral law) is no guarantee that more women will obtain seats in parliaments. Without being cynical, I must say there is an important study yet to be conducted on the strategies that political parties around the world use to escape legal quotas, in contempt of the spirit of these measures. As Sineau notes, in anticipation of the legislative elections of 2002, the French political parties based their candidate selection strategies on the following principle: "better to pay a fine than field a female candidate." A study of such strategies would lead to a better understanding of how parties sidestep sex quotas and would thus help activists and academics to develop responses to such acts of bad faith, in order to eventually increase the presence of women in parliaments.

A third and final point is that sex quotas are not limited to Closed List PR voting systems, but rather can be adopted in plurality/majority systems. This is seen in Australia (where the Labor Party adopted a quota for legislative candidates), France (where state subsidies are reduced when the percentage difference between parties' female and male candidates exceeds 2 percent), Uganda (which has reserved seats for women), and the United Kingdom (where there are all-women shortlists, and where, in Scotland and Wales, the equality measures implemented in the plurality tier have made it possible to reach new levels in the descriptive representation of women). In these countries, sex quotas have limited the negative effects of majoritarian systems on the election of women. The case of Peru reveals that it is possible to adopt sex quotas in a context where open lists are used, and that such quotas can indeed be effective. A few experiences (notably those of Belgium and South Africa) show that sex quotas can have a contagion effect.

The other political factor that has an impact on the proportion of women in parliaments is the mobilization of a country's women's movement, whether within political parties or civil society. Mexico, New Zealand, Spain, and the United Kingdom are places where women have successfully mobilized within political parties to promote the goal of further feminizing the legislature; Australia, South Africa, Uganda, and the United States are examples of countries where these mobilizations have occurred in civil society. This activism inside and beyond political parties is often directed at promoting sex quotas and fortifying the financial capacities of women wishing to take the leap into politics (as in Australia and the United States). There are also countries where the women's movement has hardly mobilized on electoral turf (in Hungary, for example).

The case studies in this book have also allowed us to examine a whole range of political factors that, depending on the specific contexts of each country, improve or limit women's abilities to be elected to national parliaments: among others, a postconflict climate favourable to the political involvement of women (Afghanistan, South Africa, and Uganda); a low turnover rate that has the same effect by limiting the number of competitive ridings (the United Kingdom and the United States); electoral financing procedures that only a certain profile of candidate (typically male) can satisfy (Japan); a bipartisan system that reduces women's chances by heightening the competitiveness of parliamentary seats (Hungary and the United States); a redefinition of electoral ridings that favours incumbent MPs, who are mostly men (United States); a feminization of leadership that, by offering models, can promote the political roles of women (New Zealand and Peru); and a leader or political party that, for various reasons, wants to increase the presence of women in legislative assemblies (Japan and Peru). It goes without saying that other studies are necessary to identify and better understand the political factors that favor or work against the election of women to parliaments.

As mentioned at the opening of this Conclusion, socioeconomic factors have perhaps the least clear influence on women's access to parliamentary arenas. This is unsurprising, given that statistical studies analyzing the impact of a range of socioeconomic variables on the election of women have produced contradictory results (see among others Moore and Shackman 1996; Norris 2004: 186; Oakes and Almquist 1993; Paxton 1997; Reynolds 1999; Tremblay 2007). Commenting on the case of South Africa, Britton goes as far as to state that "socioeconomic development is not essential for democracy." Japan also offers a counter example: a highly socioeconomically developed country with just 9.4 percent of seats in its Diet filled by women, in 2007 Japan is ranked one hundred and first out of 189 in the Inter-Parliamentary Union's (IPU's) classification of the proportion of women the lower or single houses parliaments. The same point can be made in relation to France (with women making up just 12.2 percent of the Assemblée nationale, France occupies the eighty-eighth position in the IPU ranking), the United Kingdom (19.7 percent; fifty-fourth position), and the United States (16.3 percent, seventieth position).

Despite contradictory evidence at the general level, several of the contributions in this book find explanations for the low parliamentary representation of women in particular socioeconomic factors. Thus, the authors of the chapters on Japan and the United Kingdom point out that in their countries women always trail behind men in terms of many socioeconomic indicators, such as participation in the labour force, access to the prestigious professions that are typical of career paths leading into politics, and wealth. Moreover, a gender division of labour exists almost everywhere in the world, under which women do the majority of child rearing and homemaking activities. Women also tend to reproduce these private tasks in their salaried activities, a phenomenon Sapiro (1984) calls the privatization of women. For all these reasons, women have fewer resources (financial, of course, but also in terms of time, networks, and so on) to invest in politics. In Uganda, for example, Gretchen Bauer explains that female candidates face obvious disadvantages; with fewer resources and no history of past favours or services to constituents, candidates are not able to win votes in situations where a certain amount of generosity is expected of them. In sum, a review of studies on the impact of socioeconomic factors on the percentage of women in legislatures indicates that there is a lack of consensus on these effects. Yet neither can we claim that these factors have no influence. Additional study is therefore most definitely necessary.

By contrast, there is little doubt about the impact of cultural factors on women's access to parliaments. For example, the chapter on France highlights the fact that women's more restricted access to education (notably to the *grandes écoles,* which are important pools for political recruitment) limits their ability to be elected to politics. Presenting politics as a setting that is more suited to men than to women, gender roles are influential in turning away those women who might otherwise wish to take on representative mandates in parliament (see the chapters on Afghanistan, Belgium, France, Ireland, Japan, and Uganda, for example). In the same vein, many authors (including those presenting case studies in this volume on Australia, Peru, South Africa, Spain, and the United States) see social acceptance of egalitarian gender roles as an important factor partly explaining the political success of women. This is an observation that appears in several other studies as well (Inglehart and Norris 2003: 140; Norris and Inglehart 2005; Paxton and Kunovich 2003). In part, it is the heightened awareness of the inequalities women face that have allowed measures favouring the election of women to be adopted, as we saw in the case of Afghanistan. Religion is another cultural factor that impedes women's full participation in politics (see the contribution on Spain, for example). This telling excerpt from the chapter on Afghanistan clearly illustrates the barriers posed by a patriarchal interpretation of religion and gender roles: "I am under a *burqa;* people cannot recognise me. Men can go to the mosque and talk in public. Women must talk to individuals. You cannot have that same large gathering." Added to this are the threats made against the physical safety of defiant women: threats that are motivated by the conviction that a woman's place is not in the Wolesi Jirga.

In sum, this work has sought to provide a more nuanced analysis of what is often seen as a direct connection between voting systems and the proportion of women legislators. In particular, it is common within the field of women and electoral politics to encounter the belief that PR systems are synonymous with high proportions of women in legislatures and that the reverse is true for majoritarian systems. In fact, things are much more complicated. If this book has at all challenged this simplistic but nevertheless popular reasoning, then it has succedeed in its goal.

Bibliography

Abirafeh, Lina. 2005. "Lessons from Gender-Focused International Aid in Post-Conflict Afghanistan … Learned?" *Series Gender in International Cooperation* 7. Bonn: Friedrich-Ebert-Stiftung. http://www.library.fes.de/pdf-files/iez/02978.pdf (accessed July 2006).

Achin, Catherine. 2005. *Le "mystère de la chambre basse": Comparaison des processus d'entrée des femmes au Parlement. France-Allemagne, 1945–1952* [The "mystery of the lower house" : A comparison of women's entry process into parliament. France-Germany, 1945–1952]. Paris: Dalloz.

Ágora Democrática. 2007. *Un vistazo a la participación política de la mujer* [An overview of women's political participation]. Ágora Democrática: Lima.

Ahikire, Josephine. 2004. "Towards Women's Effective Participation in Electoral Processes: A Review of the Ugandan Experience." *Feminist Africa*, 3. http://www.feministafrica.org/03-2004/2level.html (accessed April 2007).

Aimer, Peter. 1997. "Leaders and Outcomes: The Clark Factor in 1996." In *From Campaign to Coalition: The 1996 MMP Election*, edited by Jonathan Boston, Stephen Levine, Elizabeth McLeay, and Nigel Roberts, pp. 129–144. Palmerston North: Dunmore.

Almunia, Joaquín. 2001. *Memorias políticas* [Political memoires]. Madrid: Punto de Lectura.

American National Election Studies. http://www.electionstudies.org (accessed April 2007).

Amnesty International. 2005. "Women Fight for Rights in Afghan Elections." *The Wire*, October. http://www.amnesty.org/web/wire.nsf/print/October2005Afghanistan (accessed July 2006).

Andersen, Kristi, and Stuart J. Thorson. 1984. "Congressional Turnover and the Election of Women." *Western Political Quarterly* 37, no. 1:143–156.

Antić, Milica G. 2003. "Factors Influencing Women's Presence in Slovene Parliament." In *Women's Access to Political Power in Post-Communist Europe*, edited by Richard E. Matland and Kathleen A. Montgomery, pp. 267–284. Oxford: Oxford University Press.

Arredondo, Estela. 1982. *Sociedad, política y estado* [Society, politics, and the state]. Mexico City: Centro de Investigación y Docencia Economicas.

Asahi Senkyo Taikan. Various years. Tokyo: Asahi Shimbunsha.

Asahi Shimbun. Tokyo, Japan. Various issues.

Asia Foundation. 2004. *Voter Education Planning Survey: Afghanistan 2004 National Elections. A Report Based on a Public Opinion Poll*, July. http://www.asiafoundation.org/pdf/afghan_voter-ed04.pdf (accessed July 2006).

Asian Network for Free Elections (ANFREL). 2005. *ANFREL's Preliminary Statement on Wolesi Jirga and Provincial Council Elections.* http://www.anfrel.org (accessed July 2006).

Astelarra, Judith. 2005. *Veinte años de políticas de igualdad* [Twenty years of gender equality policies]. Madrid: Cátedra.

Baldauf, Scott. 2006. "Afghan Parliament Debates Chaperones for Women." *Christian Science Monitor*, February 15. http://www.csmonitor.com/2006/0215/p04s01-wosc.htm (accessed July 2006).

———. 2005. "Afghan Ballots Carry Mullahs, Jihadis, Women." *Christian Science Monitor*, July 15. http://www.csmonitor.com/2005/0915/p01s03-wosc.html (accessed July 2006).

Baldez, Lisa. 2004a. "Elected Bodies: The Gender Quota Law for Legislative Candidates in Mexico." *Legislative Studies Quarterly* 29, no. 2:231–258.

———. 2004b. "Elected Bodies II: The Impact of Gender Quotas in Mexico." Paper presented at the "Pathways to Power: Political Recruitment and Democracy in Latin America Conference," Wake Forest University, April 2–4. http://www.wfu.edu/politics/conference/baldezWFU.pdf (accessed April 2007).

Ballington, Julie. 2005. "Ten Years of Progress: Enhancing Women's Political Participation." In International IDEA, *Ten Years of Supporting Democracy Worldwide*, pp. 113–124. Stockholm: International IDEA.

———. ed. 2004. *The Implementation of Quotas: African Experiences.* Stockholm: International IDEA.

———. 1999. "Party Representation—The Women's Profile." In *The Election Bulletin*, 6th ed. (1) Women's Net, August. http://www.womensnet.org.za/election/eb6-esystem.htm (accessed November 2000).

Ballington, Julie, and Richard Matland. 2004. *Political Parties and Special Measures: Enhancing Women's Participation in Electoral Processes.* Geneva: United Nations, Office of the Special Adviser on Gender Issues and Advancement of Women. http://www.idea.int/gender/loader.cfm?url=/commonspot/security/getfile.cfm&PageID=3839 (accessed April 2007).

Barker, Fiona, Jonathan Boston, Stephen Levine, Elizabeth McLeay, and Nigel S. Roberts. 2001. "An Initial Assessment of the Consequences of MMP in New Zealand." In *Mixed-Member Electoral Systems: The Best of Both Worlds?* edited by Matthew Soberg Shugart and Martin P. Wattenberg, pp. 297–322. New York: Oxford University Press.

Bauer, Gretchen. 2008. "'50/50 by 2020': Comparing Electoral Gender Quotas for Parliament in East and Southern Africa." *International Feminist Journal of Politics* (forthcoming).

Bauer, Gretchen, and Hannah E. Britton, eds. 2006a. *Women in African Parliaments.* Boulder, CO: Lynne Rienner.

———. 2006b. "Women in African Parliaments: A Continental Shift?" In *Women in African Parliaments*, edited by Gretchen Bauer and Hannah E. Britton, pp. 1–30. Boulder, CO: Lynne Rienner.

BBC News. 2005. "Afghan Election Guide." *BBC News Online*, October 3. http://news.bbc.co.uk/2/hi/south_asia/4251580.stm (accessed July 2006).

Beckwith, Karen. 1992. "Comparative Research and Electoral Systems: Lessons from France and Italy." *Women & Politics* 12, no.3: 1–33.

Beer, Caroline C. 2003. *Electoral Competition and Institutional Change in Mexico.* Notre Dame: University of Notre Dame Press.

Benoit, Kenneth. 2005. "Hungary: Holding Back the Tiers." In *The Politics of Electoral Systems*, edited by Michael Gallagher and Paul Mitchell, pp. 231–252. Oxford: Oxford University Press.

Berch, Neil. 1996. "The 'Year of the Woman' in Context: A Test of Six Explanations." *American Politics Quarterly* 24, no. 2:169–193.

Bledsoe, Timothy, and Mary Herring. 1990. "Victims of Circumstances: Women in Pursuit of Political Office." *American Political Science Review* 84, no. 1:213–223.

Blondet, Cecilia. 1999. *Percepción ciudadana sobre la participación de la mujer: El poder político en la mira de las mujeres* [Citizens' perceptions of women's participation: Political power in the cross hairs of women]. Lima: Instituto de Estudios Peruanos.

Blondet, Cecilia, and Carmen Montero. 1994. *La situación de la mujer en el Perú 1980–1994* [The situation of women in Peru, 1980–1994]. Lima: Instituto de Estudios Peruanos.

Britton, Hannah E. 2005. *From Resistance to Governance: Women in the South African Parliament.* Urbana: University of Illinois Press.

———. 2002. "Coalition Building, Election Rules, and Party Politics: South African Women's Path to Parliament." *Africa Today* 49, no. (4): 32–67.

———. 2001. "New Struggles, New Strategies: Emerging Patterns of Women's Political Participation in the South African Parliament." *International Politics* 38, no. 2:173–199.

Bruhn, Kathleen. 2003. "Whores and Lesbians: Political Activism, Party Strategies, and Gender Quotas in Mexico." *Electoral Studies* 22, no. 1:101–119.

Budge, Ian, Ivor Crewe, David Mckay, and Ken Newton. 2004. *The New British Politics.* London: Pearson Longman.

Burrell, Barbara. 2005 "Campaign Financing: Women's Experience in the Modern Era." In *Women and Elective Office: Past, Present, and Future*, 2nd ed., edited by Sue Thomas and Clyde Wilcox, pp. 26–40. New York: Oxford University Press.

Byanyima, W. Karagwa. 1992. "Women in Political Struggle in Uganda." In *Women Transforming Politics: Worldwide Strategies for Empowerment*, edited by Jill Bystydzienski, pp. 129–142. Bloomington: Indiana University Press.

Cahill-Kennedy, Mary T. 2004. *Equality for Women Measure Project Final Report.* Dublin: Fine Gael. http://www.ewm.ie (accessed April 2007).

Campbell, Rosie, Sarah Childs, and Joni Lovenduski. 2006 "Equality Guarantees and the Conservative Party." *Political Quarterly* 7, no. 1:18–27.

Campbell, Rosie, and Joni Lovenduski. 2005. "Winning Women's Votes." In *Britain Votes 2005*, edited by Pippa Norris and Christopher Wlezien, pp. 181–197. Oxford: Oxford University Press.

Carey, John M. 2005. "Legislative Organization." Draft paper, April. http://www.dartmouth.edu/~jcarey/Carey_Legis_Org.pdf (accessed July 2006).

Carey, John M., Richard G. Niemi, Lynda W. Powell, and Gary F. Moncrief. 2006. "The Effects of Term Limits on State Legislatures: A New Survey of the 50 States." *Legislative Studies Quarterly* 31, no. 1:105–134.

Carey, John M., and Matthew Soberg Shugart. 1995. "Incentives to Cultivate a Personal Vote: A Rank Ordering of Electoral Formulas." *Electoral Studies* 14, no. 4:417–439.

Carroll, Susan J. 1994. *Women as Candidates in American Politics*, 2nd ed., Bloomington: Indiana University Press.

Carroll, Susan J., and Krista Jenkins. 2001. "Unrealized Opportunity: Term Limits and the Representation of Women in State Legislatures." *Women and Politics* 23, no. 4:1–30.

Catt, Helena. 1997. "Women, Maori and Minorities: Microrepresentation and MMP." In *From Campaign to Coalition: The 1996 MMP Election*, edited by Jonathan Boston, Stephen Levine, Elizabeth McLeay, and Nigel Roberts, pp. 199–205. Palmerston North, New Zealand: Dunmore Press .

Caul, Miki. 2001. "Political Parties and the Adoption of Candidate Gender Quotas: A Cross-National Analysis." *Journal of Politics* 63, no. 4:1214–1229.

———. 1999. "Women's Representation in Parliament: The Role of Political Parties." *Party Politics* 5, no. 1:79–98.

Caul Kittilson, Miki. 2006. *Challenging Parties, Changing Parliaments. Women and Elected Office in Contemporary Western Europe.* Columbus: Ohio State University Press.

Celis, Karen, and Petra Meier. 2006. *De macht van het geslacht. Gender, politiek en beleid in België* [The power of sex: Gender, politics, and policies in Belgium]. Leuven, Belgium: Acco.

Center for American Women and Politics. http://www.cawp.rutgers.edu/ (accessed April 2007).

Centre for the Advancement of Women in Politics: http://www.qub.ac.uk/cawp/ (accessed April 2007).

Centro de Investigaciones Sociológicas. 2006. Study Number 2,636, March. http://www.cis.es (accessed August 2006).

Chaney, Paul. 2004. "Women and Constitutional Change in Wales." *Regional and Federal Studies* 14, no. 2:281–303.

Childs, Sarah. 2005. "Political Parties." In *Developments in British Politics 8*, edited by Patrick Dunleavy, Richard Heffernan, Philip Cowley, and Colin Hay, pp. 56–76, Basingstoke, UK: Macmillan.

———. 2004. *New Labour's Women MPs: Women Representing Women.* London: Routledge.

———. 2003. "The Sex Discrimination (Election Candidates) Act 2002 and Its Implications." *Representation: The Journal of Representative Democracy* 39, no. 2:83–93.

Childs, Sarah, Joni Lovenduski, and Rosie Campbell. 2005. *Women at the Top 2005. Changing Numbers, Changing Politics?* London: Hansard Society.

Clarke, Harold, David Sanders, Marianne Stewart, and Paul Whiteley. 2004. *Political Choice in Britain.* Oxford: Oxford University Press.

Cock, Jacklyn. 1991. *Colonels and Cadres: War and Gender in South Africa.* Cape Town: Oxford University Press.

Cournède, Boris. 2006. *Removing Obstacles to Employment for Women in Ireland.* OECD Working Paper No. 39. http://www.olis.oecd.org/olis/2006doc.nsf/ linkto/ ECO-WKP(2006)39 (accessed May 2007).

Craeghs, Jo., and Wilfried Dewachter. 1998. *Vrouwen verkozen: Een eerste onderzoek naar de betekenis van de evenredige vertegenwoordiging, de hoofdvakstem en de plaatsvervanging* [Women elected: A first investigation of the significance of proportional representation, the list vote and the substitutes]. Leuven, Belgium: KUL.

Curtin, Jennifer. 2006. "Advancing Women's Interests in Formal Politics: The Politics of Presence and Proportional Representation in the Antipodes." In *The Politics of Women's Interests. New Comparative Perspectives*, edited by Louise Chappell and Lisa Hill, pp. 93–110. Abingdon, UK: Routledge.

———. 2002. "Women's Voting Patterns: Australia and New Zealand Compared." *Women Talking Politics: Newsletter of the Aotearoa/New Zealand Women and Politics Network*. New issue 5:1–3.

Curtin, Jennifer, and Kelly Sexton. 2004. "Are Quotas Contagious? Promoting Women's Parliamentary Presence in Australia." Paper presented at the annual meeting of the Canadian Political Science Association, University of Winnipeg.

Cutts, David, Sarah Childs, and Edward Fieldhouse. 2007. "This is What Happens When You Don't Listen." *Party Politics* (forthcoming).

Dahlerup, Drude, ed. 2006a. *Women, Quotas and Politics.* London: Routledge.

———. 2006b. "Introduction." In *Women, Quotas and Politics*, edited by Drude Dahlerup, pp. 3–31. London: Routledge.

———. 2006c. "Conclusion." In *Women, Quotas and Politics*, edited by Drude Dahlerup, pp. 293–307. London: Routledge.

Dahlerup, Drude, and Lenita Freidenvall. 2005. "Quotas as a 'Fast Track' to Equal Representation for Women: Why Scandinavia is No Longer the Model." *International Feminist Journal of Politics* 7, no. 1:26–48.

Dalton, Russell J. 2000. "The Decline of Party Identifications." In *Parties Without Partisans*, edited by Russell J. Dalton and Martin P. Wattenberg, pp. 19–36. Oxford: Oxford University Press.

Darcy, R., and James R. Choike. 1986. "A Formal Analysis of Legislative Turnover: Women Candidates and Legislative Representation." *American Journal of Political Science* 30, no. 1:237–255.

Darcy, R., and David L. Nixon. 1996. "Women in the 1946 and 1993 Japanese House of Representatives Elections: The Role of the Election System." *Journal of Northeast Asian Studies* 15, no. 1:3–19.

Darcy, R., Susan Welch, and Janet Clark. 1994. *Women, Elections, & Representation*, 2nd ed. Lincoln: University of Nebraska Press.

Davidson-Schmich, Louise K. 2006. "Implementation of Political Party Sex Quotas. Evidence from the German *Länder* 1990–2000." *Party Politics* 12, no. 2:211–232.

Davis, Rebecca Howard. 1997. *Women and Power in Parliamentary Democracies.* Lincoln: University of Nebraska Press.

De Pablo Masa, Antonio. 1976. "La familia española en cambio" [The Spanish family in transition]. In *Estudios sociológicos sobre la situación social de España* [Sociological studies on the social situation of Spain], edited by Fundación Foessa, pp. 345–405. Madrid: Euramérica.

Department of Constitutional Affairs (DCA). 2005. "General Election 5th May 2005 Briefing Information," April. http://www.dca.gov.uk/elections/gen-elec-brief-info.pdf (accessed April 2007).

Deschouwer, Kris, and Petra Meier. 2004. *Antitrustwetgeving of aanfluiting van de democratie: hoe Vlaamse politici denken over genderquota* [Antitrust regulation or a travesty of democracy: How Flemish politicians think about gender quota]. Brussels: Ministerie van de Vlaamse Gemeenschap.

———. 2002. *Tussen wens en werkelijkheid: reële en mogelijke impact van quotawetten op kieslijsten* [In between wishful thinking and reality: The impact of quota]. Brussels: Ministerie van de Vlaamse Gemeenschap.

Devere, Heather, and Sharyn Graham. 2006. "The Don and Helen New Zealand Election 2005: A Media A-Gender?" *Pacific Journalism Review* 12, no. 1:65–86.

Dolan, Kathleen. 2005. "How the Public Views Women Candidates." In *Women and Elective Office: Past, Present, and Future*, 2nd ed., edited by Sue Thomas and Clyde Wilcox, pp. 41–59. New York: Oxford University Press.

Duverger, Maurice. 1955. *The Political Role of Women.* Paris: UNESCO.

Economist Intelligence Unit (EIU). 2006. *Country Profile Uganda.* London: EIU. http://www.eiu.com (accessed April 2007).

Ederberg, Linda, Maja Tjernstrom, and Ray Kennedy. 2006. "South Africa: Case Study on Floor-Crossing." In *ACE Encyclopaedia*, ACE Electoral Knowledge Network, 1–2. http:ace.at.org/ace-en/topics/pc/pcy/pcy_za (accessed April 2007).

El País. May 18, 1997, 31.

Electoral Commission [New Zealand]. 2006. Unpublished data. Wellington: Electoral Commission. http://www.elections.org.nz (accessed April 2007).

———. 2002. *The New Zealand Electoral Compendium.* Wellington: Electoral Commission.

——— 1999. *The New Zealand Electoral Compendium.* Wellington: Electoral Commission.

Engstrom, Richard L. 1987. "District Magnitudes and the Election of Women to the Irish Dail." *Electoral Studies* 6, no. 2: 123–132.

Erzeel, Silvia et al. (2006), *Belgische partijen en sekse-gelijkheid: veranderingen en weerstand* [Belgian parties and sex-equality: Changes and resistance]. Brussels: VUB; Louvain-La-Neuve: UCL.

Esfandiari, Golnaz. 2005a. "Afghanistan: Interview with UN Special Reporter on Violence against Women." *Radio Free Europe*, July 26. http://www.rferl.org (accessed July 2006).

———. 2005b. "Afghanistan: Threats, Intimidation Reported against Female Candidates." *Radio Free Europe*, August 12. http://www.rferl.org (accessed July 2006).

EU Election Observation Mission (EU EOM). 2005. "Afghanistan : Parliamentary and Provincial Council Elections 18 September." Final report. http://ec.europa.eu/comm/external_relations/human_rights/eu_election_ass_observ/afghanistan/final_report.pdf (accessed July 2006).

European Commission. 1997. *Equal Opportunities for Women and Men in the European Union: Annual Report 1997.* Brussels: European Commission.

Farkas, E. János, and Ágnes Vajda. 1991. "Az 1990-es parlamenti választások képvisel&macmillan;jelöltjeinek társadalmi jellemz&macmillan;i" [Social characteristics of the candidates at the 1990 parliamentary elections]. In *Magyarország politikai évkönyve* [Political Yearbook of Hungary], edited by Sándor Kurtán, Péter Sándor and László Vass , pp. 87–99. Budapest: DKMK.

Farrell, David M. 2001. *Electoral Systems. A Comparative Introduction.* Basingstoke, UK: Palgrave Macmillan.

Farrell, David, and Ian McAllister. 2005. *The Australian Electoral System: Origins, Variations and Consequences.* Sydney: University of NSW Press.

———. 2000. "Through a Glass Darkly: Understanding the World of STV." In *Elections in Australia, Ireland and Malta under the Single Transferable Vote: Reflections on an Embedded Institution*, edited by Shaun Bowler and Bernard Grofman, pp. 17–36. Ann Arbor: University of Michigan Press.

Fernández Poncela, Anna María. 2000. "Candidaturas Federales En La Elección Del 2000: Formalidades Y Realidades" [Federal candidacies for the 2000 elections: Formalities and realities]. In *La Mujer En El Proceso Electoral 2000: Balance Y Prospectiva* [Women in the 2000 electoral process: Balance and prospectives], edited by Rosario Román Pérez, pp. 33–42. Hermosillo, Sonora, Mexico: Grupo Ciudadano por la No Violencia "Ania, Ania."

Ferrara, Federico, Erik S. Herron, and Misa Nishikawa. 2005. *Mixed Electoral Systems. Contamination and Its Consequences.* Basingstoke, UK: Palgrave Macmillan.

Fianna Fail. 2005. *Independent Gender Equality Audit and Fianna Fail Gender Equality Action Plan 2004–2014.* Dublin: Fianna Fail. http://www.qub.ac.uk/cawp/research/FiannaFailreport.pdf (accessed April 2007).

Fiers, Stefaan et al. 2006. *De trajecten van vrouwen in de politiek in België* [The trajectories of women in Belgian politics]. Brussels: ULB; Leuven, Belgium: KUL.

Fox, Richard L., and Jennifer Lawless. 2004. "Entering the Arena? Gender and the Decision to Run for Office." *American Journal of Political Science* 48, no. 2:262–280.

Francisco, Ronald A. 2000. *The Politics of Regime Transitions.* Boulder, CO: Westview.

Funk, Nanette, and Magda Mueller, eds. 1993. *Gender Politics and Post-Communism. Reflections from Eastern Europe and the Former Soviet Union.* New York and London: Routledge.

Gall, Carlotta. 2006a. "Afghan Lawmakers Review Court Nominees." *New York Times*, May 17. http://www.nytimes.com (accessed July 2006).

———. 2006b. "Taliban Threat Is Said to Grow in Afghan South." *New York Times*, May 3. http://www.nytimes.com (accessed July 2006).

Gallagher, Michael. 2005. "Conclusion." In *The Politics of Electoral* Systems, edited by Michael Gallagher and Paul Mitchell, pp. 535–578. Oxford: Oxford University Press.

Gallagher, Michael, Michael Laver, and Peter Mair. 2005. *Representative Government in Modern Europe*, 4th ed. New York: McGraw-Hill.

Gallagher, Michael, and Michael Marsh. 1988. *Candidate Selection in Comparative Perspective: The Secret Garden of Politics.* London: Sage.

Gallagher, Michael, and Paul Mitchell. 2005a. "Introduction to Electoral Systems." In *The Politics of Electoral* Systems, edited by Michael Gallagher and Paul Mitchell, pp. 3–23. Oxford: Oxford University Press.

———. 2005b. "Appendix A." In *The Politics of Electoral* Systems, edited by Michael Gallagher and Paul Mitchell, pp. 579–597. Oxford: Oxford University Press.

———, eds. 2005c. *The Politics of Electoral Systems.* Oxford: Oxford University Press.

———. 2005d. "Appendix D." In *The Politics of Electoral* Systems, edited by Michael Gallagher and Paul Mitchell, p. 621. Oxford: Oxford University Press.

Galligan, Yvonne. 2005. "Ireland." In *Sharing Power: Women, Parliament, Democracy*, edited by Yvonne Galligan and Manon Tremblay, pp. 63–77. Aldershot, UK: Ashgate.

———. 2003. "Candidate Selection: More Democratic or More Centrally Controlled?" In *How Ireland Voted 2002*, edited by Michael Gallagher, Michael Marsh, and Paul Mitchell. Basingstoke, UK: Palgrave Macmillan.

Galligan, Yvonne, Kathleen Knight, and Una Nic Giolla Choille. 2000. "Pathways to Power: Women in the Oireachtas 1919–2000." In *Women in Parliament: Ireland 1918–2000*, edited by Maedhbh McNamara and Paschal Mooney, pp. 27–69. Dublin: Wolfhound.

Galligan, Yvonne, Michael Laver, and Gemma Carney. 1999. "The Effects of Candidate Gender on Voting in Ireland, 1997." *Irish Political Studies* 14:118–122.

Gastrow, Shelagh. 1987. "Helen Suzman." In *Who's Who in South African Politics*, pp. 302–304. Johannesburg: Raven.

Geller, Chris. 2005. "Single Transferable Vote with Borda Elimination: Proportional Representation, Moderation, Quasi-Chaos and Stability." *Electoral Studies* 24, no. 2:265–280.

GenderLinks. http://www.genderlinks.org.za/article.php?a_id=290 (accessed April 2007).

Gertzog, Irwin N. 2002. "Women's Changing Pathways to the U.S. House of Representatives." In *Women Transforming* Congress, edited by Cindy Simon Rosenthal, pp. 95–118. Norman: University of Oklahoma Press.

Ghufran, Nasreen. 2006. "Afghanistan in 2005: The Challenges of Reconstruction." *Asian Survey* 46, no. 1:85–94.

Ginwala, Frene. 1992. "Non-Racial Democracy—Soon; Non-Sexism—How?" In *Proceedings of the National Workshop*, April 25–26. Johannesburg: Women's National Coalition.

Goetz, Anne Marie. 2003. "The Problem with Patronage: Constraints on Women's Political Effectiveness in Uganda." In *No Shortcuts to Power: African Women in Politics and Policy* Making, edited by Anne Marie Goetz and Shireen Hassim, pp. 110–139. London: Zed Books.

Goodson, Larry. 2005. "Bullets, Ballots, and Poppies in Afghanistan." *Journal of Democracy* 16, no. 1:24–38.

Gouws, Amanda. 2004. "Women and the 2004 Election." In *Election Update 2004 South Africa Number 9*, edited by Jackie Kalley, Khabele Matlosa, and Denis Kadima, pp. 2–3. Johannesburg: Electoral Institute of South Africa. http://www.eisa.org.za/WEP/southafrica.htm (accessed April 2007).

Guéraiche William. 1997. "Des femmes politiques à la Libération: vers de nouvelles représentations féminines?" [Women politicians in the liberation: Toward new feminine representations?], *Temps modernes* 593:96–111.

Guinier, Lani. 1991. "No Two Seats: The Elusive Quest for Political Equality." *Virginia Law Review* 77, no. 8:1413–1514.

Hassim, Shireen. 2006. *Women's Organizations and Democracy in South Africa: Contesting Authority.* Madison: University of Wisconsin Press.

Hayes, Bernadette, Ian McAllister, and Donley T. Studlar. 2000. "Gender, Postmaterialism, and Feminism in Comparative Perspective." *International Political Science Review* 21, no. 4:425–439.

Hibbing, John R., and Elizabeth Theiss-Morse. 1995. *Congress as Public Enemy: Public Attitudes toward American Political Institutions.* New York: Cambridge University Press.

Hinojosa, Magda. 2005. *Sex and the Cities: Candidate Selection Processes and Women's Political Representation in Chile and Mexico.* PhD thesis, Harvard University.

Hirczy, Wolfgang. 1995. "STV and the Representation of Women." *PS: Political Science and Politics* 28, no. 4:711–713.

Hondeghem, Annie, and Sarah Nelen. 2000. "Een beleid op weg: Situering van het gelijke-kansenbeleid in België" [Policies emerging: Situating Belgian equal opportunities policies]. *Tijdschrift voor genderstudies* 3, no. 1:36–48.

Htun, Mala. 2005. "Case Study: Latin America. Women, Political Parties and Electoral Systems in Latin America." In *Women in Parliament: Beyond Numbers. A Revised Edition,* edited by Julie Ballington and Azza Karam, pp. 112–121. Stockholm: International IDEA. http://www.idea.int/publications/wip2/upload/Latin_ America.pdf (accessed April 2007).

———. 2002. "Mujeres y poder político en Latinoamérica" [Women and political power in Latin America]. In *Mujeres en el parlamento: más allá de los números* [Women in parliament: Beyond numbers], edited by Myriam Méndez-Montalvo and Julie Ballington, pp. 18–43. Stockholm: International IDEA.

Htun, Mala N., and Mark P. Jones. 2002. "Engendering the Right to Participate in Decision-Making: Electoral Quotas and Women's Leadership in Latin America." In *Gender and the Politics of Rights and Democracy in Latin America,* edited by Nikki Craske and Maxine Molyneux, pp. 32–56. Basingstoke, UK: Palgrave Macmillan.

Huddy, Leonie, Francis K. Neely, and Marilyn R. Lafay. 2000. "Trends: Support for the Women's Movement." *Public Opinion Quarterly* 64, no. (3): 309–350.

Human Rights Watch (HRW). 2005. *Campaigning Against Fear. Women's Participation in Afghanistan's 2005 Elections.* http://www.hrw.org/backgrounder/ wrd/afghanistan0805/index.htm (accessed July 2006).

———. 2004. *Special Report: Women and Elections in Afghanistan.* http://www.hrw.org/campaigns/afghanistan/election2004.htm (accessed July 2006).

Hung-Mao, Tien. 1996. *Taiwan's Electoral Politics and Democratic Transition.* Armonk, NY: M. E. Sharpe.

Ilonszki, Gabriella. 2005. "Women in Politics: The European Union and Hungary." In *Changing Roles. Report on the Situation of Women and Men in Hungary,* edited by Ildikó Nagy, Tiborné Pongrácz, and I. György Tóth, pp. 57–69. Budapest: TÁRKI.

———. 1999. "Legislative Recruitment: Personnel and Institutional Development in Hungary, 1990–1994." In *Elections to the Hungarian National Assembly* 1994, edited by Gábor Tóka and Zsolt Enyedi, pp. 82–107. Berlin: Sigma.

Ilonszki, Gabriella, and Milica G. Antić 2003. "National vs Gender Differences." In *Women in Parliamentary Politics. Hungarian and Slovene Cases Compared,* edited by Milica G. Antić and Gabriella Ilonszki, pp. 117–150. Ljubljana, Slovenia: Peace Institute.

Ilonszki, Gabriella, Ida B. Kelemen, and Zsuzsanna Széles. 2003. *Fordulóponton. Képvisel&macmillan;n&macmillan;k 1998–2002* [At a turning point. Female MPs 1998–2002]. Budapest: OS.

Inglehart, Ronald, and Pippa Norris. 2003. *Rising Tide: Gender Equality and Cultural Change around the World.* Cambridge: Cambridge University Press.

Instituto IDES. 1988. *Las españolas ante la política* [Spanish women in front of politics]. Madrid: Instituto de la Mujer.

Instituto de la Mujer. 2006. *Mujeres en cifras* [Statistics on women]. Madrid: Instituto de la Mujer. http://www.mtas.es (accessed July 2006).

———. 1994. *La mujer en cifras, una década, 1982–1992* [Statistics on women, a decade, 1982–1992]. Madrid: Instituto de la Mujer.

International Crisis Group (ICG). 2006. "Afghanistan's New Legislature: Making Democracy Work?" *Asia Report,* no. 116, May 15. http://www.crisisgroup.org/home/index.cfm?id=4108&l=1 (accessed July 2006).

———. 2005a. "Afghanistan Elections: Endgame or New Beginning?" *Asia Report,* no. 101 (July 21). http://www.crisisgroup.org/home/index.cfm?id=3579 (accessed July 2006).

———. 2005b. "Political Parties in Afghanistan." *Asia Report,* no. 39 (June 2). http://www.icg.org (accessed July 2006).

International Institute for Democracy and Electoral Assistance (International IDEA). http://www.idea.int (accessed April 2007).

Inter-Parliamentary Union (IPU). http://www.ipu.org.

Irin News. 2005. "Afghanistan: Tough Road for Women Standing for Election." *Irin News.* http:/www.irinnews.org (accessed July 2006).

Jackson, Keith, and Alan McRobie. 1998. *New Zealand Adopts Proportional Representation: Accident? Design? Evolution?* Aldershot, UK: Ashgate.

Jacobson, Gary. 2004. *The Politics of Congressional Elections,* 6th ed. New York: Longman.

Jalalzai, Freshta, and Ron Synovitz. 2005 "Afghanistan Women Candidates Face Attacks." *Monitor.* http://www.albionmonitor.com/0509a/afghanwomencandidate.html. (accessed July 2006).

Japan, Jichisho, Senkyobu. 2000. *Shugiingiin sosenkyo saikosaibansho saibankan kokumin shinsa, kekkacho* [General election for the House of Representatives and Supreme Court retention, data, and results]. Tokyo: Jichisho senkyobu.

Japan, Naikaku, Danjo kyodo Sankaku Kyoku. 2006. *Danjo kyodo sankaku hakusho, heisei 18 nenban* [White paper on gender equality, 2006 annual edition]. http://www.gender.go.jp/whitepaper/h18/web/danjyo/mokuji/zu_mkj.htm (accessed July 2006).

Jenson, Jane, and Mariette Sineau. 1995. *Mitterrand et les Françaises: un rendez-vous manqué* [Mitterrand and French women: A missed date]. Paris: Presses de Sciences Po.

———. 1994. "The Same or Different? An Unending Dilemma for French Women." In *Women and Politics Worldwide,* edited by Barbara J. Nelson and Najma Chowdhury, pp. 243–260. New Haven: Yale University Press.

Jenson, Jane, and Celia Valiente. 2003. "Comparing Two Movements for Gender Parity: France and Spain." In *Women's Movements Facing the Reconfigured State,* edited by

Lee Ann Banaszak, Karen Beckwith, and Dieter Rucht, pp. 69–93. New York: Cambridge University Press.

Johnson, Jo. 2005. "Afghan Women Offer Electorate Moral Choice." *Financial Times Online*, September 17. http://www.news.ft.com (accessed January 2006).

Joint Electoral Management Body (JEMB). 2005a. *Final Report National Assembly and Provincial Council Elections 2005*, December. http://www.jemb.org/pdf/JEMBS%20MGT%20Final%20Report%202005-12-12.pdf (accessed July 2006).

———. 2005b. "Interview with Masooda Jalal." http://www.jemb.org/interview_masoodaj.htm (accessed July 2006).

Joint Electoral Management Body of the *Wolesi Jirga* and Provincial Council Elections, Afghanistan. http://www.jemb.org (accessed July 2006).

Jouhette, Sylvain, and Fabrice Romans. 2006. "EU Labour Force Survey, Principal Results 2005." *Statistics in Focus: Population and Social Conditions*, 13. http://epp.eurostat.ec.europa.eu/portal/page?_pageid=0,1136184,0_45572592&_dad=portal&_schema=PORTAL (accessed April 2007).

Jurado Nacional de Elecciones [Peru] (JNE). 2006. "Resolución No. 1163-2006-JNE."

Kandiyoti, Deniz. 2005. *The Politics of Gender and Reconstruction in Afghanistan*. UNRISD Occasional Paper No. 4, February. http://www.unrisd.org/publications/opgp4 (accessed July 2005).

———. 2004. "Political Fiction Meets Gender Myth: Post-Conflict Reconstruction, 'Democratization' and Women's Rights. *IDS Bulletin* 35, no. 4:134–136.

Kennedy, Geraldine, ed. 2002. *The Irish Times Nealon's Guide to the 29th Dail and Seanad*. Dublin: Gill & Macmillan.

Kenworthy, Lane, and Melissa Malami. 1999. "Gender Inequality in Political Representation: A Worldwide Comparative Analysis." *Social Forces* 78, no. 1:235–268.

Kincaid, Diane. 1978. "Over His Dead Body: A Positive Perspective on Widows in the U.S. Congress." *Western Political Quarterly* 31, no. 1:96–104.

Klesner, Joseph L. 2006. "Institutionalizing Mexico's New Democracy." In *Changing Structure of Mexico: Political, Social, and Economic Prospects*, edited by Laura Randall, pp. 384–405. Armonk, NY: M. E. Sharpe.

Kohn, Walter S. G. 1980. *Women in National Legislatures: A Comparative Study of Six Countries*. New York: Praeger.

Kreile, Renate. 2005. "Befreiung durch Krieg? Frauenrechte in Afghanistan zwischen Weltordnungspolitik und Identitätspolitik" [Liberation through war? Women in Afghanistan between world order politics and identity politics], *Zeitschrift Internationale Politik und Gesellschaft (IPG)* 1:102–120.

Krook, Mona Lena, Joni Lovenduski, and Judith Squires. 2006. "Western Europe, North America, Australia and New Zealand. Sex Quotas in the Context of Citizenship Models." In *Women, Quotas and Politics*, edited by Drude Dahlerup, pp. 194–221. London: Routledge.

Kunovich, Sheri, and Pamela Paxton. 2005. "Pathways to Power: The Role of Political Parties in Women's National Political Representation." *American Journal of Sociology* 111, no. 2:505–552.

Lane, John C. 1995. "The Election of Women under Proportional Representation: The Case of Malta." *Democratization* 2, no. 2:140–157.

Larserud, Stina, and Rita Taphorn. 2007. *Designing for Equality. Best-Fit, Medium-Fit and Non-Favourable Combinations of Electoral Systems and Gender Quotas.* Stockholm: International IDEA.

Lawless, Jennifer. 2003. *Women and Elections: Do They Run? Do They Win? Does It Matter?* PhD thesis, Stanford University.

Lawless, Jennifer L., and Richard L. Fox. 2005. *It Takes a Candidate: Why Women Don't Run for Office.* New York: Cambridge University Press.

Leonard, Dick, and Roger Mortimore. 2005. *Elections in Britain.* Basingstoke, UK: Macmillan.

Levine, Stephen, and Nigel Roberts. 2006. "The General Election of 2005." In *New Zealand Government and Politics*, edited by Raymond Miller, pp. 338–352. Auckland: Oxford University Press.

Leyenaar, Monique. 2004. *Political Empowerment of Women: The Netherlands and Other Countries.* Leiden and Boston: Martinus Nijhoff.

Lijphart, Arend. 1995. "The South African Electoral System: Unusual Features and Prospects for Reform." In *Voting and Democracy Report 1995*, edited by Rob Richie. http://www.fairvote.org/reports/1995/spot4/lijphart.html (accessed April 2007).

———. 1994. *Electoral Systems and Party Systems. A Study of Twenty-Seven Democracies, 1945–1990.* Oxford: Oxford University Press.

———. 1984. *Democracies. Patterns of Majoritarian and Consensus Government in Twenty-One Countries.* New Haven, CT: Yale University Press.

Lodge, Tom. 2004. "The Context: How the System Works." In *Election Update 2004 South Africa Number 1*, edited by Wole Olaleye, Jackie Kalley, Khabele Matlosa, and Claude Kabemba, pp. 2–7. Johannesburg: Electoral Institute of South Africa.

Lovenduski, Joni. 2005. *Feminizing Politics.* Cambridge: Polity.

Lovenduski, Joni et al. 2005. *State Feminism and Political Representation.* Cambridge: Cambridge University Press.

Lovenduski, Joni, and Pippa Norris. 1993. *Gender and Party Politics.* London: Sage.

Mackay, Fiona, Fiona Myers, and Alice Brown. 2003. "Towards a New Politics." In *Women Making Constitutions: New Politics and Comparative* Perspectives, edited by Alexandra Dobrowolsky and Vivien Hart, pp. 84–98. Basingstoke, UK: Palgrave Macmillan.

Magone, José M. 2004. *Contemporary Spanish Politics.* London: Routledge.

Majtenyi, Cathy. 2005. "Critics Slam End to Term Limits for Uganda's President." *VOANews.Com* (Nairobi), June 29. http://www.voanews.com (accessed April 2007).

Massicotte, Louis, and André Blais. 1999. "Mixed Electoral Systems: A Conceptual and Empirical Survey." *Electoral Studies* 18, no. 3:341–366.

Matembe, Miria. 2006. "Participating in Vain: The Betrayal of Women's Rights in Uganda." Paper presented to the Reagan-Fascell Democracy Fellows, Washington, D.C., May 16.

Mateo Diaz, Mercedes. 2005. *Representing Women? Female Legislators in West European Parliaments.* Colchester: ECPR Press.

Matland, Richard E. 2006. "Electoral Quotas: Frequency and Effectiveness." In *Women, Quotas and* Politics, edited by Drude Dahlerup, pp. 275–292. London: Routledge.

———. 2005. "Enhancing Women's Political Participation: Legislative Recruitment and Electoral Systems." In *Women in Parliament: Beyond Numbers. A Revised Edition*, edited by Julie Ballington and Azza Karam, pp. 93–111. Stockholm: International IDEA.

———. 2003. "Women's Representation in Post-Communist Europe." In *Women's Access to Political Power in Post-Communist Europe*, edited by Richard E. Matland and Kathleen A. Montgomery, pp. 321–342. Oxford: Oxford University Press.

———. 1998a. "Women's Representation in National Legislatures: Developed and Developing Countries." *Legislatives Studies Quarterly* 23, no. 1:109–125.

———. 1998b. "Enhancing Women's Political Participation: Legislative Recruitment and Electoral Systems." In *Women in Parliament: Beyond Numbers*, edited by Azza Karam et al., pp. 65–88. Stockholm: International IDEA.

———. 1995. "How the Election System Structure Has Helped Women Close the Representation Gap." In *Women in Nordic Politics: Closing the* Gap, edited by Lauri Karvonen and Per Selle, pp. 281–309. Aldershot, UK: Dartmouth.

———. 1993. "Institutional Variables Affecting Female Representation in National Legislatures: The Case of Norway." *Journal of Politics* 55, no. 3:737–755.

Matland, Richard E., and Deborah Dwight Brown. 1992. "District Magnitude's Effect on Female Representation in U.S. State Legislatures." *Legislative Studies Quarterly* 17, no. 4:469–492.

Matland, Richard E., and David C. King. 2002. "Women as Candidates in Congressional Elections." In *Women Transforming Congress*, edited by Cindy Simon Rosenthal, pp. 119–145. Norman: University of Oklahoma Press.

Matland, Richard E., and Kathleen A. Montgomery. 2003a. "Recruiting Women to National Legislatures: A General Framework with Applications to Post-Communist Democracies." In *Women's Access to Political Power in Post-Communist Europe*, edited by Richard E. Matland and Kathleen A. Montgomery, pp. 19–42. Oxford: Oxford University Press.

———, eds. 2003b. *Women's Access to Political Power in Post-Communist Europe*. Oxford: Oxford University Press.

Matland, Richard E., and Donley T. Studlar. 2004. "Determinants of Legislative Turnover: A Cross-National Analysis." *British Journal of Political Science* 34, no. 1:87–108.

———. 1996. "The Contagion of Women Candidates in Single-Member District and Proportional Representation Electoral Systems: Canada and Norway." *Journal of Politics* 58, no. 3:707–733.

Matland, Richard E., and Michelle M. Taylor. 1997. "Electoral System Effects on Women's Representation: Theoretical Arguments and Evidence from Costa Rica." *Comparative Political Studies* 30, no. 2:186–210.

McAllister, Ian. 2006. "Women's Electoral Representation in Australia." In *Representing Women in Parliament: A Comparative Study*, edited by Marian Sawer, Manon Tremblay, and Linda Trimble, pp. 27–46. London: Routledge.

———. 2002. "Political Parties in Australia: Party Stability in a Utilitarian Society." In *Political Parties at the Millennium: Adaptation and Decline in Democratic Societies*, edited by Paul Webb, David Farrell, and Ian Holliday, pp. 22–40. Oxford: Oxford University Press.

————. 1991. "Party Adaptation and Factionalism within the Australian Party System." *American Journal of Political Science* 35, no. 1:206–227.

McAllister, Ian, and Donley T. Studlar. 2002. "Electoral Systems and Women's Representation: A Long-Term Perspective." *Representation: The Journal of Representative Democracy* 39, no. 1:3–14.

————. 1992. "Gender and Representation among Legislative Candidates in Australia." *Comparative Political Studies* 25, no. 3:388–411.

McGinnity, Frances, Helen Russell, James Williams, and Sylvia Blackwell. 2005. *Time-Use in Ireland 2005: Survey Report.* Dublin: Economic and Social Review.

McLean, Iain. 1991. "Forms of Representation and Systems of Voting." In *Political Theory Today*, edited by David Held, pp. 172–196. Cambridge: Polity Press.

McLeay, Elizabeth. 2006. "Climbing on: Rules, Values, and Women's Representation in the New Zealand Parliament." In *Representing Women in Parliament: A Comparative Study*, edited by Marian Sawer, Manon Tremblay, and Linda Trimble, pp. 67–82. London: Routledge.

————. 1993. "Women's Parliamentary Representation: A Comparative Perspective." In *Women and Politics in New Zealand*, edited by Helena Catt and Elizabeth McLeay, pp. 40–62. Wellington: Victoria University Press.

McRobie, Alan, ed. 1993. *Taking it to the People: The New Zealand Electoral Referendum Debate.* Christchurch: Hazard Press.

Meier, Petra. 2005. "The Belgian Paradox: Inclusion and Exclusion of Gender Issues in Politics." In *State Feminism and Political Representation*, edited by Joni Lovenduski et al., pp. 41–61. Cambridge: Cambridge University Press.

————. 2003. "Het ligt niet aan de quota: de opmars van vrouwen in de Kamer" [It's not only quota: The advance of women in the House of Representatives]. *Samenleving & Politiek* 10, no. 8:40–48.

Meintjes, Sheila. 2001. "War and Post-War Shifts in Gender Relations." In *The Aftermath: Women in Post-Conflict Transformation*, edited by Sheila Meintjes, Anu Pillay, and Meredeth Turshen, pp. 63–77. New York: Zed Books.

Meintjes, Sheila, and Mary Simons. 2002a. "Why Electoral Systems Matter to Women." In *One Woman, One Vote*, edited by Glenda Flick, Sheila Meintjes, and Mary Simons, pp. 162–175. Johannesburg: Electoral Institute of South Africa.

————. 2002b. "Women and Democracy, Women in Democracy, Gender and Democracy." In *One Woman, One Vote: The Gender Politics of South African Elections*, edited by Glenda Flick, Sheila Meintjes, and Mary Simons, pp. 11–23. Johannesburg: Electoral Institute of South Africa.

Méndez, Mónica, and Julián Santamaría. 2001. "La ley de la disparidad ideológica curvilínea de los partidos políticos: El caso del PSOE" [The curvilinear law on ideological disparity of political parties: The case of the PSOE]. *Revista Española de Ciencia Política* 4 (April): 35–69.

Miller, Raymond. 2005. *Party Politics in New Zealand.* South Melbourne: Oxford University Press.

Mizrahi, Yemile. 2003. *From Martyrdom to Power: The Partido Acción Nacional in Mexico.* Notre Dame: University of Notre Dame Press.

Molinar Horcasitas, Juan, and Jeffrey A. Weldon. 2001. "Reforming Electoral Systems in Mexico." In *Mixed-Member Electoral Systems: The Best of Both Worlds?* edited by

Matthew Soberg Shugart and Martin P. Wattenberg, pp. 209–230. New York: Oxford University Press.

Montgomery, Kathleen A., and Gabriella Ilonszki. 2003. "Weak Mobilization, Hidden Majoritarianism, and Resurgence of the Right: A Recipe for Female Under-Representation in Hungary." In *Women's Access to Political Power in Post-Communist Europe*, edited by Richard E. Matland and Kathleen A. Montgomery, pp. 105–129. Oxford: Oxford University Press.

Moore, Gwen, and Gene Shackman. 1996. "Gender and Authority: A Cross-National Study." *Social Science Quarterly* 77, no. 2:275–288.

Mora, Guadalupe Vallejo. 2006. "En el PRI, Mujeres Son 'Adversarias Reales' De Los Hombres" [In the PRI, women are "real adversaries" for men]. *Cimacnoticias*, January 4. http://www.cimacnoticias.com/noticias/06ene/06010408.html (accessed April 2007).

Morna, Colleen Lowe, ed. 2004. *Ringing Up the Changes: Gender in Southern African Politics.* Johannesburg: Gender Links.

Moser, Robert G. 2001. "The Effects of Electoral Systems on Women's Representation in Post-Communist States." *Electoral Studies* 20, no. 3:353–369.

Muhumuza, Rodney. 2006. "Women Legislators Come of Age." *The Monitor* (Kampala), March 8.

Mujer, Coordinación General de la Comisión Nacional de la. 2000. "Memoria: Mujeres En El Poder" [Compilation: Women in power]. Paper presented at the "Mujeres en el Poder Conference," Mexico City.

Mujeres [Women], 1994, 13:22–23.

Mulumba, Badru. 2005. "Succession, an Issue That Was Not Allowed to be Debated." *Daily Monitor* (Kampala), June 29. http://www.monitor.co.ug (accessed April 2007).

Murray, Rainbow. 2004. "Why Didn't Parity Work? A Closer Examination of the 2002 Election Results." *French Politics* 2, no. 3:347–362.

Nacif, Benito. 2002. "Understanding Party Discipline in the Mexican Chamber of Deputies: The Centralized Party Model." In *Legislative Politics in Latin America*, edited by Scott Morganstern and Benito Nacif, pp. 254–284. New York: Cambridge University.

———. 1997. "Electoral Institutions and Single Party Politics in the Mexican Chamber of Deputies." Mexico City: Centro de Investigación y Docencia Economicas.

National Economic and Social Forum (NESF). 2006. *Creating a More Inclusive Labour Market.* NESF Report No. 33, National Economic and Social Development Office, Dublin.

National Women's Council of Ireland. 2007. General election website. http://www.nwci.ie/highlights/election_2007 (accessed April 2007).

Nealon, Ted. 1997. *Nealon's Guide to the 28th Dail and Seanad, Election 97.* Dublin: Gill & Macmillan.

———. 1993. *Nealon's Guide to the 27th Dail and Seanad, Election 92.* Dublin: Gill & Macmillan.

Niemi, Richard G., and John Fuh-sheng Hsieh. 2002. "Counting Candidates: An Alternative to the Effective N." *Party Politics* 8, no. 1:75–100.

Niven, David. 1998. "Party Elites and Women Candidates: The Shape of Bias." *Women & Politics* 19, no. 2:57–80.

Nixon, David, and R. Darcy. 1996. "Special Elections and the Growth of Women's Representation in the U.S. House of Representatives." *Women and Politics* 16, no. 4:99–107.

Nordlund, Anja Taarup. 2004. *Demands for Electoral Gender Quotas in Afghanistan and Iraq.* Working Paper Series 2004/2, the Research Program on Gender Quotas. http://www.statsvet.su.se/quotas/a_nordlund_wps_2004_2.pdf (accessed July 2006).

Nordstoga Hanssen, Kari. 2005. "Towards Multiparty System in Uganda: The Effect on Female Representation in Politics." *Chr. Michelsen Institute Research Notes,* Bergen, CMI. http://www.cmi.no/pdf/?file=/publications/2006/wp/wp2006-9.pdf (accessed April 2007).

Norris, Pippa. 2004. *Electoral Engineering: Voting Rules and Political Behavior.* Cambridge: Cambridge University Press.

———. 2001. "Women's Power at the Ballot Box." In International IDEA, *Voter Turnout from 1945 to 2000: A Global Report on Political Participation.* Stockholm: International IDEA.

———. 2000. "Women: Representation and Electoral Systems." In *The International Encyclopedia of Elections,* edited by Richard Rose, pp. 348–351. Washington, D.C.: Congressional Quarterly Press.

———. 1997a. "Choosing Electoral Systems: Proportional, Majoritarian and Mixed Systems." *International Political Science Review* 18, no. 3:297–312.

———. 1997b. "Conclusions: Comparing Passages to Power. In *Passages to Power: Legislative Recruitment in Advanced Democracies,* edited by Pippa Norris, pp. 209–231. Cambridge: Cambridge University Press.

———. 1997c. *Passages to Power: Legislative Recruitment in Advanced Democracies.* Cambridge: Cambridge University Press.

———. 1997d. "Introduction: Theories of Recruitment." In *Passages to Power: Legislative Recruitment in Advanced Democracies,* edited by Pippa Norris, pp. 1–14. Cambridge: Cambridge University Press.

———. 1992. "Electoral Systems and the Parliamentary Recruitment of Women." In *Political Leadership in Democratic* Societies, edited by Anthony Mughan and Samuel C. Patterson, pp. 136–144. Chicago: Nelson-Hall.

———. 1987. *Politics and Sexual Equality: The Comparative Position of Women in Western Democracies.* Boulder, CO: Lynne Rienner.

———. 1985. "Women's Legislative Participation in Western Europe." *West European Politics* 8, no. 4:90–101.

———. n.a. *Implementing Women's Representation in Afghanistan's Electoral Law: Options for Reserved Seats.* http://www.ksghome.harvard.edu/~pnorris/Acrobat/Afghanistan%20electoral%20law%20Norris.pdf (accessed July 2006).

Norris, Pippa, R. J. Carty, Lynda Erickson, Joni Lovenduski, and Marian Simms. 1990. "Party Selectorates in Australia, Britain and Canada: Prolegomena for Research in the 1990s." *Journal of Commonwealth & Comparative Politics* 28, no. 2:219–245.

Norris, Pippa, and Mark Franklin. 1997. "Social Representation." *European Journal of Political Research* 32, no. 2:185–210.

Norris, Pippa, and Ronald Inglehart. 2005. "Women as Political Leaders Worldwide: Cultural Barriers and Opportunities." In *Women and Elective Office: Past, Present, and Future*, 2nd ed., edited by Sue Thomas and Clyde Wilcox, pp. 244–263. New York: Oxford University Press.

———. 2001. "Cultural Obstacles to Equal Representation." *Journal of Democracy* 12, no. 3:126–140.

Norris, Pippa, and Joni Lovenduski. 1995. *Political Recruitment. Gender, Race, and Class in the British Parliament.* Cambridge: Cambridge University Press.

———. 1989. "Pathways to Parliament." *Talking Politics* 1, no. 3:90–94.

Norris, Pippa, and Christopher Wlezien. 2005. "Introduction: The Third Blair Victory." *Parliamentary Affairs* 58, no. 4:657–683.

Nowacki, Dawn. 2003. "Women in Russian Regional Assemblies: Losing Ground." In *Women's Access to Political Power in Post-Communist Europe*, edited by Richard E. Matland and Kathleen A. Montgomery, pp. 173–195. Oxford: Oxford University Press.

Oakes, Ann, and Elizabeth Almquist. 1993. "Women in National Legislatures." *Population Research and Policy Review* 12, no. 1:71–81.

Ogai, Tokuko. 1996. "Stars of Democracy: The First Thirty-Nine Female Members of the Japanese Diet." *U.S.-Japan Women's Journal. English Supplement* 11:81–117.

O'Kelly, Michael. 2000. "Gender and Voter Appeal in Irish Elections 1948–1997." *Economic and Social Review* 31, no. 3:249–265.

Ondercin, Heather, and Susan Welch. 2005. "Women Candidates for Congress." In *Women and Elective Office: Past, Present, and Future*, 2nd ed., edited by Sue Thomas and Clyde Wilcox, pp. 60–80. New York: Oxford University Press.

Palmer, Barbara, and Dennis Simon. 2006. *Breaking the Political Glass Ceiling: Women and Congressional Elections.* New York: Routledge.

Pankhurst, Donna. 2002. "Women and Politics in Africa: The Case of Uganda." In *Women, Politics and Change*, edited by Karen Ross, pp. 119–128. Oxford: Oxford University Press.

Paxton, Pamela. 1997. "Women in National Legislatures: A Cross-National Analysis." *Social Science Research* 26, no. 4:442–464.

Paxton, Pamela, Melanie Hughes, and Jennifer L. Green. 2006. "The International Women's Movement and Women's Political Representation, 1893–2003." *American Sociological Review* 71, no. 6:898–920.

Paxton, Pamela, and Sheri Kunovich. 2003. "Women's Political Representation: The Importance of Ideology." *Social Forces* 82, no. 1:87–114.

Peschard, Jacqueline. 2003. "The Quota System in Latin America: General Overview." In International IDEA, *The Implementation of Quotas: Latin American Experiences*, pp. 20–29. Stockholm: International IDEA.

Pitkin, Hanna Fenichel. 1967. *The Concept of Representation.* Berkeley: University of California Press.

Rallings, Colin, and Michael Thrasher. 2005. *The 2005 General Election: Analysis of the Results.* Paper published on the Electoral Commission website. http//www. electoralcommission.org.uk/files/dms/RallingsandThrasherreport_18801-13909__E__N__S__W__.pdf (accessed April 2007).

Ramiro, Luis. 2000. *Incentivos electorales y límites organizativos: Cambio y elección de estrategias en el PCE e IU, 1986–1999* [Electoral incentives and organizational limitations: Change and choice of strategies in the PCE and the IU, 1986–1999]. PhD thesis, European University Institute.

Randall, Vicky. 1982. *Women and Politics.* London: Macmillan.

Raunio, Tapio. 2005. "Finland: One Hundred Years of Quietude." In *The Politics of Electoral Systems*, edited by Michael Gallagher and Paul Mitchell, pp. 473–489. Oxford: Oxford University Press.

Reed, Steven R. 2003. "The 1993 Election and the End of LDP One-Party Dominance." In *Japanese Electoral Politics: Creating a New Party System*, edited by Steven R. Reed, pp. 7–23. New York: Routledge.

Reilly, Ben. 1997. "Preferential Voting and Political Engineering: A Comparative Study." *Journal and Commonwealth and Comparative Politics* 35, no. 1:1–19.

Reilly, Ben, and Michael Maley. 2000. "The Single Transferable Vote and the Alternative Vote Compared." In *Elections in Australia, Ireland and Malta under the Single Transferable Vote: Reflections on an Embedded Institution*, edited by Shaun Bowler and Bernard Grofman, pp. 37–56. Ann Arbor: University of Michigan Press.

Requena, Miguel. 2005. "The Secularization of Spanish Society: Change in Religious Practice." *South European Society & Politics* 10, no. 3:369–90.

Reynolds, Andrew. 2006. "South Africa: Electoral Systems, Conflict Management, and Inclusion." In *ACE Encyclopaedia*, ACE Electoral Knowledge Network, 1–3. http://www.ace.at.org/ace-en/topics/es/esy/esy_za (accessed April 2007).

———. 1999. "Women in the Legislatures and Executives of the World: Knocking at the Highest Glass Ceiling." *World Politics* 51, no. 4:547–572.

———. 1995. "Testing Voting Systems in South Africa: Re-Running the 1994 Elections with Different Systems." In *Voting and Democracy Report* 1995, edited by Rob Richie. http://www.fairvote.org/reports/1995/spot4/reynolds.html (accessed April 2007).

Reynolds, Andrew, and Ben Reilly, eds. 1997. *The International IDEA Handbook of Electoral System Design.* Stockholm: International IDEA.

Reynolds, Andrew, Ben Reilly, and Andrew Ellis. 2005. *Electoral System Design: The New International IDEA Handbook.* Stockholm: International IDEA.

Rochon, Thomas R. 1997. *Culture Moves: Ideas, Activism, and Changing Values.* Princeton, NJ: Princeton University Press.

Rodríguez, Victoria E. 2003. *Women in Contemporary Mexican Politics.* Austin: University of Texas Press.

Rosenbluth, Frances, Rob Salmond, and Michael F. Thies. 2006. "Welfare Works: Explaining Female Legislative Representation." *Politics & Gender* 2, no. 2:165–192.

Ruiz Jiménez, Antonia María. 2006. *De la necesidad, virtud: La transformación "feminista" del Partido Popular en perspectiva comparada, 1977–2004* [To make a virtue of necessity: The "feminist" transformation of the People's Party in comparative perspective, 1977–2004]. Madrid: Centro de Estudios Políticos y Constitucionales.

Rule, Wilma. 2000. "Comparing Systems of Election and Representation." In *The U.S. House of Representatives: Reform or Rebuild?* edited by Joseph F. Zimmerman and Wilma Rule, pp. 114–125. Westport, CT: Praeger.

———. 1996. "Response to Wolfgang Hirczy" [STV and the Representation of Women]. *PS: Political Science and Politics* 29, no. 2:143.

———. 1994a. "Women's Underrepresentation and Electoral Systems." *PS. Political Science & Politics* 27, no. 4:689–692.

———. 1994b. "Parliaments of, by, and for the People: Except for Women?" In *Electoral Systems in Comparative Perspective: Their Impact on Women and Minorities*, edited by Wilma Rule and Joseph F. Zimmerman, pp. 15–30. Westport: Greenwood.

———. 1988. "Why Women Don't Run: The Critical Contextual Factors in Women's Legislative Recruitment." *Western Political Quarterly* 34, no. 1:60–77.

———. 1987. "Electoral Systems, Contextual Factors and Women's Opportunity for Election to Parliament in Twenty-Three Democracies." *Western Political Quarterly* 40, no. 3:477–498.

Rule, Wilma, and Pippa Norris. 1992. "Anglo and Minority Women's Underrepresentation in Congress: Is the Electoral System the Culprit?" In *United States Electoral Systems: Their Impact on Women and Minorities*, edited by Wilma Rule and Joseph F. Zimmerman, pp. 41–54. New York: Praeger.

Rule, Wilma, and Matthew Shugart. 1995. "The Preference Vote and Election of Women: Women Win More Seats in Open List PR" http://www.fairvote.org/reports/1995/chp7/rule.html (accessed May 2007).

Rule, Wilma, and Joseph F. Zimmerman, eds. 1994. *Electoral Systems in Comparative Perspective. Their Impact on Women and Minorities.* Westport, CT: Greenwood.

———. 1992. *United States Electoral Systems: Their Impact on Women and Minorities.* New York: Praeger.

Russell, Diane. 1989. *Lives of Courage: Women for a New South Africa.* Oakland, CA: Basic Books.

Russell, Meg, Fiona Mackay, and Laura McAllister. 2002. "Women's Representation in the Scottish Parliament and National Assembly for Wales." *Journal of Legislative Studies* 8, no. 2:49–76.

Saint-Germain, Michelle A. 1994. "The Representation of Women and Minorities in the National Legislatures of Costa Rica and Nicaragua." In *Electoral Systems in Comparative Perspective: Their Impact on Women and Minorities*, edited by Wilma Rule and Joseph F. Zimmerman, pp. 211–221. Westport, CT: Greenwood.

Salmond, Rob. 2006. "Proportional Representation and Female Parliamentarians." *Legislative Studies Quarterly* 31, no. 2:175–204.

———. 2003. "Choosing Candidates: Labour and National in 2002." In *New Zealand Votes: The General Election of 2002*, edited by Jonathan Boston, Stephen Church, Stephen Levine, Elizabeth McLeay, and Nigel Roberts, pp. 192–206. Wellington: Victoria University of Wellington Press.

Sanbonmatsu, Kira. 2006. "State Elections: Where Do Women Run? Where Do Women Win?" In *Gender and Elections: Shaping the Future of American Politics*, edited by Susan J. Carroll and Richard L. Fox, pp. 189–214. New York: Cambridge University Press.

Sánchez Ferriz, Remedio. 2000. "Las mujeres en las Cortes Generales y en los Parlamentos de las Comunidades Autónomas' [Women in central-state and regional parliaments]. In *Mujer y Constitución en España* [Women and Constitution in Spain], edited by Centro de Estudios Políticos y Constitucionales, pp. 203–234. Madrid: Centro de Estudios Políticos y Constitucionales.

Sánchez Hernández, María F. 2003. *Liderazgo político de mujeres: Desde la transición hacia las cuotas (Estudio documental)* [Female political leadership: From the transition to democracy to quotas (a documentary study)]. Sevilla, Spain: Instituto Andaluz de la Mujer.

Sanshu Ryoin Meikan [A directory of the national diet]. 1990. Tokyo: Nihon Kokusei Chosakai.

Sapiro, Virginia. 1984. *The Political Integration of Women. Roles, Socialization, and Politics.* Urbana: University of Illinois Press.

Sartori, Giovanni. 1997. *Comparative Constitutional Engineering: An Inquiry into Structures, Incentives and Outcomes. Second Edition.* New York: New York University Press.

———. 1994. *Comparative Constitutional Engineering: An Inquiry into Structures, Incentives and Outcomes.* Basingstoke, UK: Macmillan.

Sawer, Marian, ed. 2001. *Elections Full, Free and Fair.* Sydney: Federation Press.

———. 2000. "A Question of Heartland." In *The Machine: Labor Confronts the Future*, edited by John Warhurst and Andrew Parkin, pp. 264–280. Sydney: Allen and Unwin.

———. 1997. "Mirroring the Nation? Electoral Systems and the Representation of Women." *Current Affairs Bulletin* 73, no. 5:8–12.

Sawer, Marian, and Marian Simms. 1993. *A Woman's Place: Women and Politics in Australia.* Sydney: Allen and Unwin.

Schmidt, Gregory D. 2006. "All the President's Women: Fujimori and Gender Equity in Peruvian Politics." In *The Fujimori Legacy: The Rise of Electoral Authoritarianism in Latin America*, edited by Julio Carrión, pp. 150–177. University Park: Pennsylvania State Press.

———. 2005. "Is Closed List PR Really Optimal for the Election of Women? A Cross-National Analysis." Paper presented at the annual meeting of the American Political Science Association, Washington, D.C.

———. 2004. *Peru: The Politics of Surprise.* New York: McGraw-Hill Primis Online.

———. 2003a. "The Implementation of Gender Quotas in Peru: Legal Reform, Discourses and Impacts." In International IDEA, *The Implementation of Quotas: Latin American Experiences*, pp. 42–50. Stockholm: International IDEA.

———. 2003b. "Unanticipated Successes: Lessons from Peru's Experiences with Gender Quotas in Majoritarian Closed List and Open List PR Systems." In International IDEA, *The Implementation of Quotas: Latin American Experiences*, pp. 120–133. Stockholm: International IDEA.

———. 2001. "Descriptive Information for Peru." Report prepared for Mark Jones and David Samuels (primary investigators). Project for the National Science Foundation "On the Electoral Link Between Presidents and Assemblies: Coattail Effects in Presidential Democracies."

———. 1996. "Fujimori's 1990 Upset Victory in Peru: Electoral Rules, Contingencies, and Adaptive Strategies." *Comparative Politics* 28, no. 3:321–354.

Schmidt, Manfred G. 1993. "Gendered Labour Force Participation." In *Families of Nations: Patterns of Public Policy in Western Democracies*, edited by Francis G. Castles, pp. 179–238. Brookfield, VT: Dartmouth.

Schwindt-Bayer, Leslie A. 2005. "The Incumbency Disadvantage and Women's Election to Legislative Office." *Electoral Studies* 24, no. 2:227–244.

Schwindt-Bayer, Leslie A., and William Mishler. 2005. "An Integrated Model of Women's Representation." *Journal of Politics* 67, no. 2:407–428.

Scott, Joan W. 2005. *Parité! Sexual Equality and the Crisis of French Universalism.* Chicago: University of Chicago Press.

Sebestyén, István. 2003. "Országgyűlési választások: pártok, stratégiák, képviselőjelöltek és mandátumok" [Parliamentary elections: Parties, strategies, candidates and mandates]. In *Magyarország politikai évkönyve* [Political yearbook of Hungary], edited by Sándor Kurtán, Péter Sándor, and László Vass, pp. 1100–1146. Budapest: DKMKKA.

Seidman, Gay W. 1999. "Gendered Citizenship: South Africa's Democratic Transition and the Construction of a Gendered State." *Gender and Society* 13, no. 3:287–307.

Shah, Niaz A. 2005. "The Constitution of Afghanistan and Women's Rights." *Feminist Legal Studies* 13, no. 2:239–258.

Shepherd-Robinson, Laura, and Joni Lovenduski. 2002. *Women and Candidate Selection in British Political Parties.* London: Fawcett Society.

Shields, Margaret. 2001. "Women in the Labour Party during the Kirk and Rowling Years." In *Three Labour Leaders: Nordmeyer, Kirk, Rowling*, edited by Margaret Clark, pp. 125–138. Palmerston North, New Zealand: Dunmore Press.

Shugart, Matthew Soberg. 2001. "Electoral 'Efficiency' and the Move to Mixed-Member Systems." *Electoral Studies* 20, no. 2:173–193.

Shugart, Matthew Soberg, and Martin P. Wattenberg, eds. 2001a. *Mixed-Member Electoral Systems: The Best of Both Worlds?* Oxford: Oxford University Press.

———. 2001b. "Conclusion: Are Mixed-Member Systems the Best of Both Worlds?" In *Mixed-Member Electoral Systems: The Best of Both Worlds?* edited by Matthew Soberg Shugart and Martin P. Wattenberg, pp. 571–596. Oxford: Oxford University Press.

Siaroff, Alan. 2000. "Women's Representation in Legislatures and Cabinets in Industrial Democracies." *International Political Science Review* 21, no. 2:197–215.

Siemieńska, Renata. 2003. "Women in the Polish Sejm: Political Culture and Party Politics versus Electoral Rules." In *Women's Access to Political Power in Post-Communist Europe*, edited by Richard E. Matland and Kathleen A. Montgomery, pp. 217–244. Oxford: Oxford University Press.

Sineau, Mariette. 2005a. "The French Experience: Institutionalizing Parity." In *Women in Parliament: Beyond Numbers. A Revised Edition*, edited by Julie Ballington and Azza Karam, pp. 122–131. Stockholm: International IDEA.

———. 2005b. "France." In *Sharing Power: Women, Parliament, Democracy*, edited by Yvonne Galligan and Manon Tremblay, pp. 49–61. Aldershot, UK: Ashgate.

———. 2001. *Profession: femme politique. Sexe et pouvoir sous la Cinquième République* [Profession: female politician. Sex and power in the Fifth Republic]. Paris: Presses de Sciences Po.

Sineau, Mariette, and Vincent Tiberj. 2007. "Candidats et députés français en 2002. Une approche sociale de la représentation" [French candidates and deputies in 2002: A social approach of representation]. *Revue française de science politique* 57, no. 2: 163–185.

Sineau, Mariette, and Manon Tremblay. 2007. "Représentation parlementaire des femmes et système uninominal. Une comparaison France/Québec." [Women's legislative representation and single member district system: A comparison France/Quebec]. In *Genre, citoyenneté et représentation* [Gender, citizenship and representation], edited by Manon Tremblay, Thanh-Huyen Ballmer-Cao, Bérengère Marques-Pereira, and Mariette Sineau, pp. 151–169. Québec City, Paris: Les Presses de l'Université Laval.

Sinnott, Richard. 2005. "The Rules of the Electoral Game." In *Politics in the Republic of Ireland*, edited by John Coakley and Michael Gallagher, pp. 105–134. London: Routledge.

SISESIM. 2005. *Sistema De Indicadores Para El Seguimiento De La Situación De La Mujer En México* [System of indicators for the tracking of the situation of women in Mexico]. http://www.dgcnesyp.inegi.gob.mx/sisesim/sisesim.html?c=1416 (accessed April 2007).

Smits, Jozef, and Inge Thomas. 1998. "Het gebruik van de meervoudige voorkeurstem bij de parlementsverkiezingen van 21 mei 1995" [The use of multiple preferential votes at the elections of May 21, 1995]. *Res Publica* 40, no. 1:127–168.

Smits, Jozef, and Bram Wauters. 2000. "Het gebruik van de voorkeurstem bij de parlementsverkiezingen van 13 juni 1999" [The use of preferential votes at the elections of June 31, 1999]. *Res Publica* 42, no. 2–3:265–304.

Stevenson, Linda S. 1999. "Gender Politics in the Mexican Democratization Process." In *Towards Mexico's Democratization*, edited by Jorge I. Domínguez and Alejandro Poiré, pp. 57–87. New York: Routledge.

Studlar, Donley T., and Ian McAllister. 2002. "Does a Critical Mass Exist? A Comparative Analysis of Women's Legislative Representation Since 1950." *European Journal of Political Research* 41, no. 2:233–253.

———. 1991. "Political Recruitment to the Australian Legislature: Toward an Explanation of Women's Electoral Disadvantages." *Western Political Quarterly* 44, no. 2:467–485.

Studlar, Donley T., Ian McAllister, and Bernadette Hayes. 1998. "Explaining the Gender Gap in Voting: A Cross-National Analysis." *Social Science Quarterly* 79, no. 4:779–798.

Studlar, Donley T., and Susan Welch. 1991. "Does District Magnitude Matter? Women Candidates in London Local Elections." *Western Political Quarterly* 44, no. 2:457–466.

Swyngedouw, Marc, and Patrick Vander Weyden. 2006. "Het kiesstelsel en de verkiezingen" [The electoral system and elections]. In *De geschiedenis van België na 1945* [Belgian history after 1945], edited by Els Witte and Alain Meynen, pp. 197–231. Antwerp: Standaard Uitgeverij.

Taagepera, Rein. 1994. "Beating the Law of Minority Attrition." In *Electoral Systems in Comparative Perspective: Their Impact on Women and Minorities*, edited by Wilma Rule and Joseph F. Zimmerman, pp. 235–245.Westport, CT: Greenwood.

Tabe, Angel. 2006. "African Presidential Term Limits: How Uganda Extended the Status Quo." *VOANews.Com* (Washington, D.C.), May 30. http://www.voanews.com (accessed April 2007).

Tamale, Sylvia. 2004. "Introducing Quotas: Discourse and Legal Reform in Uganda." In *The Implementation of Quotas: African Experiences*, edited by Julie Ballington, pp. 38–45. Stockholm: International IDEA.

———. 1999. *When Hens Begin to Crow: Gender and Parliamentary Politics in Uganda.* Boulder, CO: Westview.

Tarrés, María Luisa. 2006. "The Political Participation of Women in Contemporary Mexico, 1980–2000." In *Changing Structure of Mexico: Political, Social, and Economic Prospects*, edited by Laura Randall, pp. 406–423. Armonk, NY: M. E. Sharpe.

Tarzi, Amin. 2005. "Afghanistan: Female Candidates Discuss Development Needs." *Radio Free Europe*, August 30. http://www.rferl.org (accessed July 2006).

Threlfall, Monica. 2005a. "Towards Parity Representation in Party Politics." In *Gendering Spanish Democracy*, edited by Monica Threlfall, Christine Cousins, and Celia Valiente, pp. 124–161. London: Routledge.

———. 2005b. "Explaining Gender Parity Representation in Spain: The Internal Dynamics of Parties." Paper presented at the "European Consortium for Political Research Conference," Budapest.

Tremblay, Manon. 2007. "Democracy, Representation, and Women: A Comparative Analysis." *Democratization* 14, no. 4:1–21.

Tremblay, Manon, and Réjean Pelletier. 2001. "More Women Constituency Party Presidents: A Strategy for Increasing the Number of Women Candidates in Canada?" *Party Politics* 7, no. 2:157–190.

Tripp, Aili Mari. Forthcoming. "Post-Conflict Societies, Quotas and the Representation of Women in Africa's Legislatures." Article manuscript.

———. 2006 "Uganda: Agents of Change for Women's Advancement?" In *Women in African Parliaments*, edited by Gretchen Bauer and Hannah E. Britton, pp. 111–132. Boulder, CO: Lynne Rienner.

———. 2000. *Women and Politics in Uganda.* Madison: University of Wisconsin Press.

Tuesta Soldevilla, Fernando. 2001. *Perú político en cifras, 1821–2001* [Peruvian politics in figures, 1821–2001], 3rd ed. Lima: Friedrich Ebert Stiftung.

Uhr, John. 2000. "Rules for Representation: Parliament and the Design of the Australian Electoral System." Research Paper No. 29, Commonwealth of Australia, Department of the Parliamentary Library. http://www.aph.gov.au/LIBRARY/Pubs/rp/1999-2000/2000rp29.htm (accessed April 2007).

UNDP (United Nations Development Programme). 2005. *Human Development Report 2005.* New York: UNDP.

———. 2004. "Afghanistan National Human Development Report 2004. Security with a Human Face: Challenges and Responsibilities." http://hdr.undp.org/docs/reports/national/AFG_Afghanistan/afghanistan_2004_en.pdf(accessed July 2006).

UNIFEM/CONMUJER (2000). *El Enfoque De Género En La Producción De Las Estadísticas Sobre Participación Política Y Toma De Decisiones En México* [The focus on gender in the production of statistics on political participation and decision making in Mexico]. Mexico City: UNIFEM/CONMUJER.

United Kingdom (House of Commons) (2006). "Factsheet M4." http://www. dca.gov.uk/elections/gen-elec-brief-info.pdf (accessed April 2007).

United Nations Office at Vienna, Centre for Social Development and Humanitarian Affairs. 1992. *Women in Politics and Decision-Making in the Late Twentieth Century.* Dordrecht, Netherlands: Martinus Nijhoff.

Uriarte, Edurne, and Cristina Ruiz. 1999. "Mujeres y hombres en las élites políticas españolas: Diferencias o similitudes?" [Female and male members of the Spanish political elite: Differences or similarities?]. *Revista Española de Investigaciones Sociológicas* 88:207–232.

Valiente, Celia. 2005. "The Women's Movement, Gender Equality Agencies and Central-State Debates on Political Representation in Spain." In *State Feminism and Political* Representation, ed. Joni Lovenduski et al., pp. 174–194. Cambridge: Cambridge University Press.

———. 2001. "Implementing Women's Rights in Spain." In *Globalization, Gender and Religion: The Politics of Women's Rights in Catholic and Muslim Contexts,* edited by Jane H. Bayes and Nayereh Tohidi, pp. 107–125. New York: Palgrave Macmillan.

Valiente, Celia, Luis Ramiro, and Laura Morales. 2005. "Spain." In *Sharing Power: Women, Parliament, Democracy,* edited by Yvonne Galligan and Manon Tremblay, pp. 189–203. Aldershot, UK: Ashgate.

Van Molle, Leen, and Eliane Gubin. 1998. *Vrouw en politiek in België* [Woman and politics in Belgium]. Tielt, Belgium: Lannoo.

Varnham, Mary. 1993. "Vote PR for More Women on the Hill." In *Taking It to the People: The New Zealand Electoral Referendum Debate,* edited by Alan McRobie, pp. 149–152. Christchurch: Hazard Press.

Verge, Tania. 2005. "Mujer y partidos políticos en España: Las estrategias de los partidos y su impacto institucional, 1978–2004" [Women and political parties in Spain: The strategies of parties and their institutional impact, 1978–2004]. Paper presented at the seventh meeting of the Asociación Española de Ciencia Política y de la Administración, Madrid.

Vincent, Louise. 1999. "A Cake of Soap: The Volksmoeder Ideology and Afrikaner Women's Campaign for the Vote." *International Journal of African Historical Studies* 32, no. 1:1–17.

Vowles, Jack. 2000. "The Impact of the 1999 Campaign." In *Left Turn: The New Zealand General Election of 1999,* edited by Jonathan Boston, Stephen Church, Stephen Levine, Elizabeth McLeay, and Nigel Roberts, pp. 141–160. Wellington: Victoria University Press.

Walker, Brian M. 1993. *Parliamentary Election Results in Ireland, 1918–1992.* Dublin: Royal Irish Academy.

Walker, Cherryl. 1990. "The Women's Suffrage Campaign." In *Women and Gender in Southern Africa to 1945,* edited by Cherryl Walker, pp. 313–345. Cape Town: David Phillip.

———. 1982. *Women and Resistance in South Africa,* 2nd ed. Cape Town: David Phillip.

Wang, Yeh-lih. 1996. "The Political Consequences of the Electoral System: Single Non Transferable Vote in Taiwan." *Issues & Studies* 32, no. 8:85–104.

Ward, Russell. 1958. *The Australian Legend.* Melbourne: Oxford University Press.

Waring, Marilyn. 1993. "Voting Reform: The Conspiracy Theory." In *Taking it to the People: The New Zealand Electoral Referendum Debate*, edited by Alan McRobie, pp. 202–204. Christchurch: Hazard Press.

Webb, Paul. 2005. "The Continuing Advance of the Minor Parties." *Parliamentary Affairs* 58, no. 4:757–775.

Webb, Richard, and Graciela Fernández Baca. 2000. *Perú en Números 2000* [Peru in numbers 2000]. Lima: Cuánto S.A.

Welch, Susan, and Donley T. Studlar. 1996. "The Opportunity Structure for Women's Candidacies and Electability in Britain and the United States." *Political Research Quarterly* 49, no. 4:861–874.

Weldon, Jeffrey A. 2001. "The Consequences of Mexico's Mixed-Member Electoral System, 1988–1997." In *Mixed-Member Electoral Systems: The Best of Both Worlds?* edited by Matthew Soberg Shugart and Martin P. Wattenberg, pp. 447–476. New York: Oxford University Press.

Wells, Julia. 1993. *We Now Demand: The History of Women's Resistance to Pass Laws in South Africa.* Johannesburg: Witwatersrand University Press.

Whiteley, Paul, Marianne Stewart, David Sanders and Harold Clarke. 2005. "The Issue Agenda and Voting in 2005." *Parliamentary Affairs* 58, no. 4:802–817.

Wieland-Karimi, Almut. 2006. *Afghanistan: Rückblick 2005, Ausblick auf 2006* [Afghanistan: Retrospective view on 2005, prospect for 2006]. Kabul: Friedrich-Ebert-Stiftung.

———. 2005. "Wahlen und Warlords—Ein Parlament und 34 Provinzräte in Afghanistan gewählt" [Elections and warlords—a parliament and 34 provincial councils elected in Afghanistan]. Short reports from the International Development Cooperation, Department Asia/Pacific, Friedrich-Ebert-Foundation. http://www.fes.de/international/asien/ (accessed July 2006).

Wilder, Andrew. 2005. *A House Divided? Analysing the 2005 Afghan Elections.* Afghan Research and Evaluation Unit (AREAU), December. http://www.areu.org.af/publications/A%20House%20Divided.pdf (accessed July 2006).

Wilson, Margaret. 1992. "Women and the Labour Party." In *The Labour Party After 75 Years*, edited by Margaret Clark, pp. 35–49.Wellington, Victoria University of Wellington, Department of Politics, Occasional Publication No. 4.

Women's National Coalition. 1994. *The Origins, History, and Process of the Women's National Coalition.* Cape Town: University of the Western Cape.

Woodward, Alison. 1998. "Politische Partizipation in Belgien: die gespaltene Frau" [Political participation in Belgium: The splintered woman]. In *Handbuch politische Partizipation von Frauen in Europa* [Handbook on women's political participation in Europe], edited by Beate Hoecker, pp. 17–40. Opladen, Germany: Leske+Budrich.

Zimmermann, Joseph F. 1994. "Equity in Representation for Women and Minorities." In *Electoral Systems in Comparative Perspective: Their Impact on Women and Minorities*, edited by Wilma Rule and Joseph F. Zimmermann, pp. 3–13. Westport, CT: Greenwood.

Index